Danger Girl™

RENEGADE

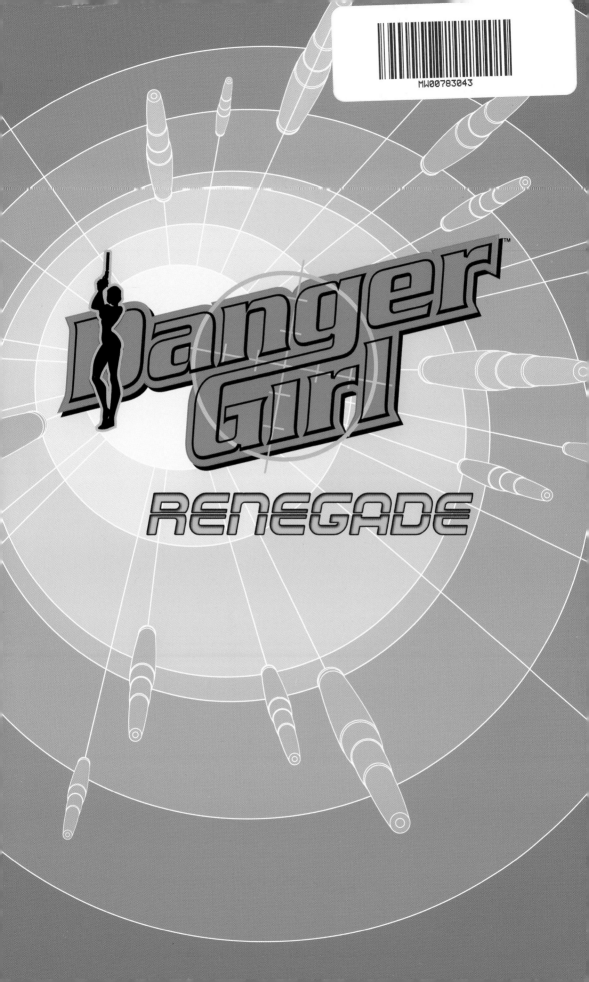

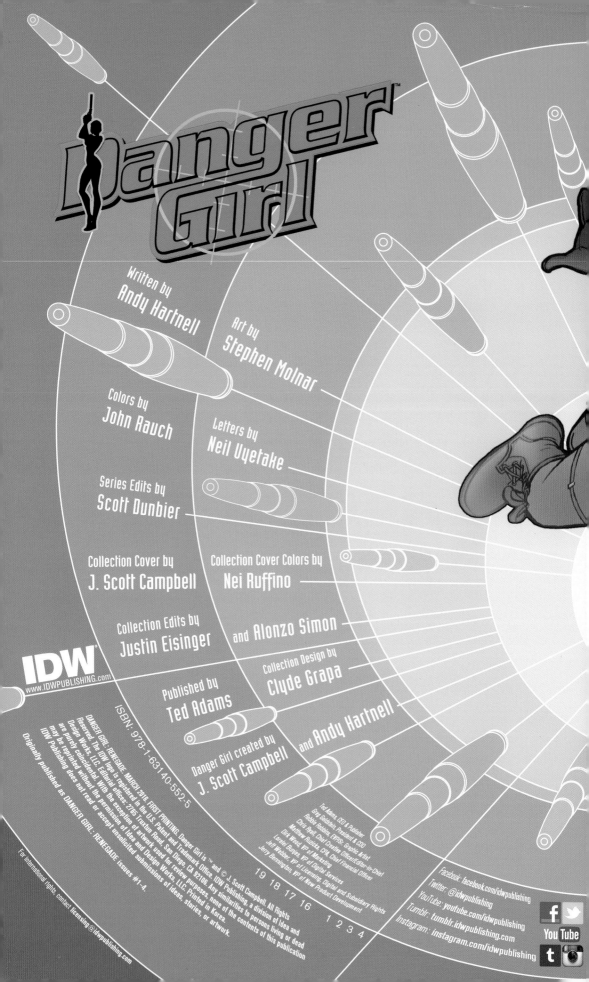

Danger Girl™

Written by
Andy Hartnell

Art by
Stephen Molnar

Colors by
John Rauch

Letters by
Neil Uyetake

Series Edits by
Scott Dunbier

Collection Cover by
J. Scott Campbell

Collection Cover Colors by
Nei Ruffino

Collection Edits by
Justin Eisinger
and Alonzo Simon

Collection Design by
Clyde Grapa

Published by
Ted Adams

Danger Girl created by
J. Scott Campbell
and Andy Hartnell

IDW®
www.IDWPUBLISHING.com

ISBN: 978-1-63140-552-5

19 18 17 16   1 2 3 4

Ted Adams, CEO & Publisher
Greg Goldstein, President & COO
Robbie Robbins, EVP/Sr. Graphic Artist
Chris Ryall, Chief Creative Officer/Editor-in-Chief
Matthew Ruzicka, CPA, Chief Financial Officer
Dirk Wood, VP of Marketing
Lorelei Bunjes, VP of Digital Services
Jeff Webber, VP of Licensing, Digital and Subsidiary Rights
Jerry Bennington, VP of New Product Development

Facebook: facebook.com/idwpublishing
Twitter: @idwpublishing
YouTube: youtube.com/idwpublishing
Tumblr: tumblr.idwpublishing.com
Instagram: instagram.com/idwpublishing

Originally published as DANGER GIRL: RENEGADE issues #1-4.

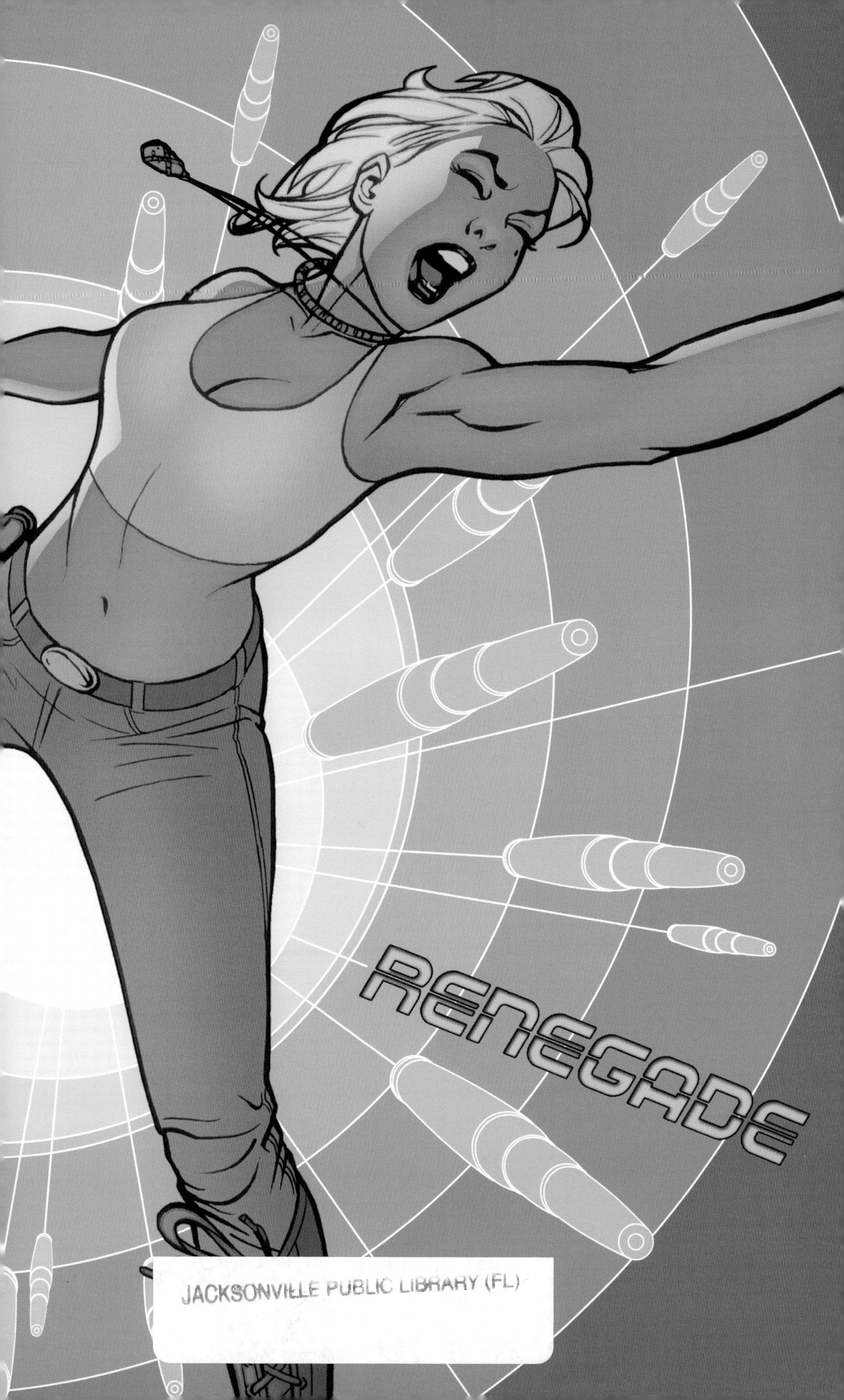
RENEGADE

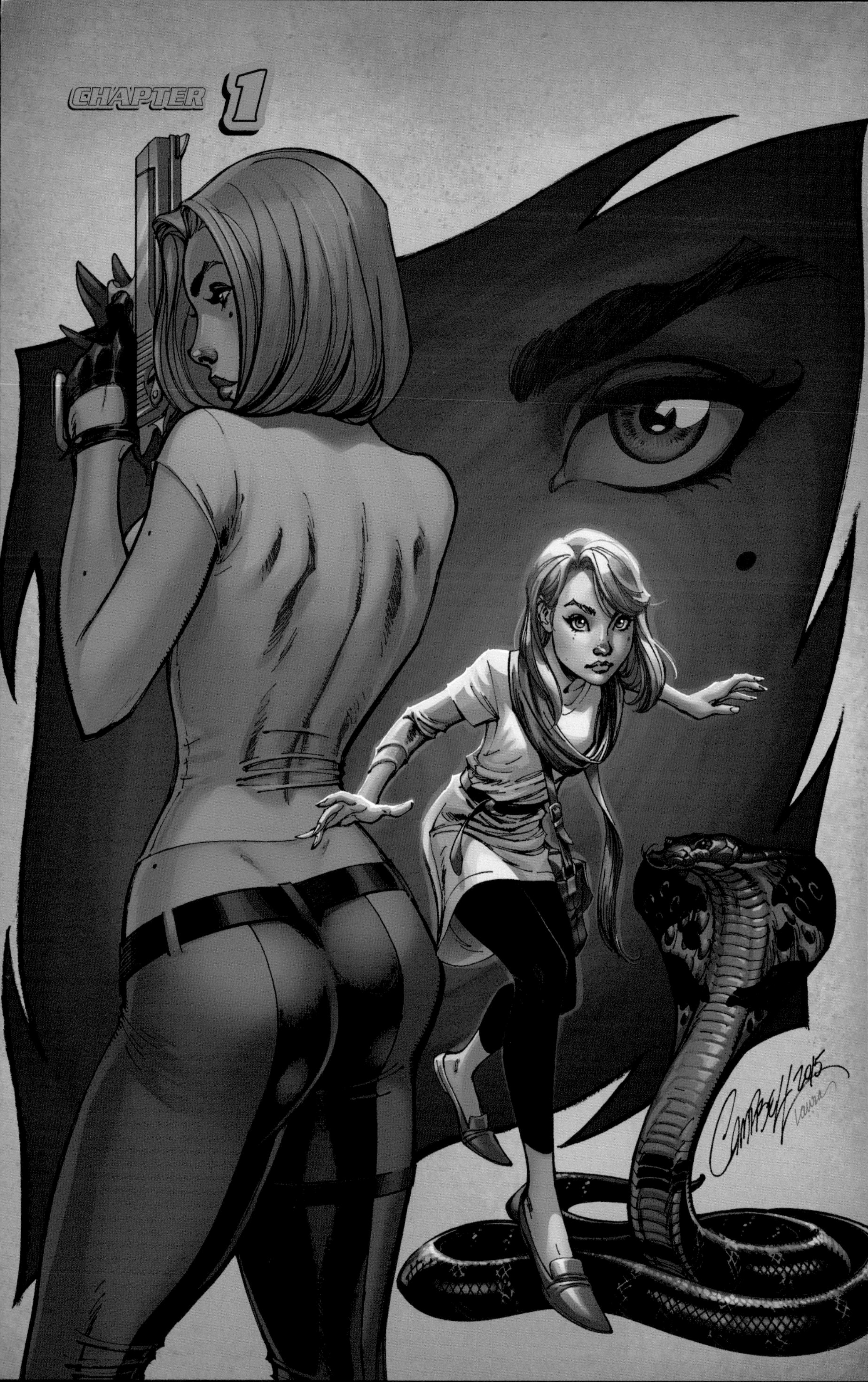
CHAPTER 1

Art by J. Scott Campbell • Colors by Laura Martin

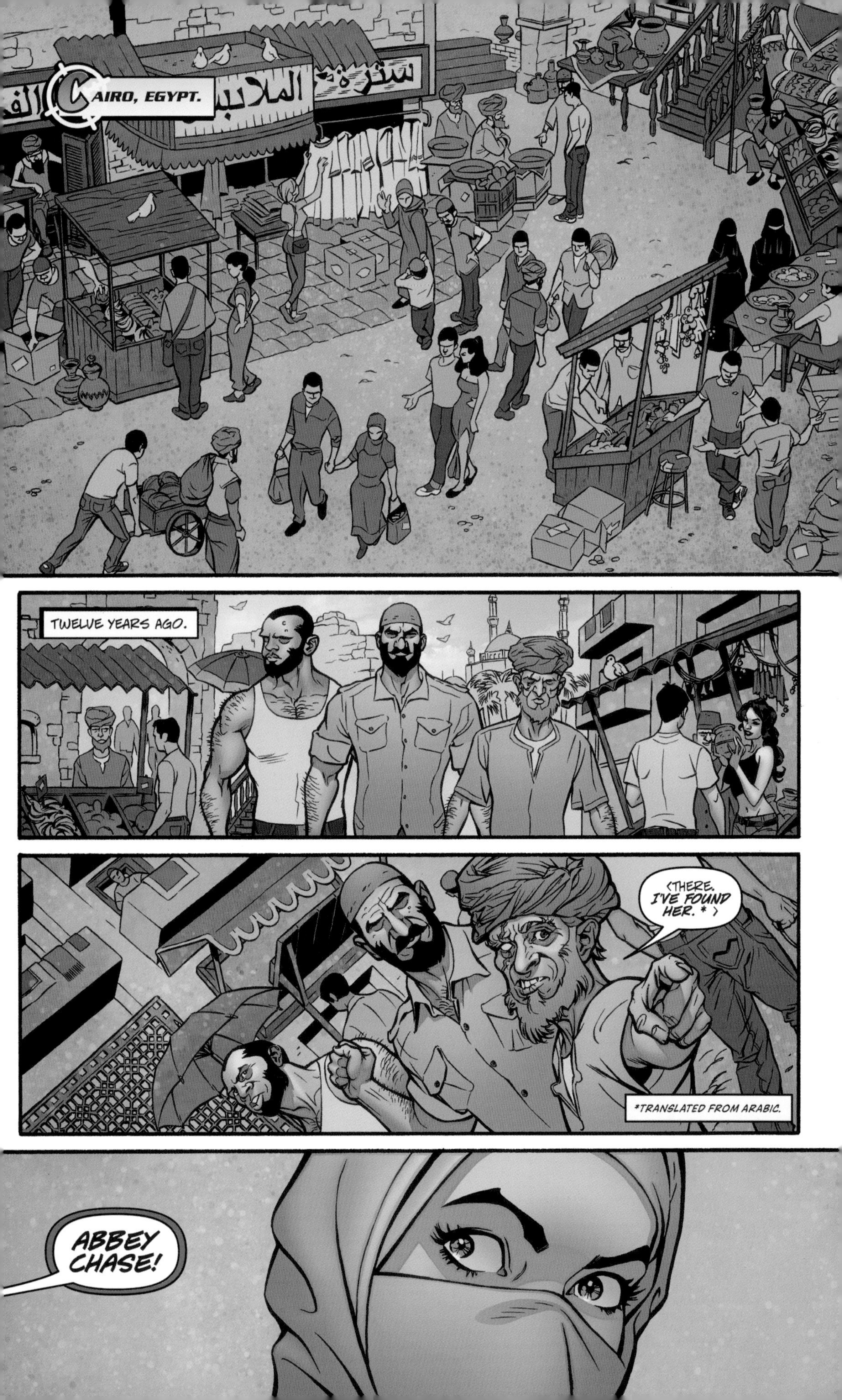
CAIRO, EGYPT.
TWELVE YEARS AGO.
<THERE. I'VE FOUND HER. * >
*TRANSLATED FROM ARABIC.
ABBEY CHASE!

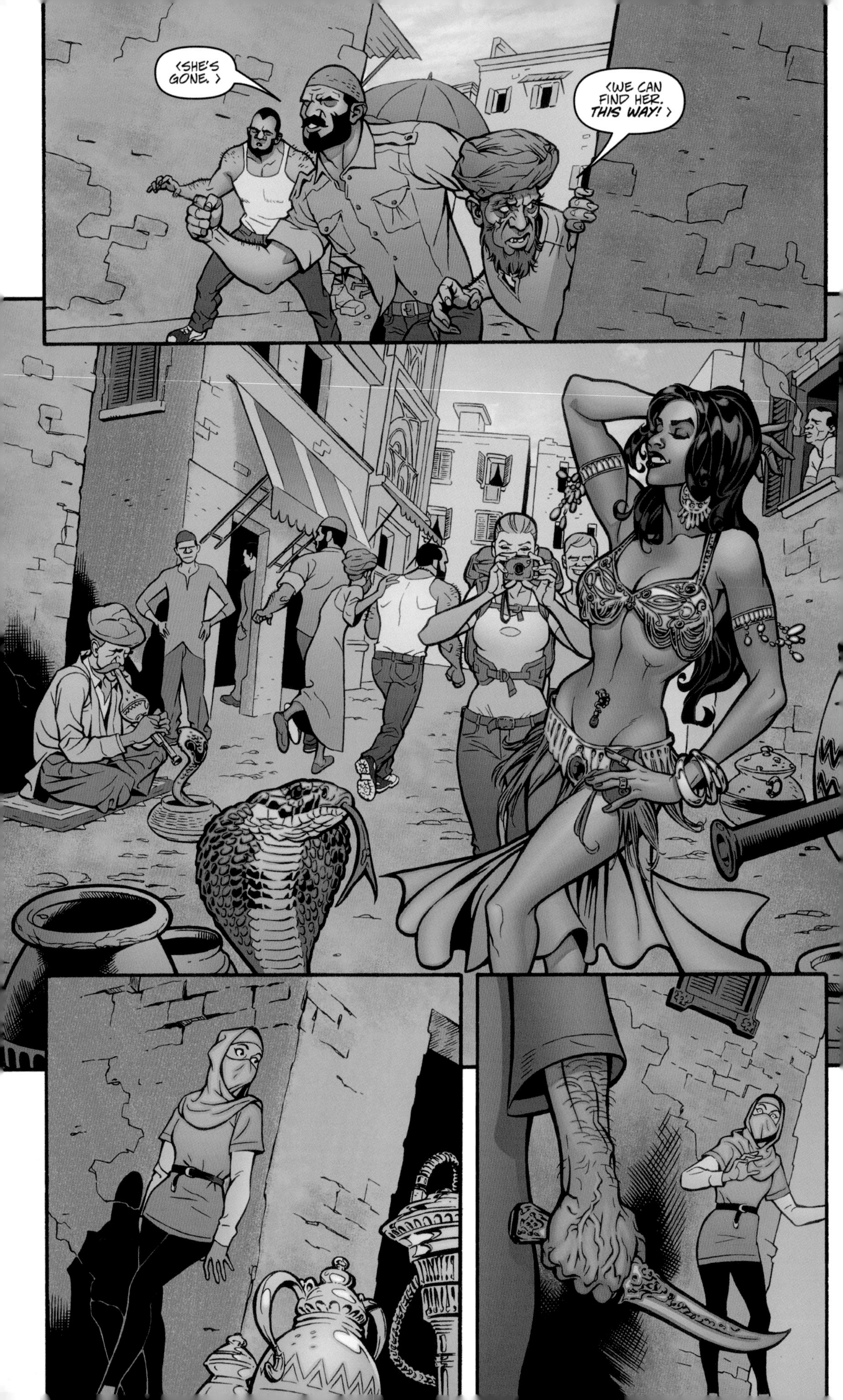
<SHE'S GONE.>
<WE CAN FIND HER. THIS WAY!>

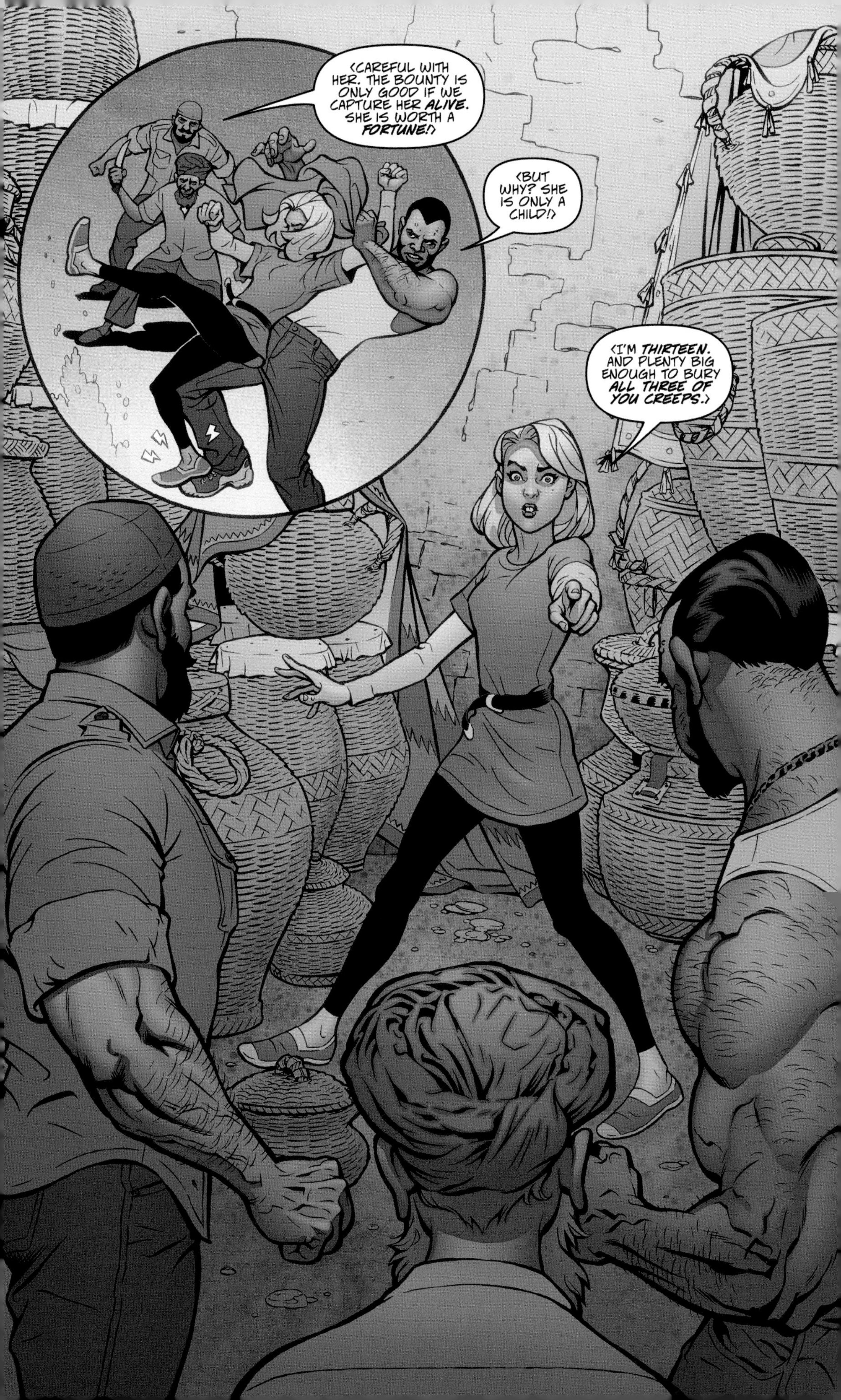
<CAREFUL WITH HER. THE BOUNTY IS ONLY GOOD IF WE CAPTURE HER **ALIVE**. SHE IS WORTH A **FORTUNE**!>
<BUT WHY? SHE IS ONLY A CHILD!>
<I'M **THIRTEEN**. AND PLENTY BIG ENOUGH TO BURY **ALL THREE OF YOU CREEPS**.>

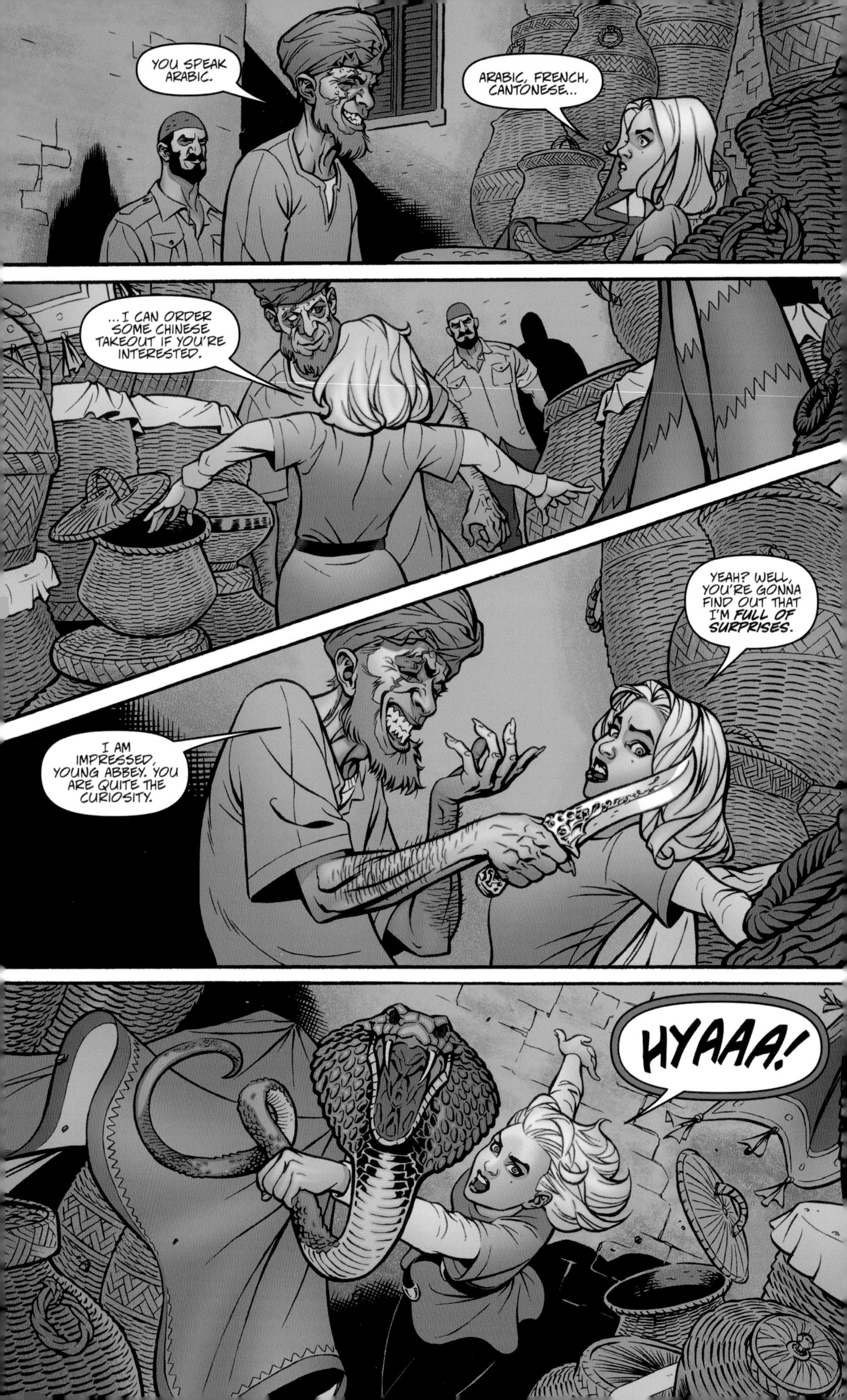
YOU SPEAK ARABIC.
ARABIC, FRENCH, CANTONESE...
...I CAN ORDER SOME CHINESE TAKEOUT IF YOU'RE INTERESTED.
I AM IMPRESSED, YOUNG ABBEY. YOU ARE QUITE THE CURIOSITY.
YEAH? WELL, YOU'RE GONNA FIND OUT THAT I'M FULL OF SURPRISES.
HYAAA!

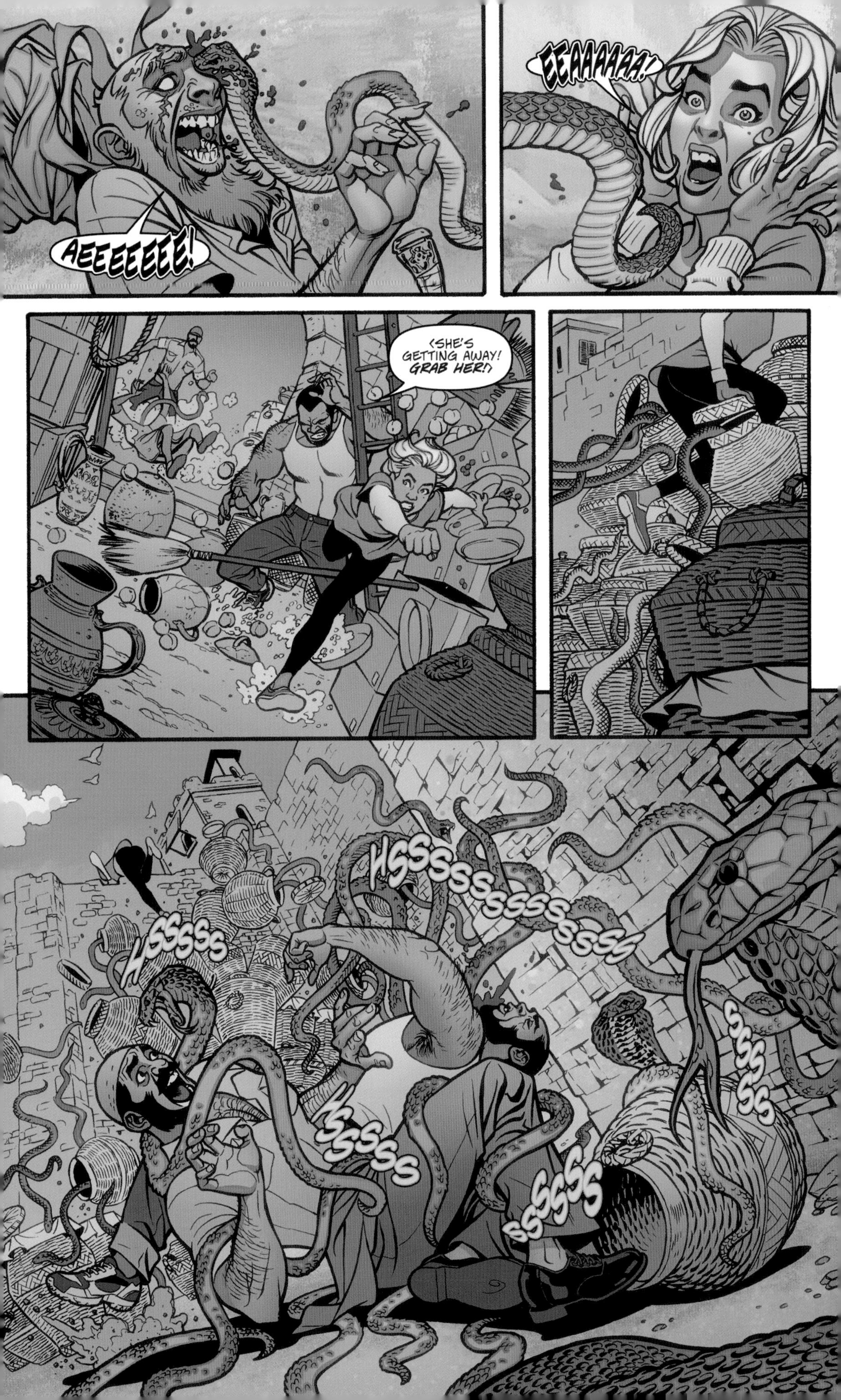
AEEEEEEE!
EEAAAAAA!
‹SHE'S GETTING AWAY! GRAB HER!›
HSSSSSSSSSSSSSSS
HSSSSS
SSSSSS
HSSSSS
SSSSSS

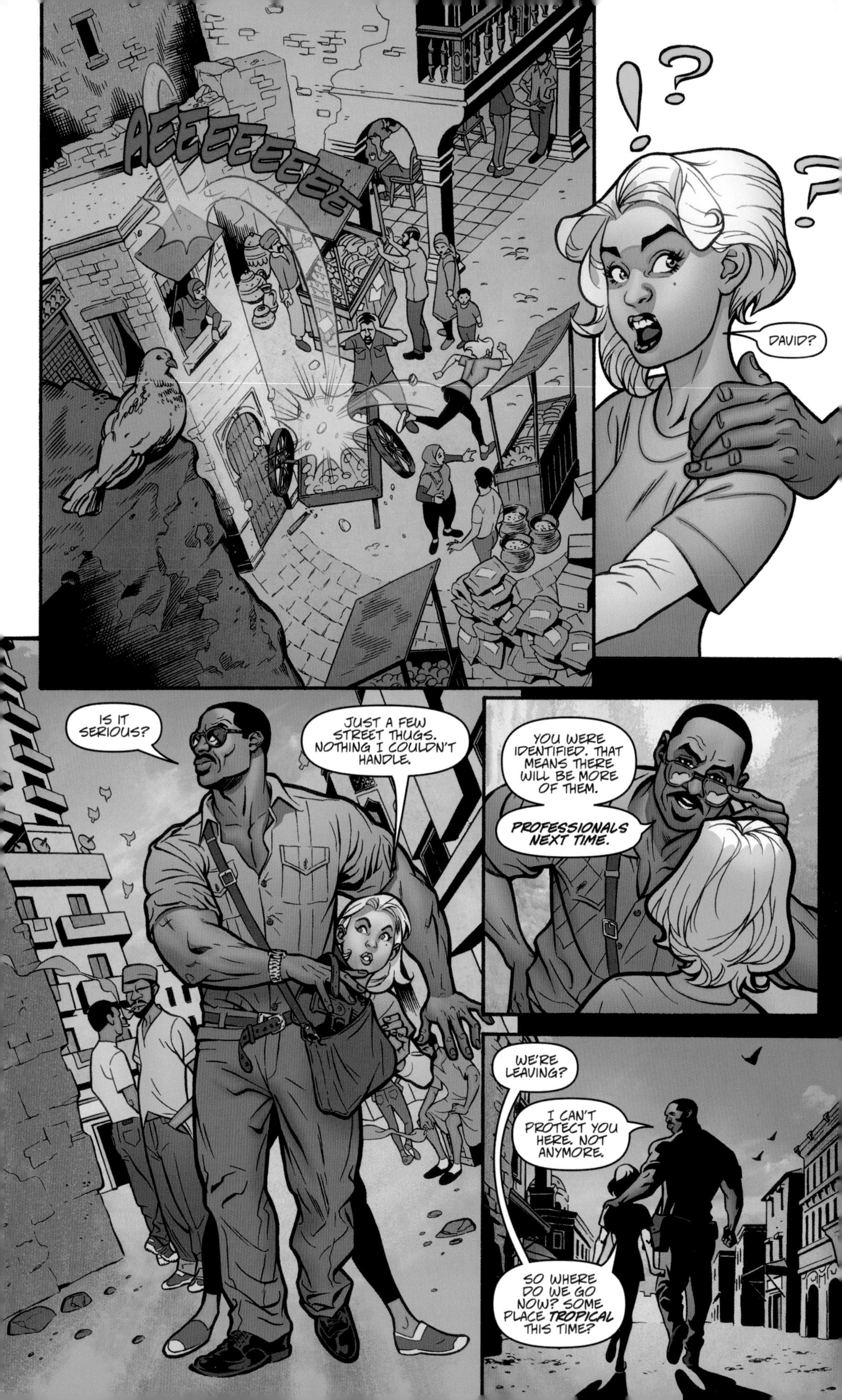
AEEEEEEEEE
!??
DAVID?
IS IT SERIOUS?
JUST A FEW STREET THUGS. NOTHING I COULDN'T HANDLE.
YOU WERE IDENTIFIED. THAT MEANS THERE WILL BE MORE OF THEM.
PROFESSIONALS NEXT TIME.
WE'RE LEAVING?
I CAN'T PROTECT YOU HERE. NOT ANYMORE.
SO WHERE DO WE GO NOW? SOME PLACE TROPICAL THIS TIME?

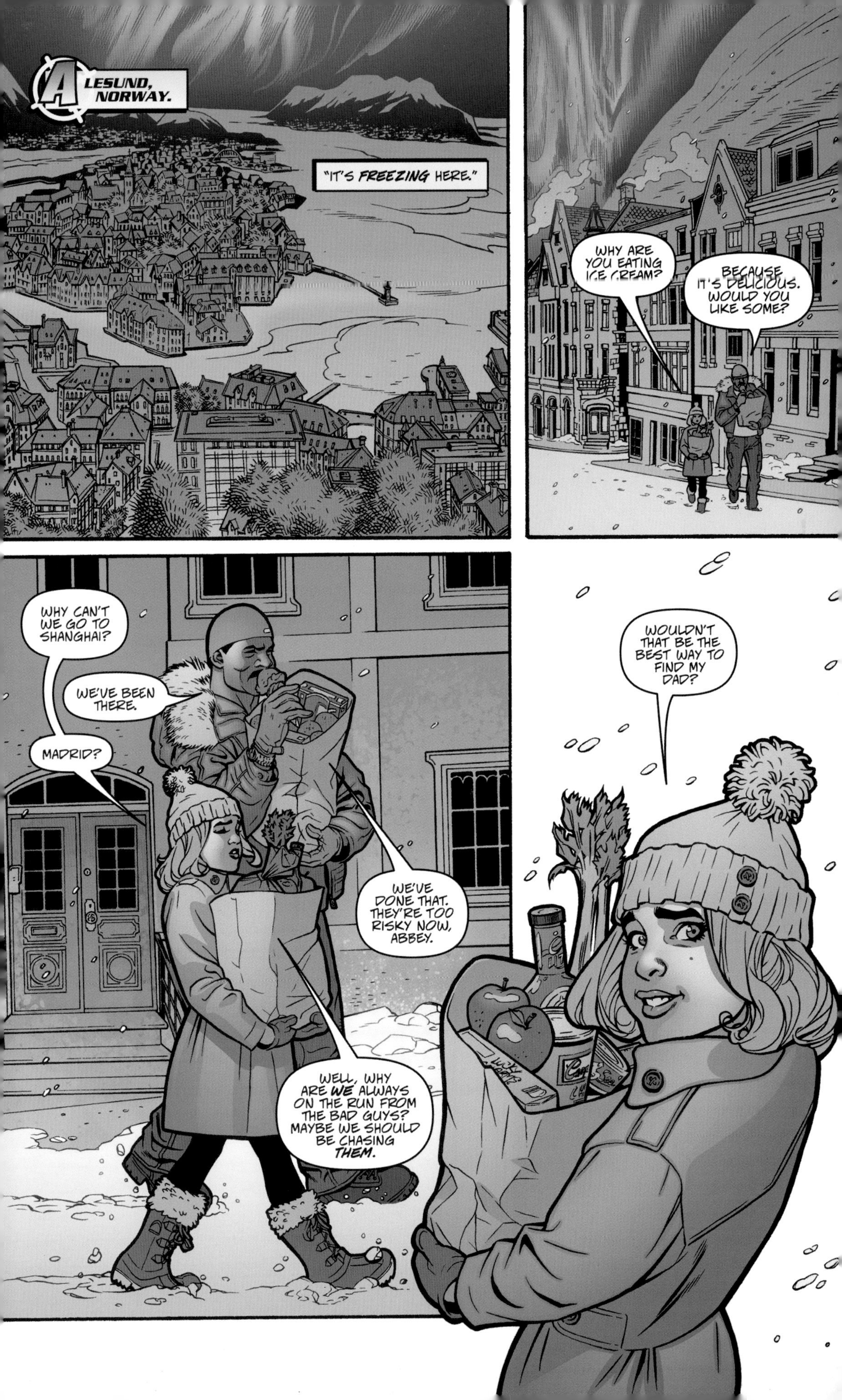

ALESUND, NORWAY.
"IT'S FREEZING HERE."
WHY ARE YOU EATING ICE CREAM?
BECAUSE IT'S DELICIOUS. WOULD YOU LIKE SOME?
WHY CAN'T WE GO TO SHANGHAI?
WE'VE BEEN THERE.
MADRID?
WE'VE DONE THAT. THEY'RE TOO RISKY NOW, ABBEY.
WELL, WHY ARE WE ALWAYS ON THE RUN FROM THE BAD GUYS? MAYBE WE SHOULD BE CHASING THEM.
WOULDN'T THAT BE THE BEST WAY TO FIND MY DAD?

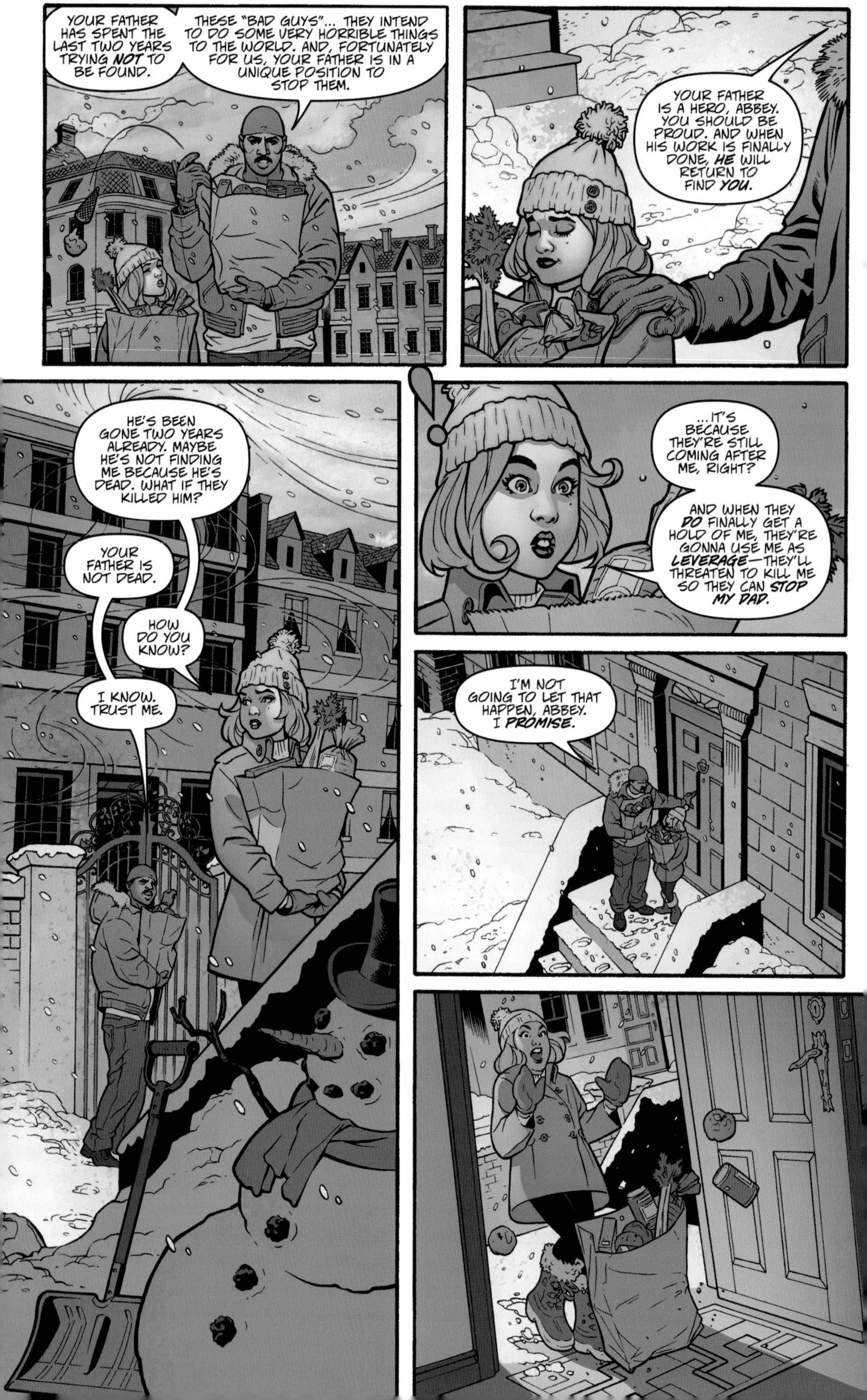
YOUR FATHER HAS SPENT THE LAST TWO YEARS TRYING NOT TO BE FOUND.
THESE "BAD GUYS"... THEY INTEND TO DO SOME VERY HORRIBLE THINGS TO THE WORLD. AND, FORTUNATELY FOR US, YOUR FATHER IS IN A UNIQUE POSITION TO STOP THEM.
YOUR FATHER IS A HERO, ABBEY. YOU SHOULD BE PROUD. AND WHEN HIS WORK IS FINALLY DONE, HE WILL RETURN TO FIND YOU.
HE'S BEEN GONE TWO YEARS ALREADY. MAYBE HE'S NOT FINDING ME BECAUSE HE'S DEAD. WHAT IF THEY KILLED HIM?
YOUR FATHER IS NOT DEAD.
HOW DO YOU KNOW?
I KNOW. TRUST ME.
!
...IT'S BECAUSE THEY'RE STILL COMING AFTER ME, RIGHT?
AND WHEN THEY DO FINALLY GET A HOLD OF ME, THEY'RE GONNA USE ME AS LEVERAGE—THEY'LL THREATEN TO KILL ME SO THEY CAN STOP MY DAD.
I'M NOT GOING TO LET THAT HAPPEN, ABBEY. I PROMISE.

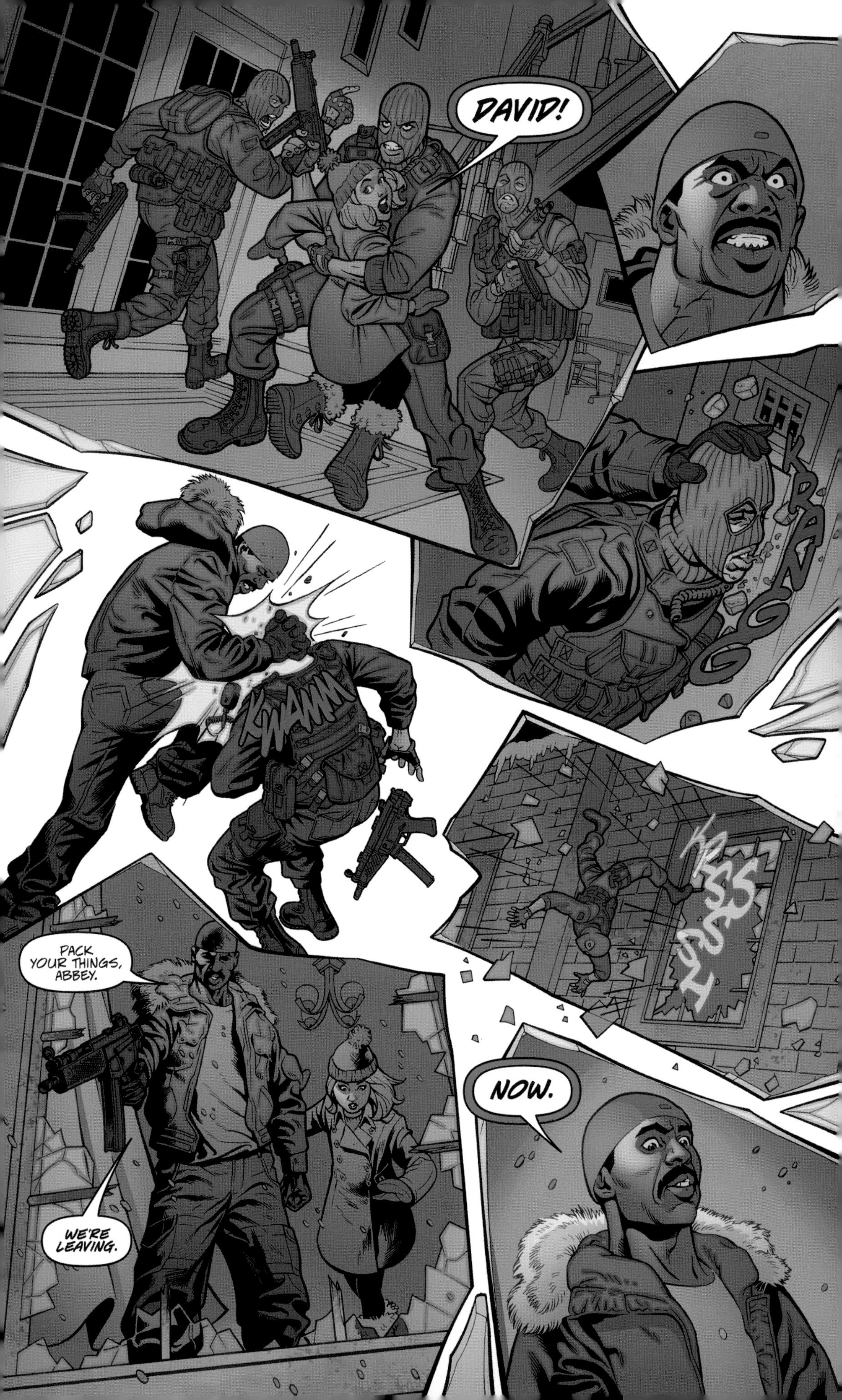
DAVID!
KWAMM
VRANGG
KRSSSH
PACK YOUR THINGS, ABBEY.
WE'RE LEAVING.
NOW.

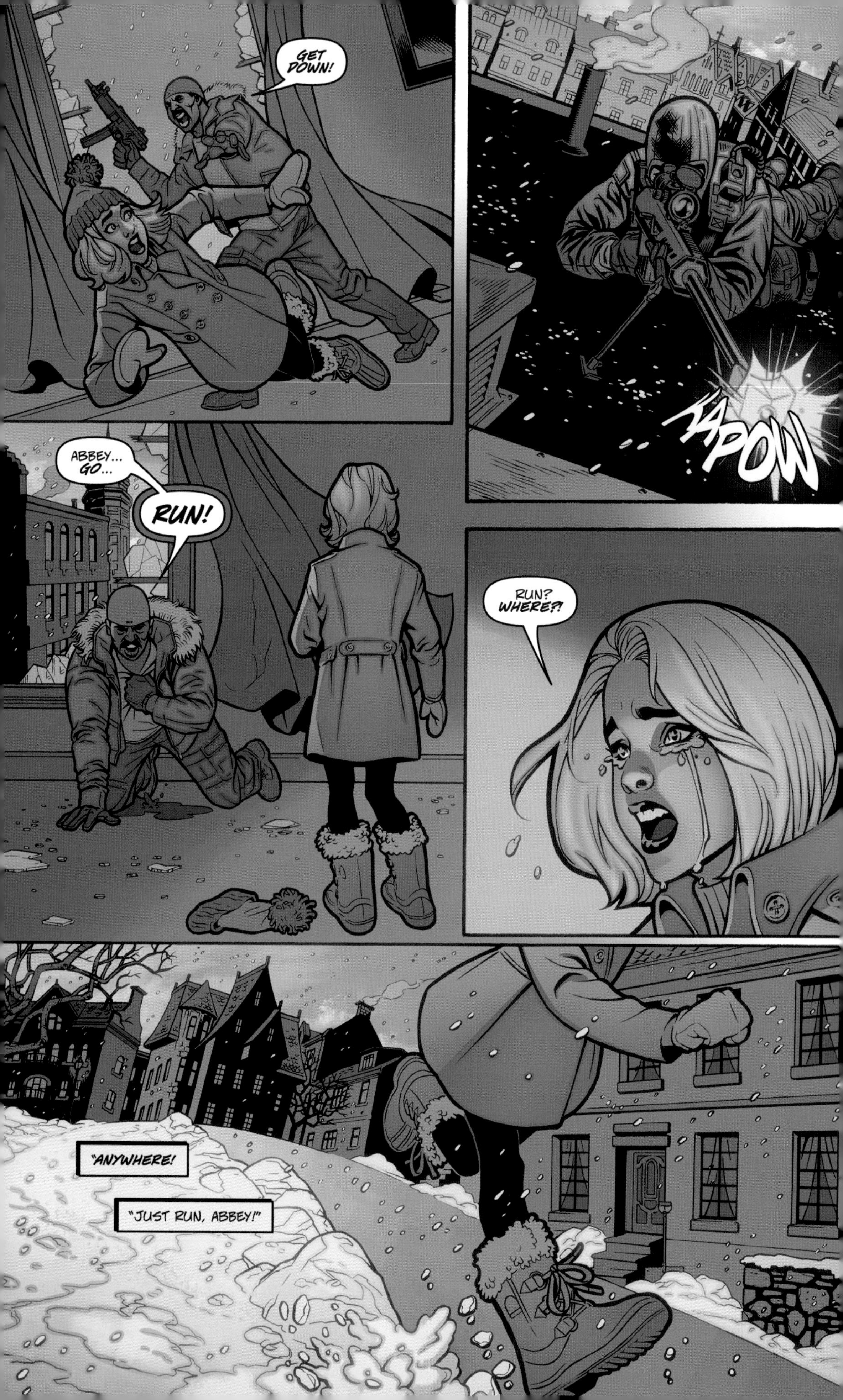
GET DOWN!
KAPOW
ABBEY... GO...
RUN!
RUN? WHERE?!
"ANYWHERE!
"JUST RUN, ABBEY!"

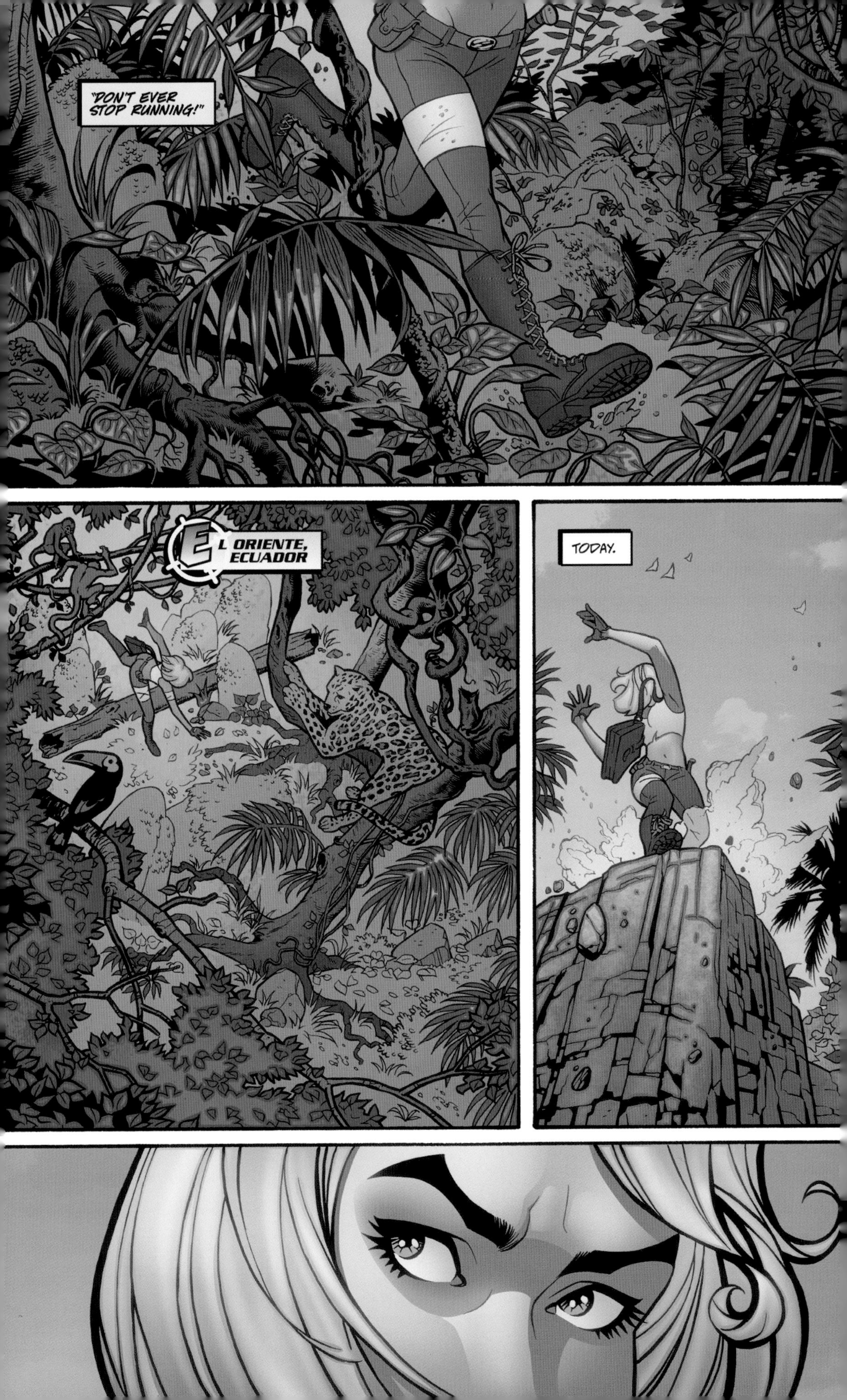
"DON'T EVER STOP RUNNING!"
EL ORIENTE, ECUADOR
TODAY.

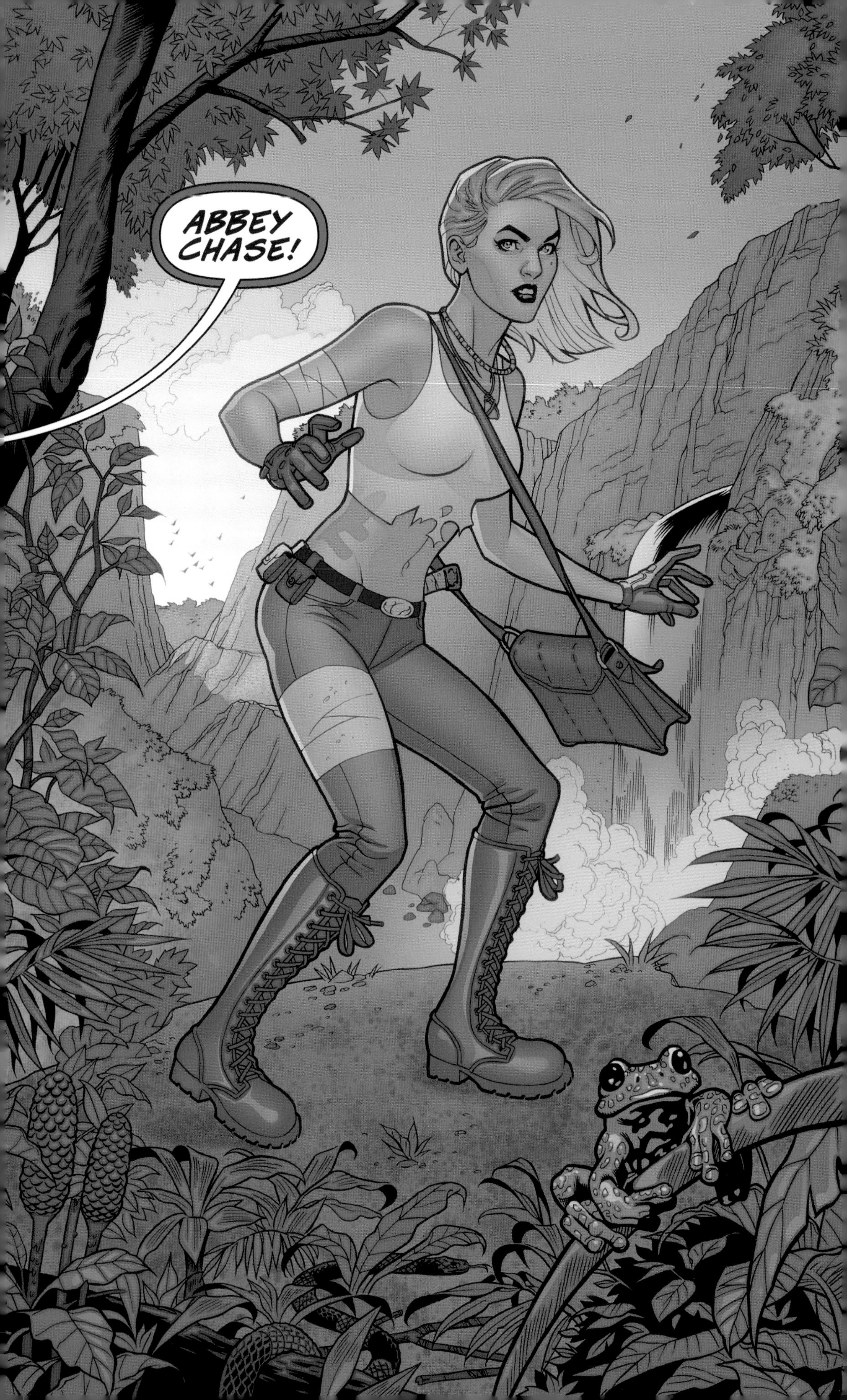
ABBEY CHASE!

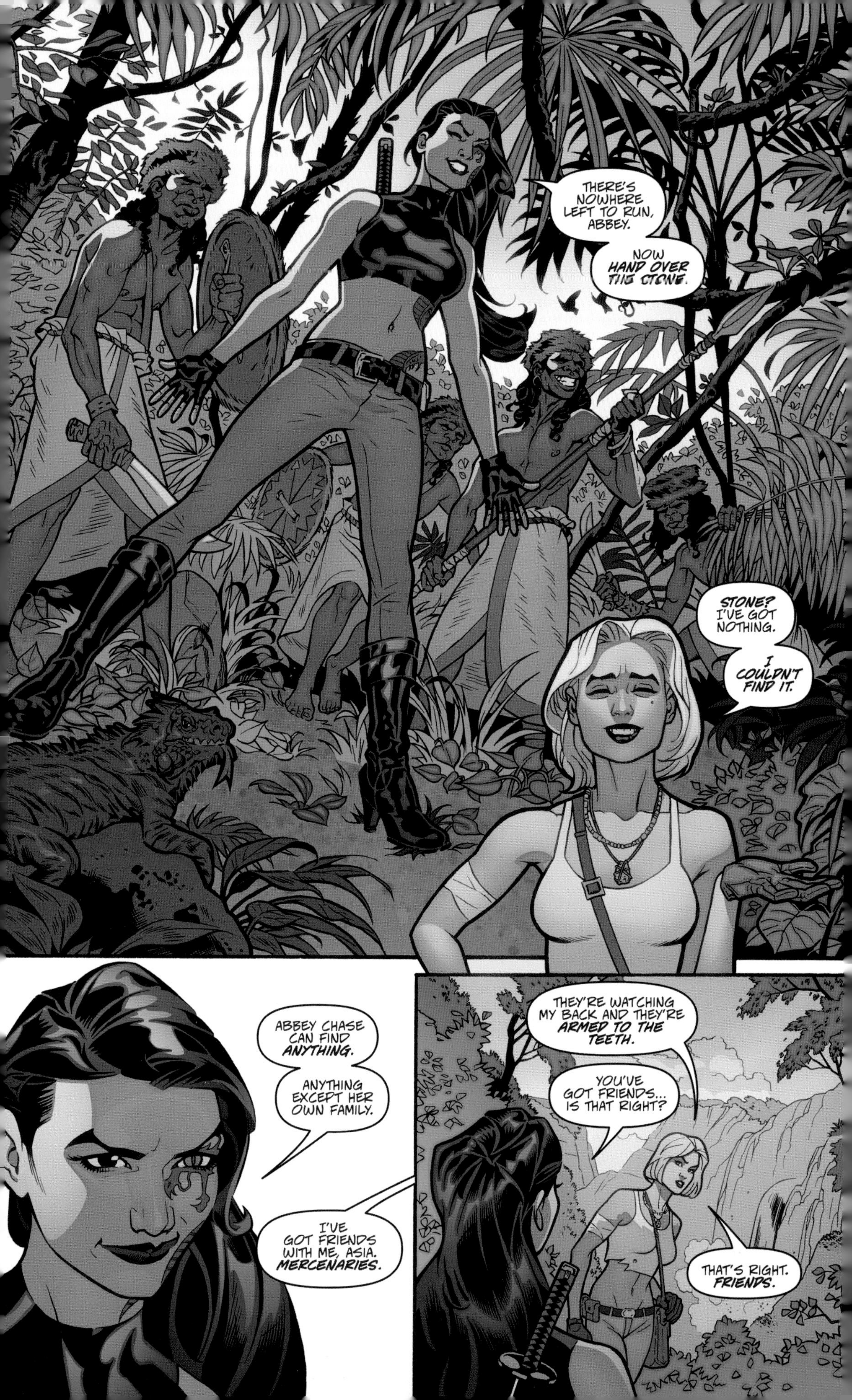

THERE'S NOWHERE LEFT TO RUN, ABBEY.
NOW HAND OVER THE STONE.
STONE? I'VE GOT NOTHING.
I COULDN'T FIND IT.
ABBEY CHASE CAN FIND ANYTHING.
ANYTHING EXCEPT HER OWN FAMILY.
I'VE GOT FRIENDS WITH ME, ASIA. MERCENARIES.
THEY'RE WATCHING MY BACK AND THEY'RE ARMED TO THE TEETH.
YOU'VE GOT FRIENDS... IS THAT RIGHT?
THAT'S RIGHT. FRIENDS.

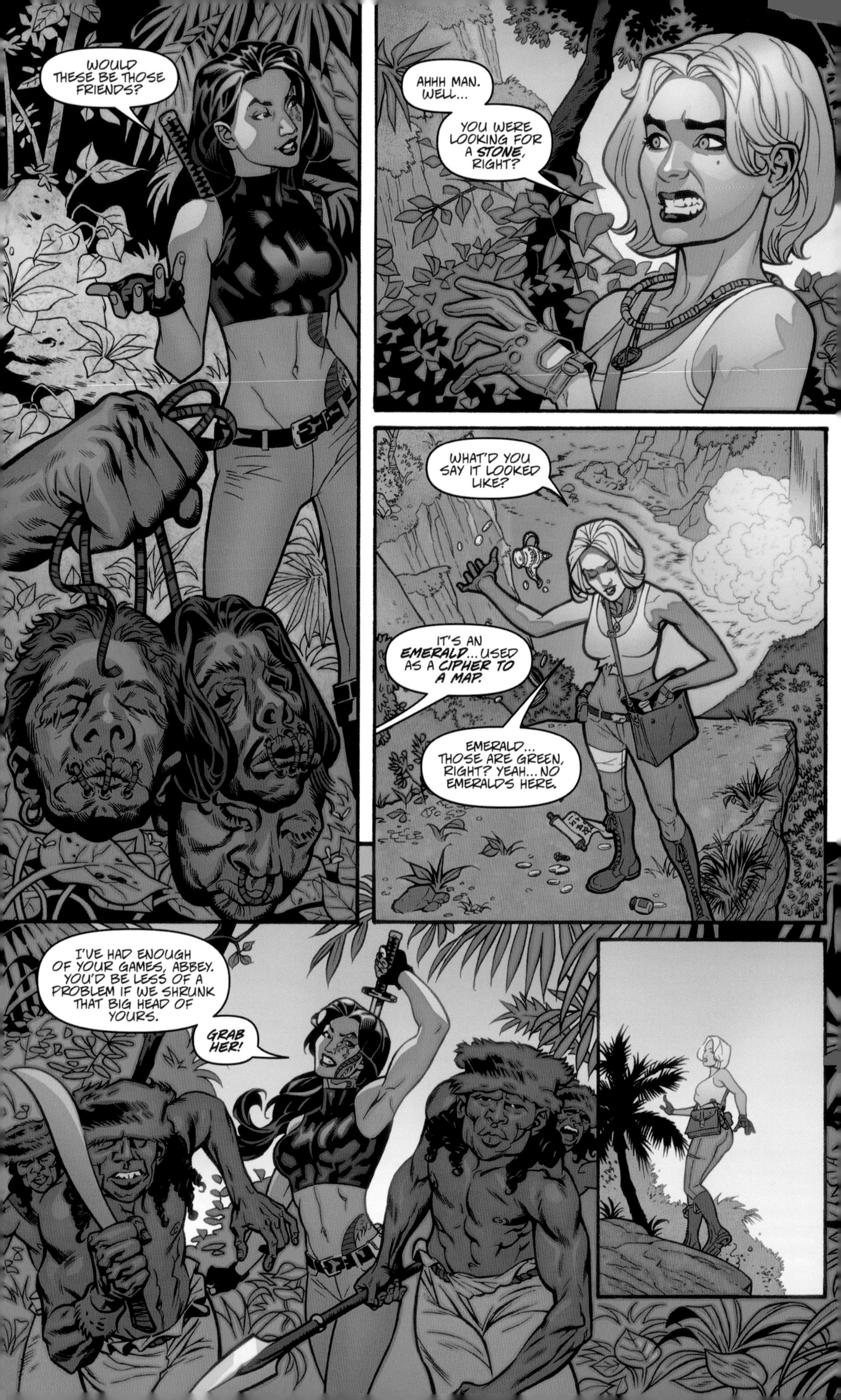
WOULD THESE BE THOSE FRIENDS?
AHHH MAN. WELL...
YOU WERE LOOKING FOR A STONE, RIGHT?
WHAT'D YOU SAY IT LOOKED LIKE?
IT'S AN EMERALD... USED AS A CIPHER TO A MAP.
EMERALD... THOSE ARE GREEN, RIGHT? YEAH... NO EMERALDS HERE.
I'VE HAD ENOUGH OF YOUR GAMES, ABBEY. YOU'D BE LESS OF A PROBLEM IF WE SHRUNK THAT BIG HEAD OF YOURS.
GRAB HER!

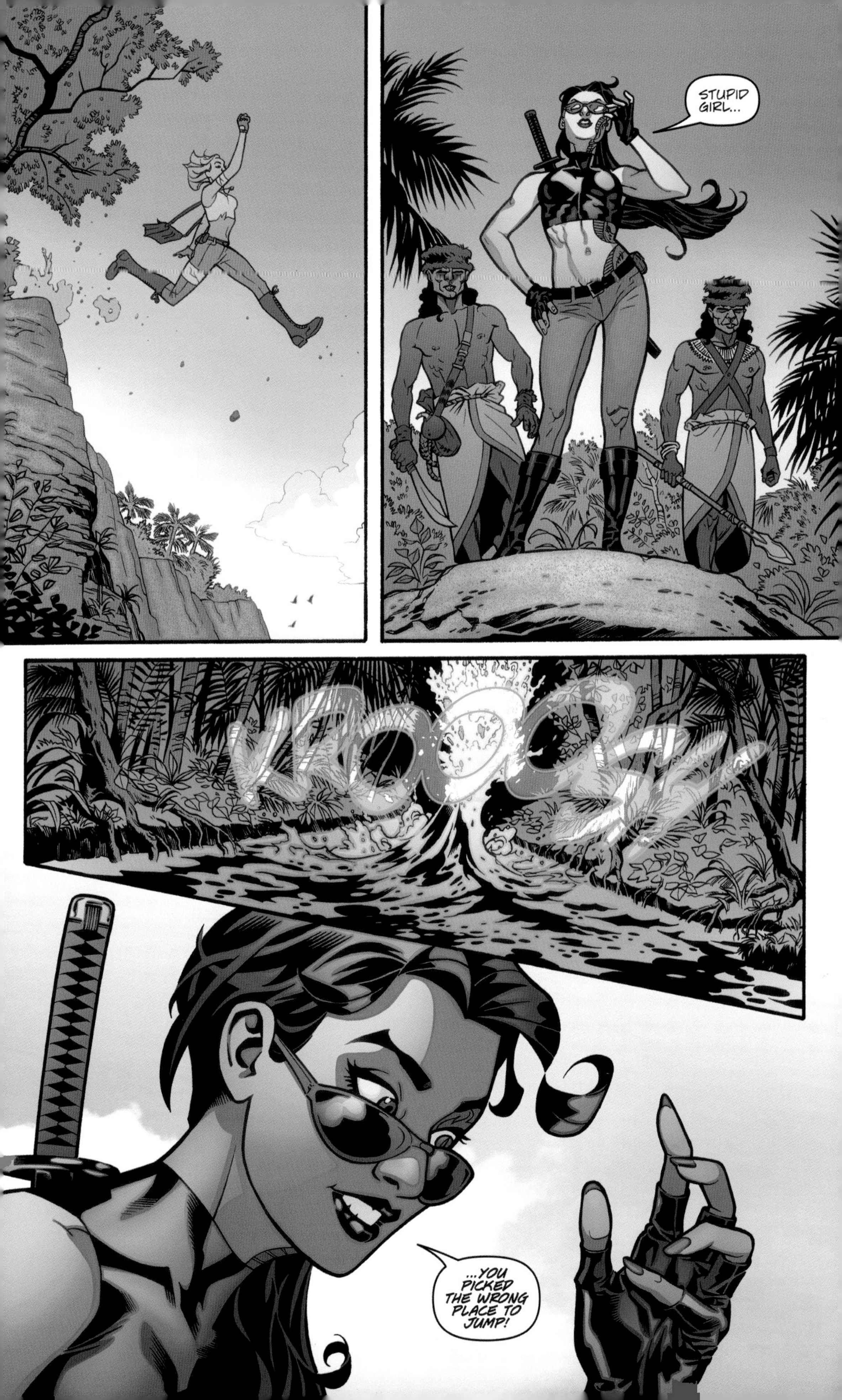
STUPID GIRL...
...YOU PICKED THE WRONG PLACE TO JUMP!

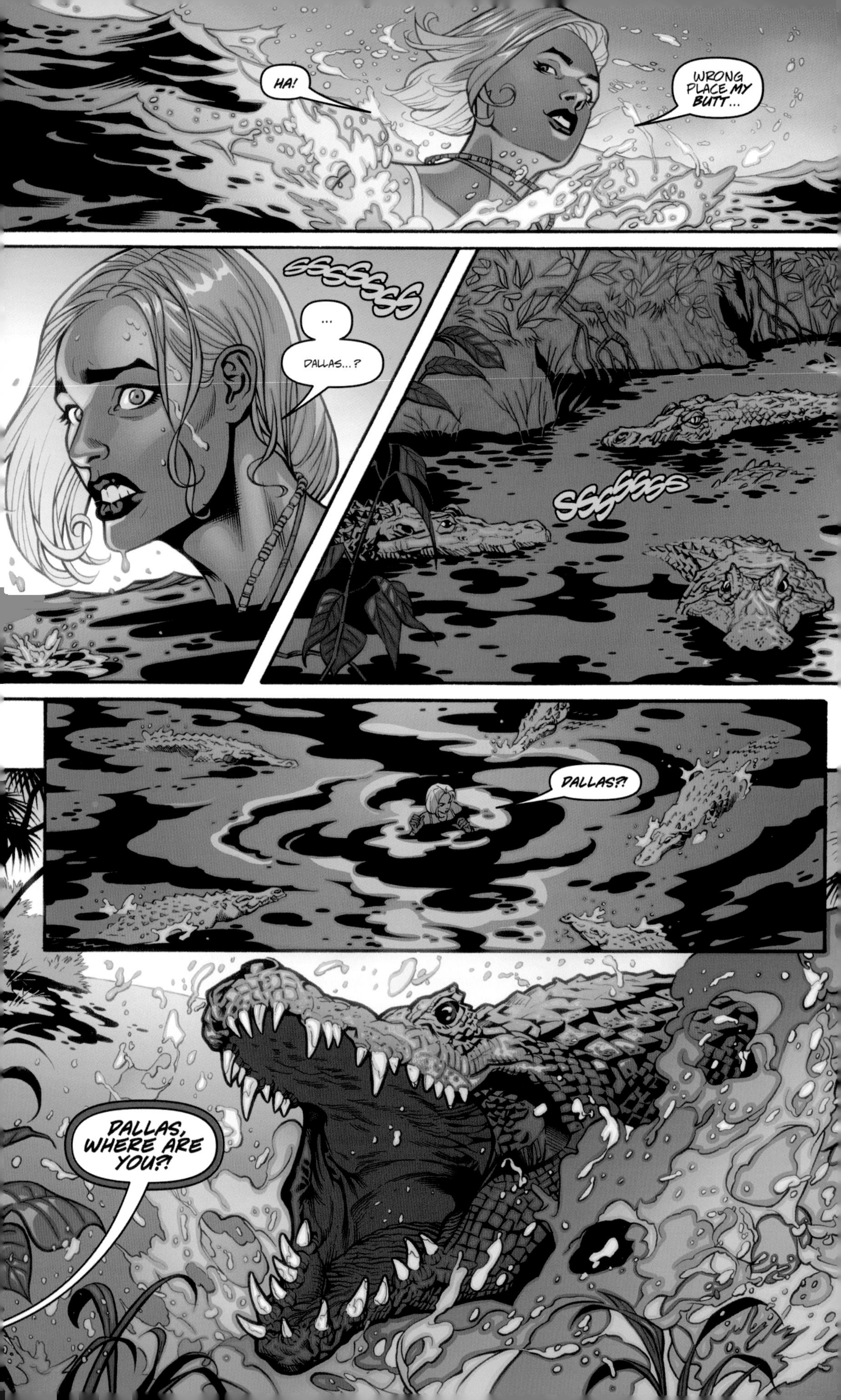
HA!
WRONG PLACE MY BUTT...
SSSSSSS
...
DALLAS...?
SSSSSSS
DALLAS?!
DALLAS, WHERE ARE YOU?!

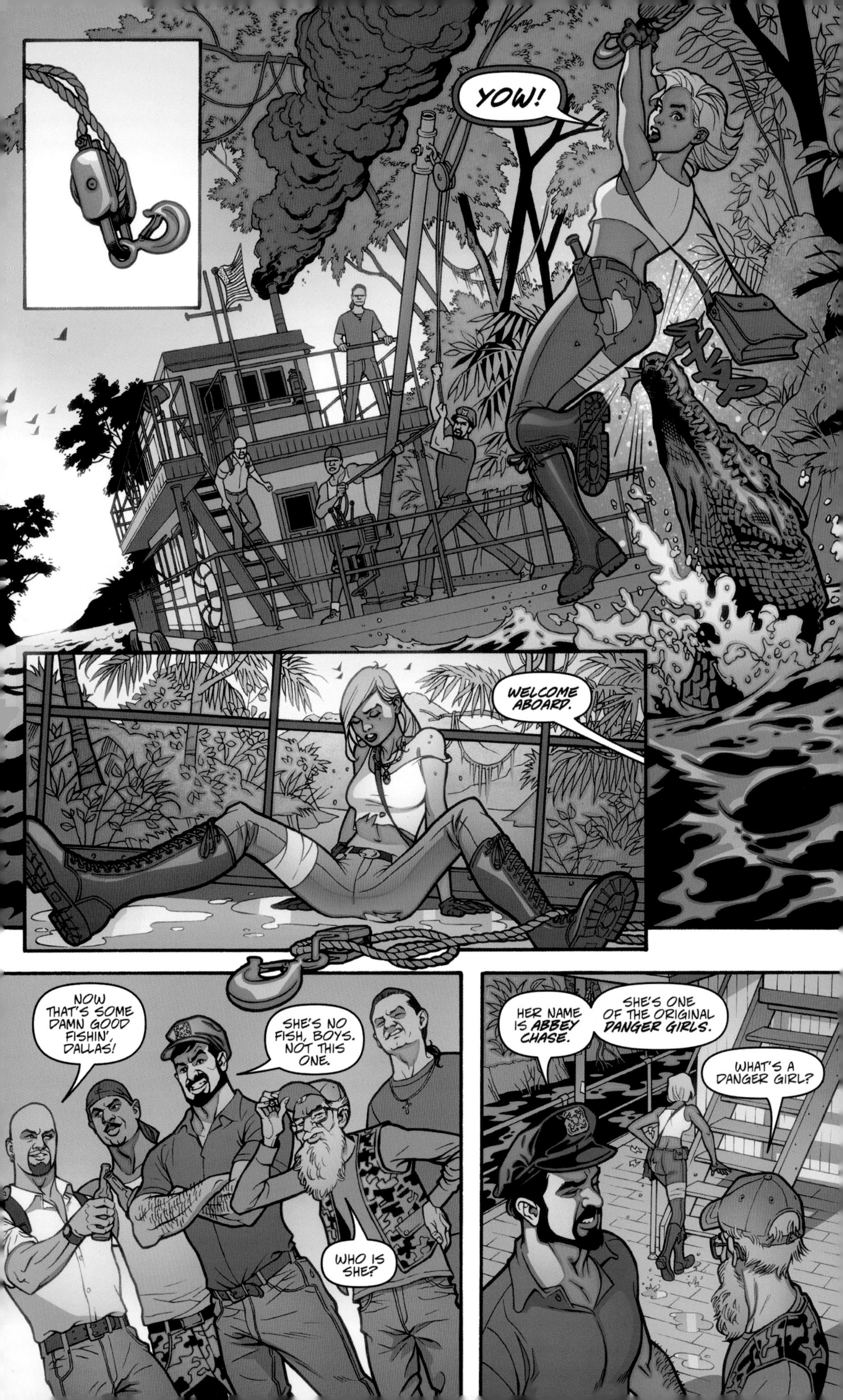
YOW!
SNAP
WELCOME ABOARD.
NOW THAT'S SOME DAMN GOOD FISHIN', DALLAS!
SHE'S NO FISH, BOYS. NOT THIS ONE.
WHO IS SHE?
HER NAME IS ABBEY CHASE.
SHE'S ONE OF THE ORIGINAL DANGER GIRLS.
WHAT'S A DANGER GIRL?

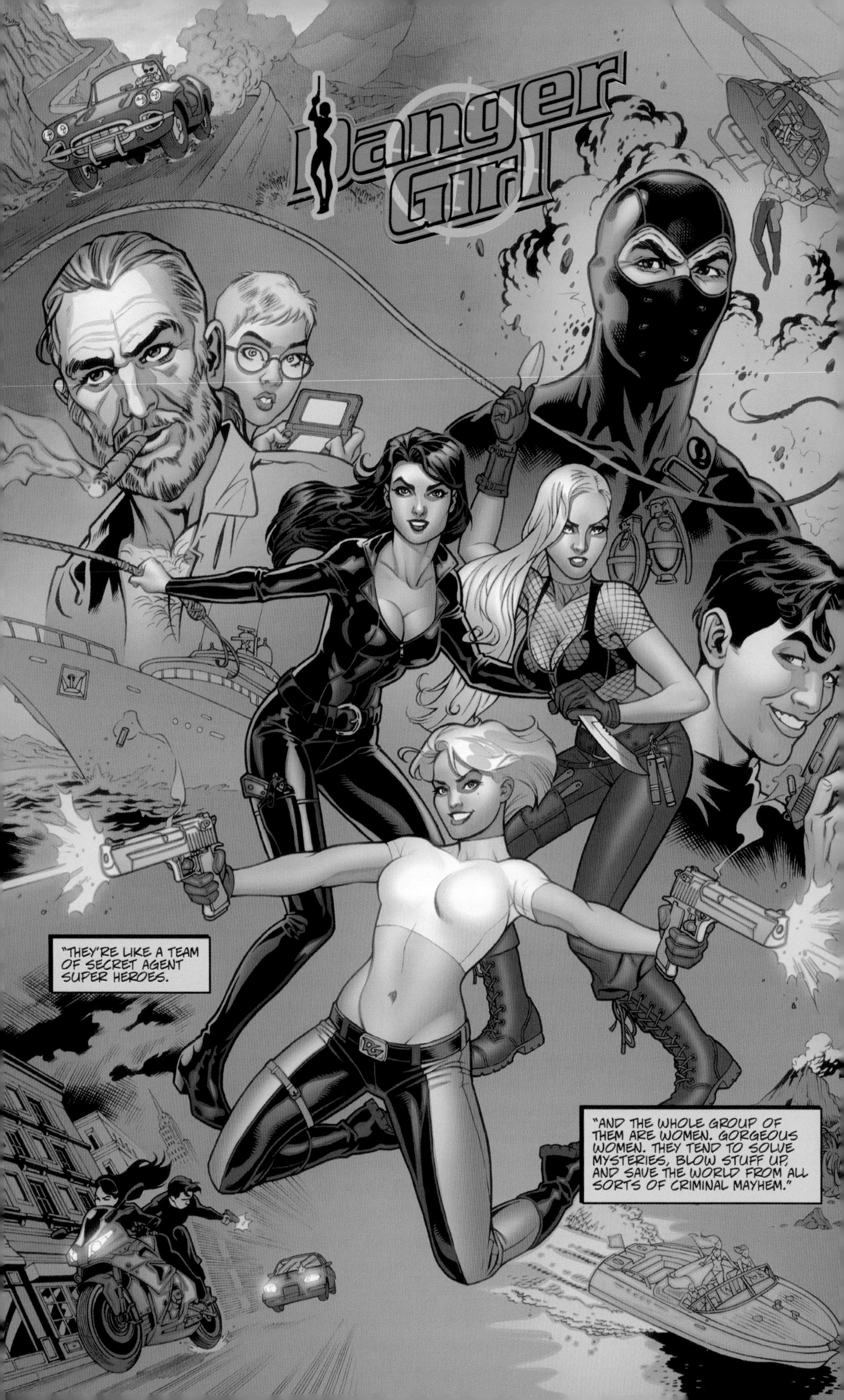
Danger Girl
"THEY'RE LIKE A TEAM OF SECRET AGENT SUPER HEROES.
"AND THE WHOLE GROUP OF THEM ARE WOMEN. GORGEOUS WOMEN. THEY TEND TO SOLVE MYSTERIES, BLOW STUFF UP, AND SAVE THE WORLD FROM ALL SORTS OF CRIMINAL MAYHEM."

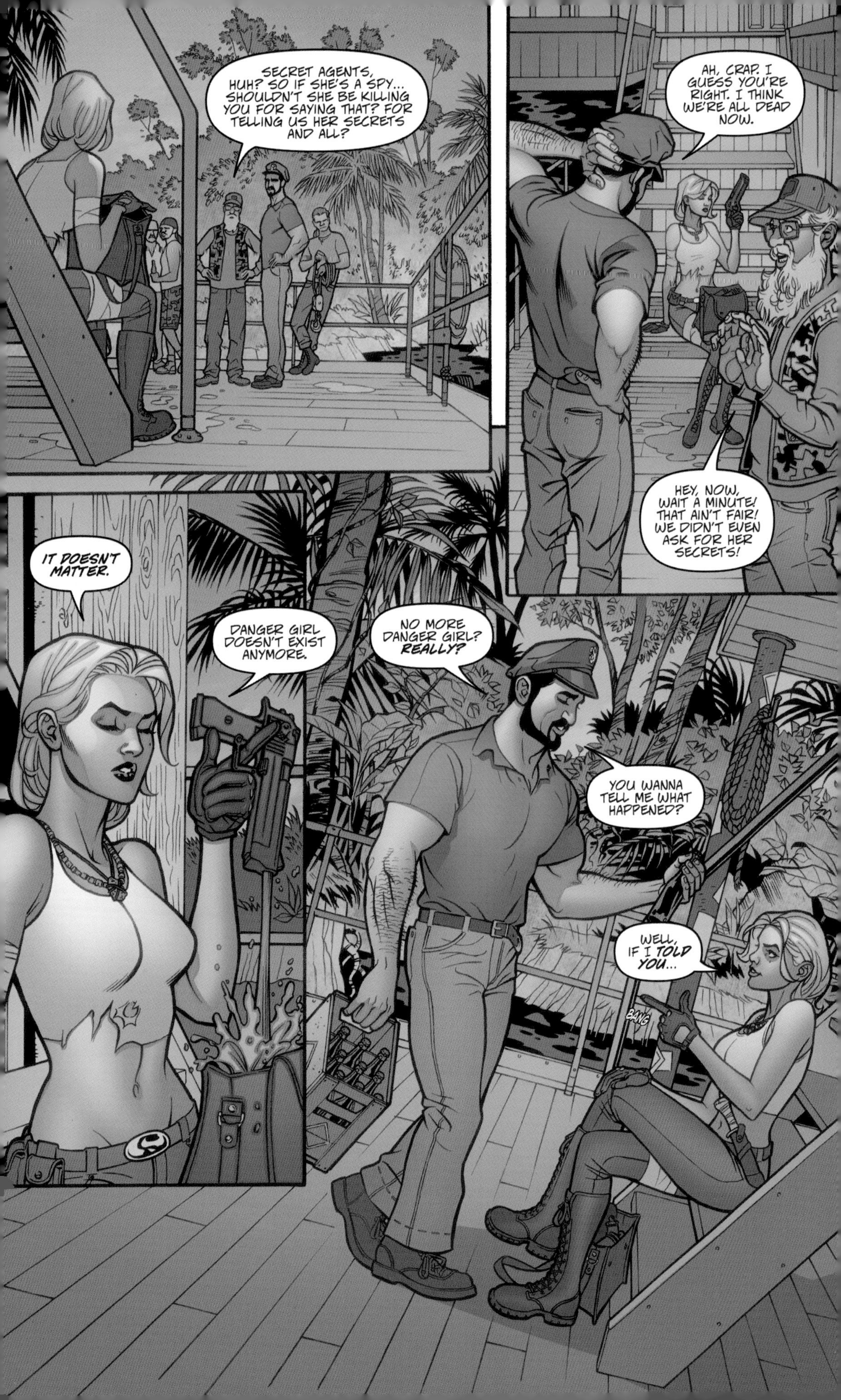
SECRET AGENTS, HUH? SO IF SHE'S A SPY... SHOULDN'T SHE BE KILLING YOU FOR SAYING THAT? FOR TELLING US HER SECRETS AND ALL?
AH, CRAP. I GUESS YOU'RE RIGHT. I THINK WE'RE ALL DEAD NOW.
HEY, NOW, WAIT A MINUTE! THAT AIN'T FAIR! WE DIDN'T EVEN ASK FOR HER SECRETS!
IT DOESN'T MATTER.
DANGER GIRL DOESN'T EXIST ANYMORE.
NO MORE DANGER GIRL? REALLY?
YOU WANNA TELL ME WHAT HAPPENED?
WELL, IF I TOLD YOU...
BANG

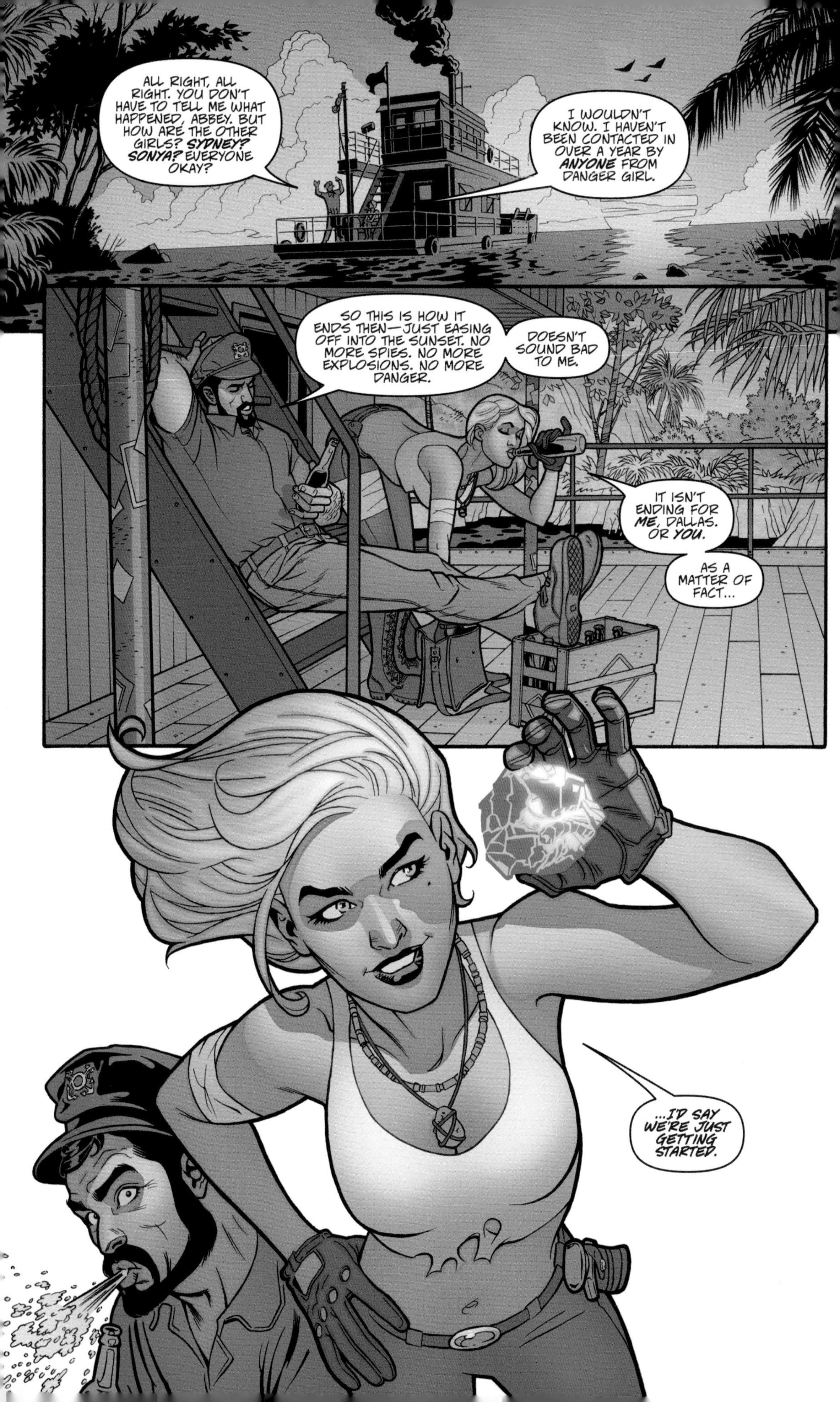
ALL RIGHT, ALL RIGHT. YOU DON'T HAVE TO TELL ME WHAT HAPPENED, ABBEY. BUT HOW ARE THE OTHER GIRLS? SYDNEY? SONYA? EVERYONE OKAY?
I WOULDN'T KNOW. I HAVEN'T BEEN CONTACTED IN OVER A YEAR BY ANYONE FROM DANGER GIRL.
SO THIS IS HOW IT ENDS THEN—JUST EASING OFF INTO THE SUNSET. NO MORE SPIES. NO MORE EXPLOSIONS. NO MORE DANGER.
DOESN'T SOUND BAD TO ME.
IT ISN'T ENDING FOR ME, DALLAS. OR YOU.
AS A MATTER OF FACT...
...I'D SAY WE'RE JUST GETTING STARTED.

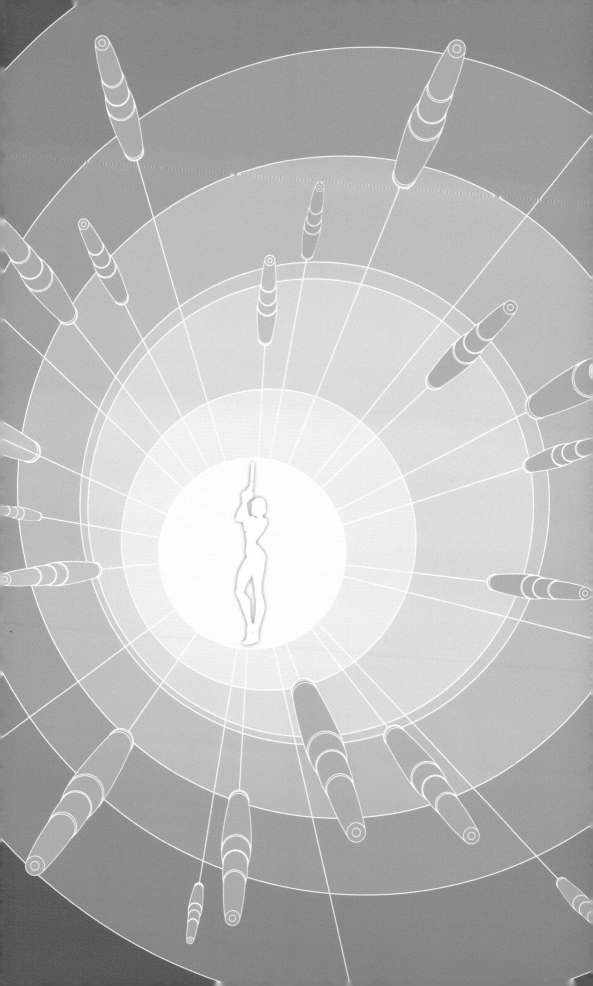

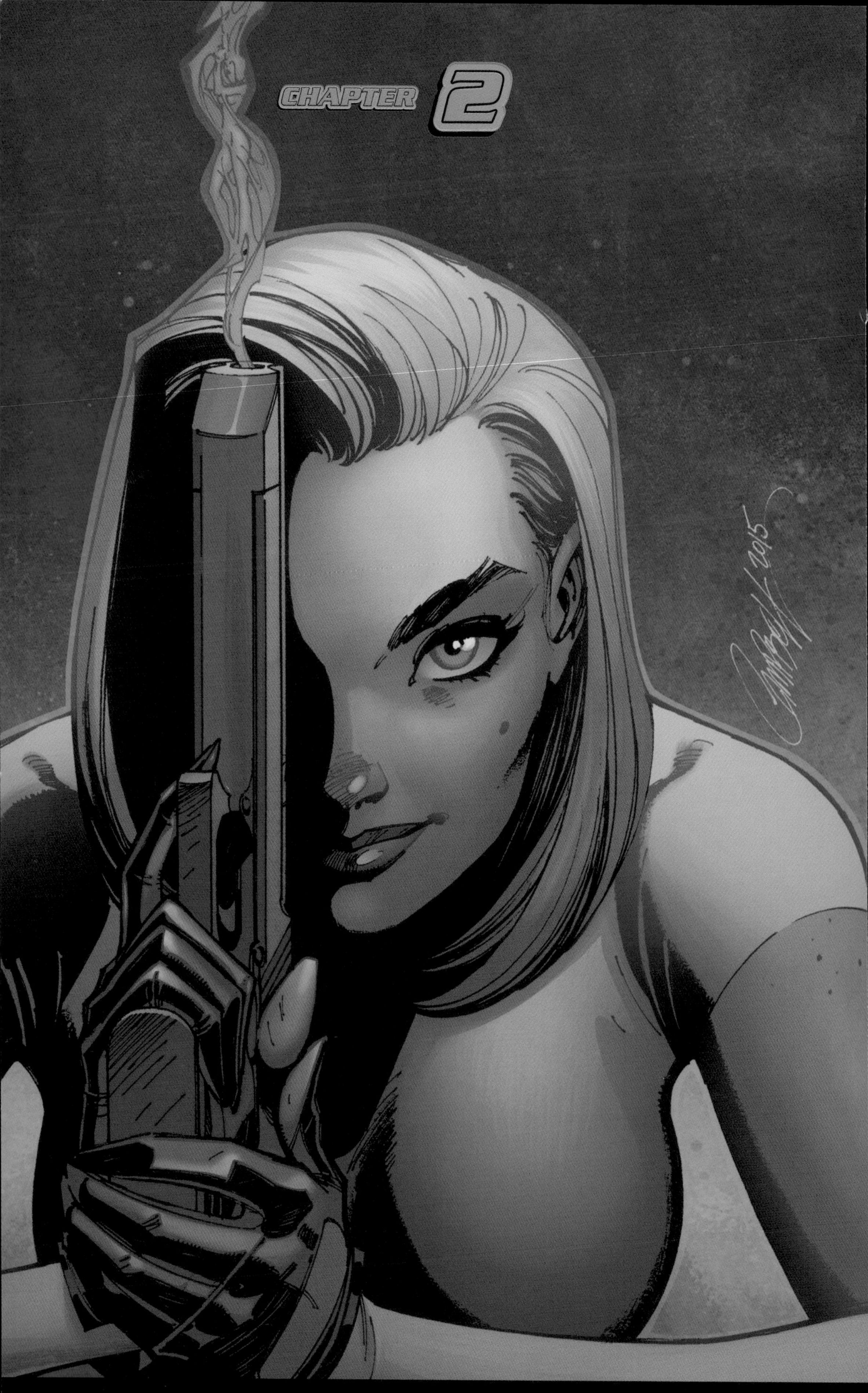
CHAPTER 2
Art by J. Scott Campbell • Colors by John Rauch

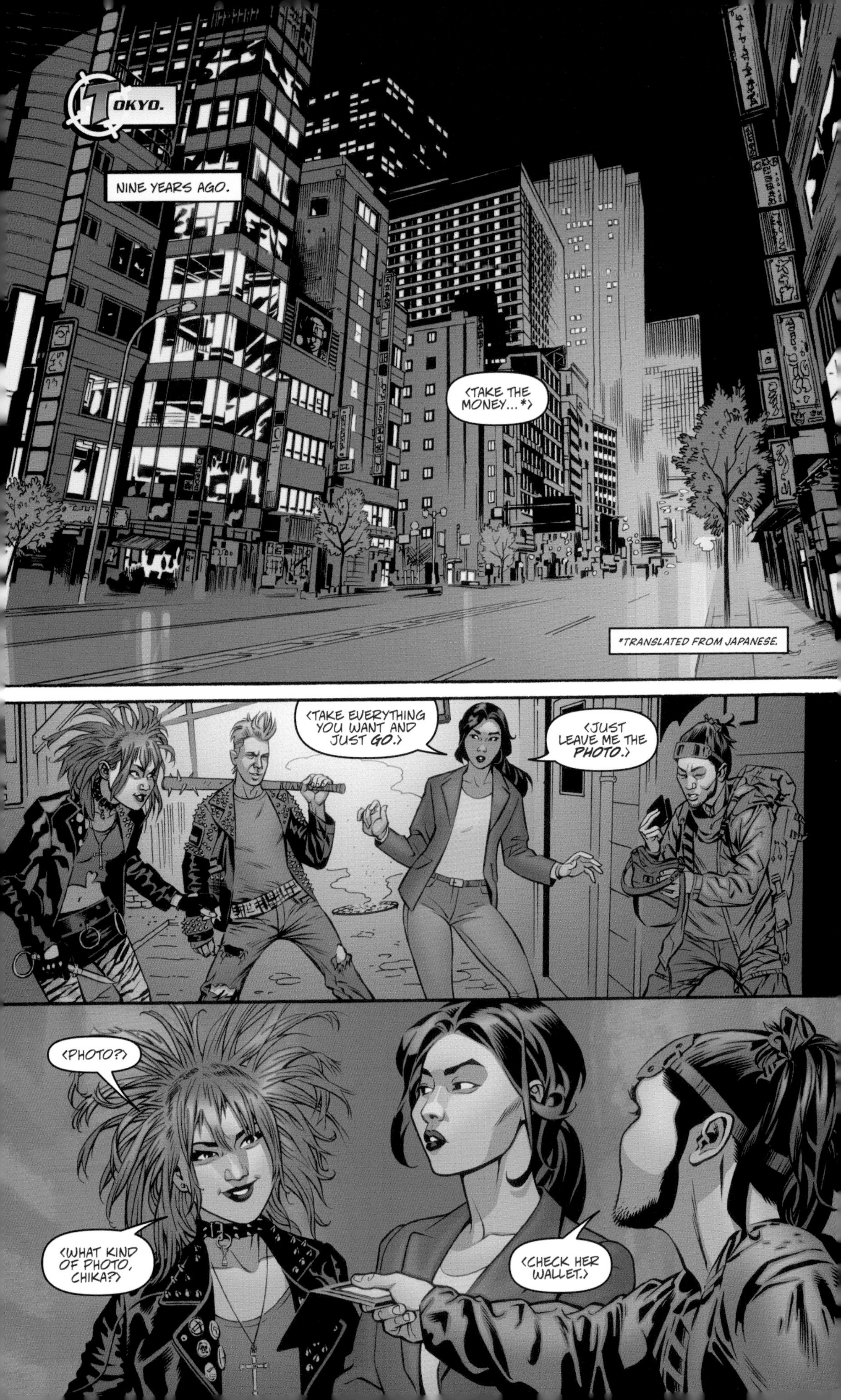
TOKYO.
NINE YEARS AGO.
<TAKE THE MONEY...*>
*TRANSLATED FROM JAPANESE.
<TAKE EVERYTHING YOU WANT AND JUST GO.>
<JUST LEAVE ME THE PHOTO.>
<PHOTO?>
<WHAT KIND OF PHOTO, CHIKA?>
<CHECK HER WALLET.>

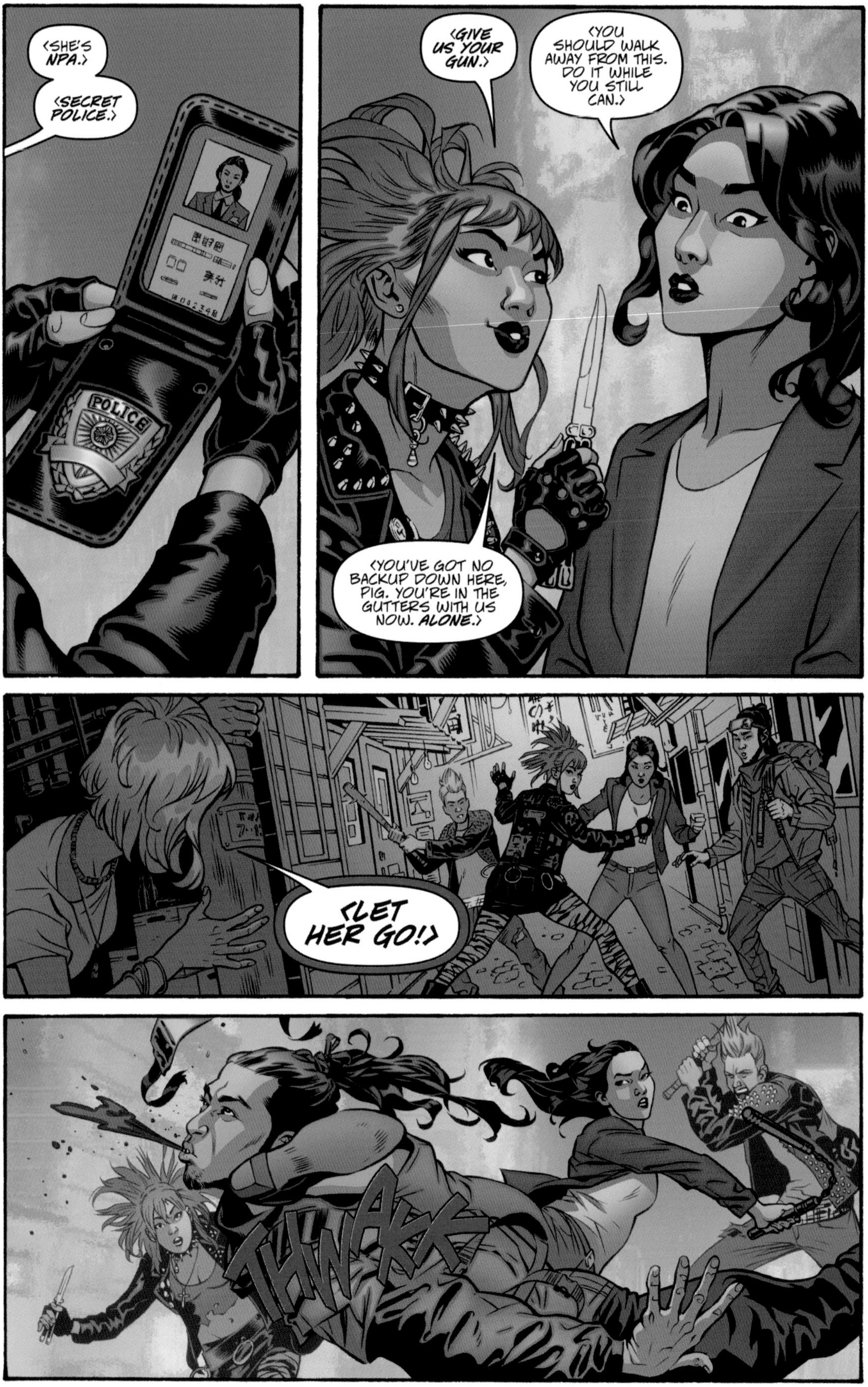
‹SHE'S NPA.›
‹SECRET POLICE.›
POLICE
‹GIVE US YOUR GUN.›
‹YOU SHOULD WALK AWAY FROM THIS. DO IT WHILE YOU STILL CAN.›
‹YOU'VE GOT NO BACKUP DOWN HERE, PIG. YOU'RE IN THE GUTTERS WITH US NOW. ALONE.›
‹LET HER GO!›
THWAKK

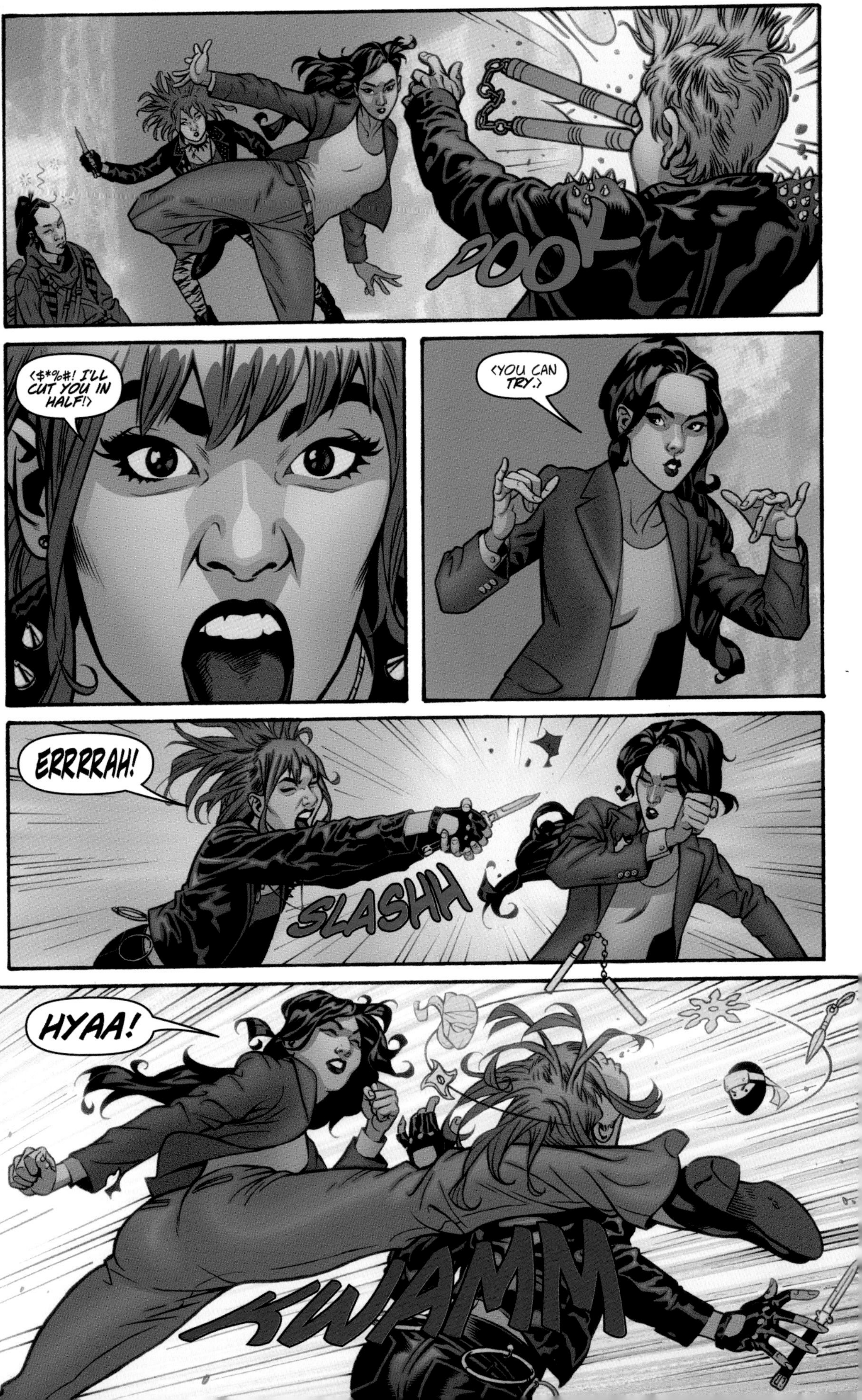
POOK
<$*%#! I'LL CUT YOU IN HALF!>
<YOU CAN TRY.>
ERRRRAH!
SLASHH
HYAA!
KWAMM

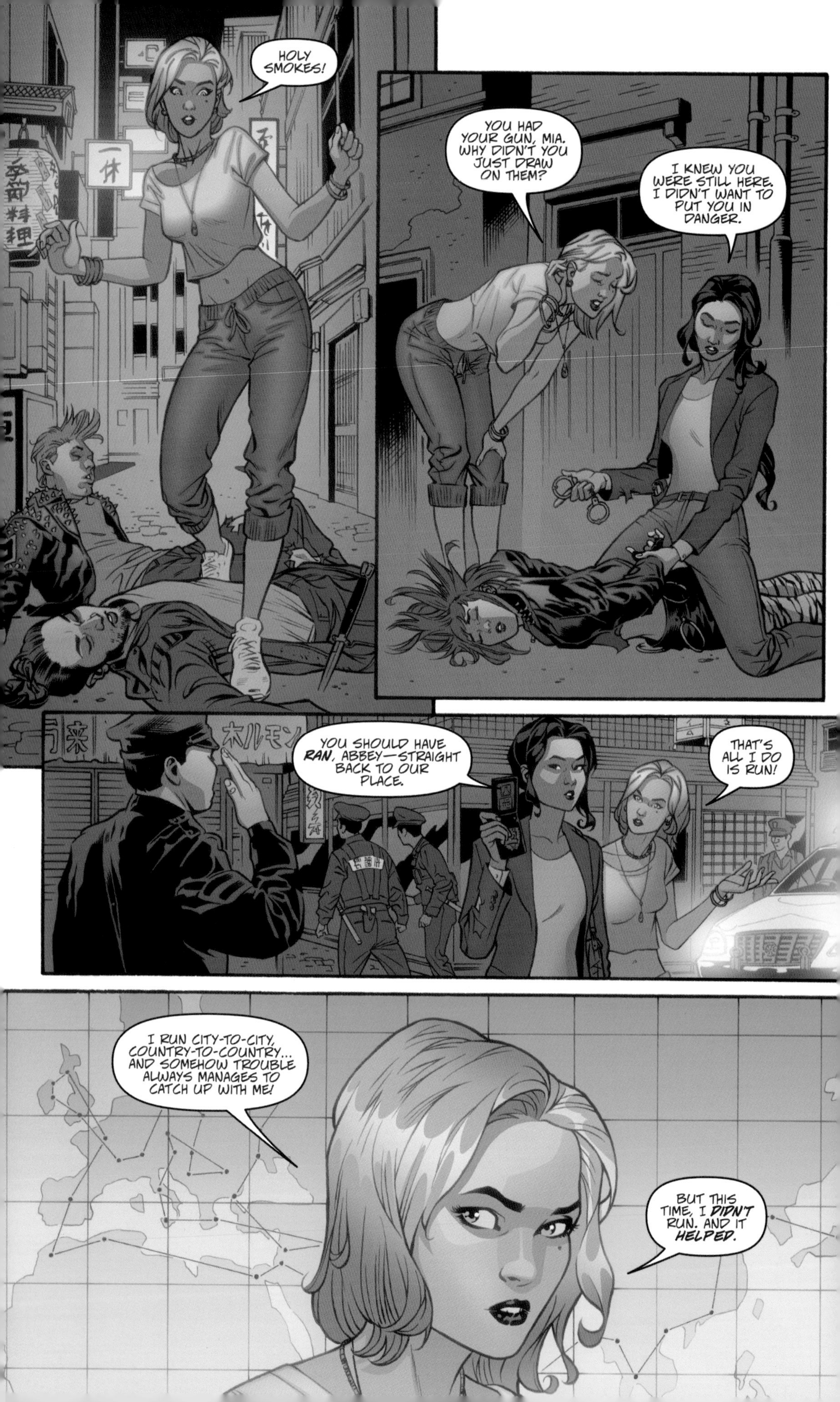
HOLY SMOKES!
YOU HAD YOUR GUN, MIA. WHY DIDN'T YOU JUST DRAW ON THEM?
I KNEW YOU WERE STILL HERE. I DIDN'T WANT TO PUT YOU IN DANGER.
YOU SHOULD HAVE ***RAN***, ABBEY—STRAIGHT BACK TO OUR PLACE.
THAT'S ALL I DO IS RUN!
I RUN CITY-TO-CITY, COUNTRY-TO-COUNTRY... AND SOMEHOW TROUBLE ALWAYS MANAGES TO CATCH UP WITH ME!
BUT THIS TIME, I ***DIDN'T*** RUN. AND IT ***HELPED***.

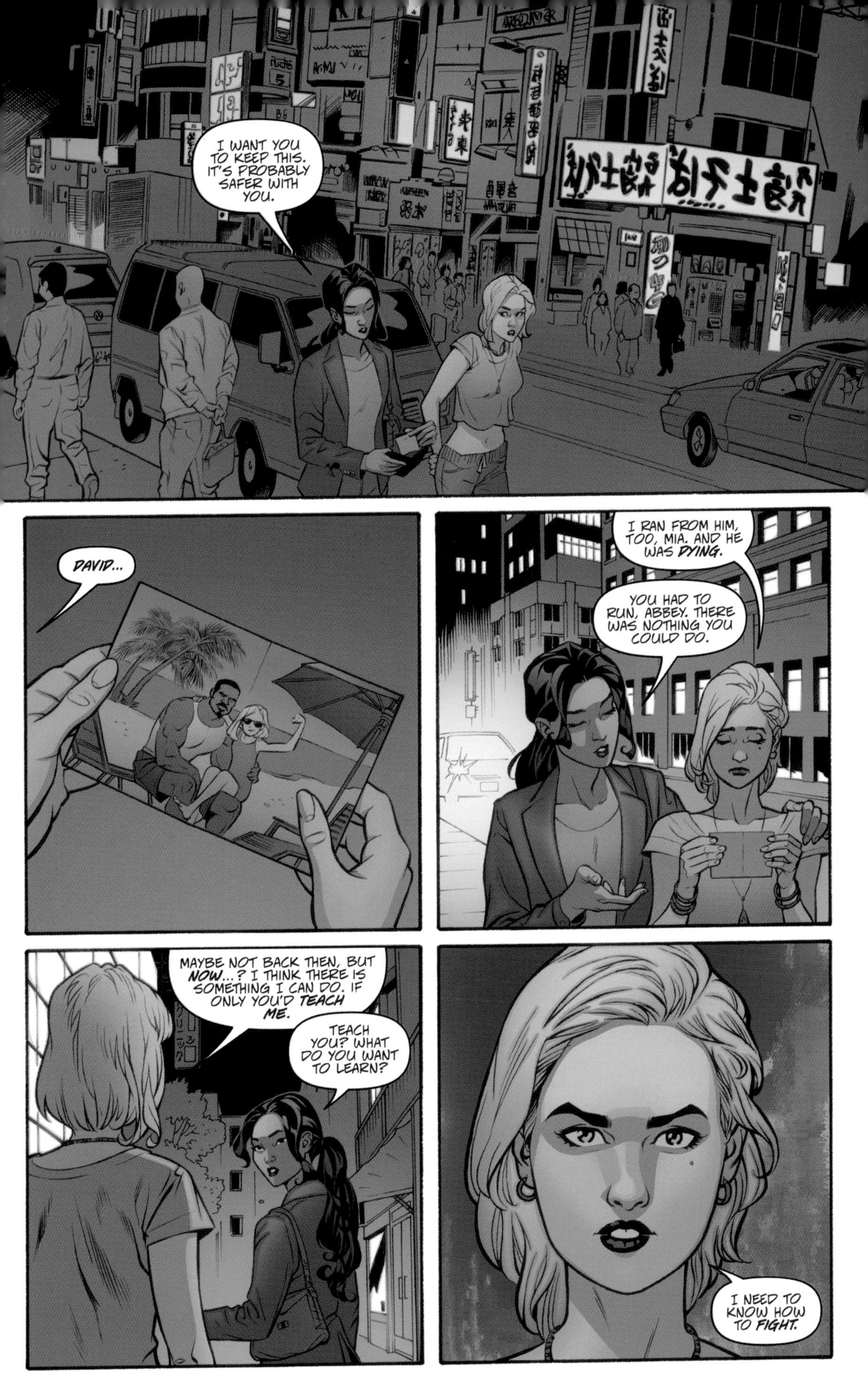
I WANT YOU TO KEEP THIS. IT'S PROBABLY SAFER WITH YOU.
DAVID...
I RAN FROM HIM, TOO, MIA. AND HE WAS DYING.
YOU HAD TO RUN, ABBEY. THERE WAS NOTHING YOU COULD DO.
MAYBE NOT BACK THEN, BUT NOW...? I THINK THERE IS SOMETHING I CAN DO. IF ONLY YOU'D TEACH ME.
TEACH YOU? WHAT DO YOU WANT TO LEARN?
I NEED TO KNOW HOW TO FIGHT.

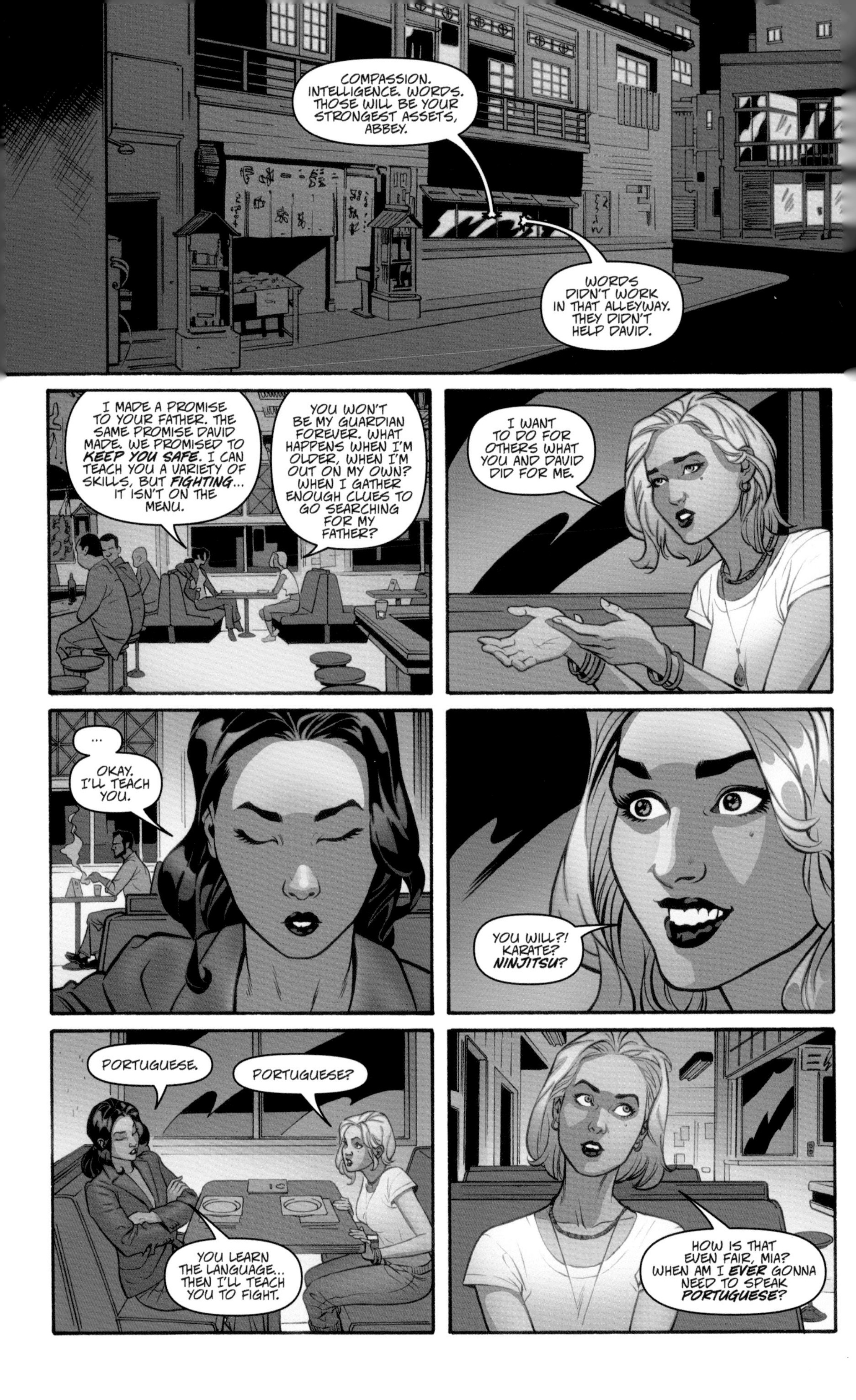

COMPASSION. INTELLIGENCE. WORDS. THOSE WILL BE YOUR STRONGEST ASSETS, ABBEY.
WORDS DIDN'T WORK IN THAT ALLEYWAY. THEY DIDN'T HELP DAVID.
I MADE A PROMISE TO YOUR FATHER. THE SAME PROMISE DAVID MADE. WE PROMISED TO KEEP YOU SAFE. I CAN TEACH YOU A VARIETY OF SKILLS, BUT FIGHTING... IT ISN'T ON THE MENU.
YOU WON'T BE MY GUARDIAN FOREVER. WHAT HAPPENS WHEN I'M OLDER, WHEN I'M OUT ON MY OWN? WHEN I GATHER ENOUGH CLUES TO GO SEARCHING FOR MY FATHER?
I WANT TO DO FOR OTHERS WHAT YOU AND DAVID DID FOR ME.
...
OKAY. I'LL TEACH YOU.
YOU WILL?! KARATE? NINJITSU?
PORTUGUESE.
PORTUGUESE?
YOU LEARN THE LANGUAGE... THEN I'LL TEACH YOU TO FIGHT.
HOW IS THAT EVEN FAIR, MIA? WHEN AM I EVER GONNA NEED TO SPEAK PORTUGUESE?

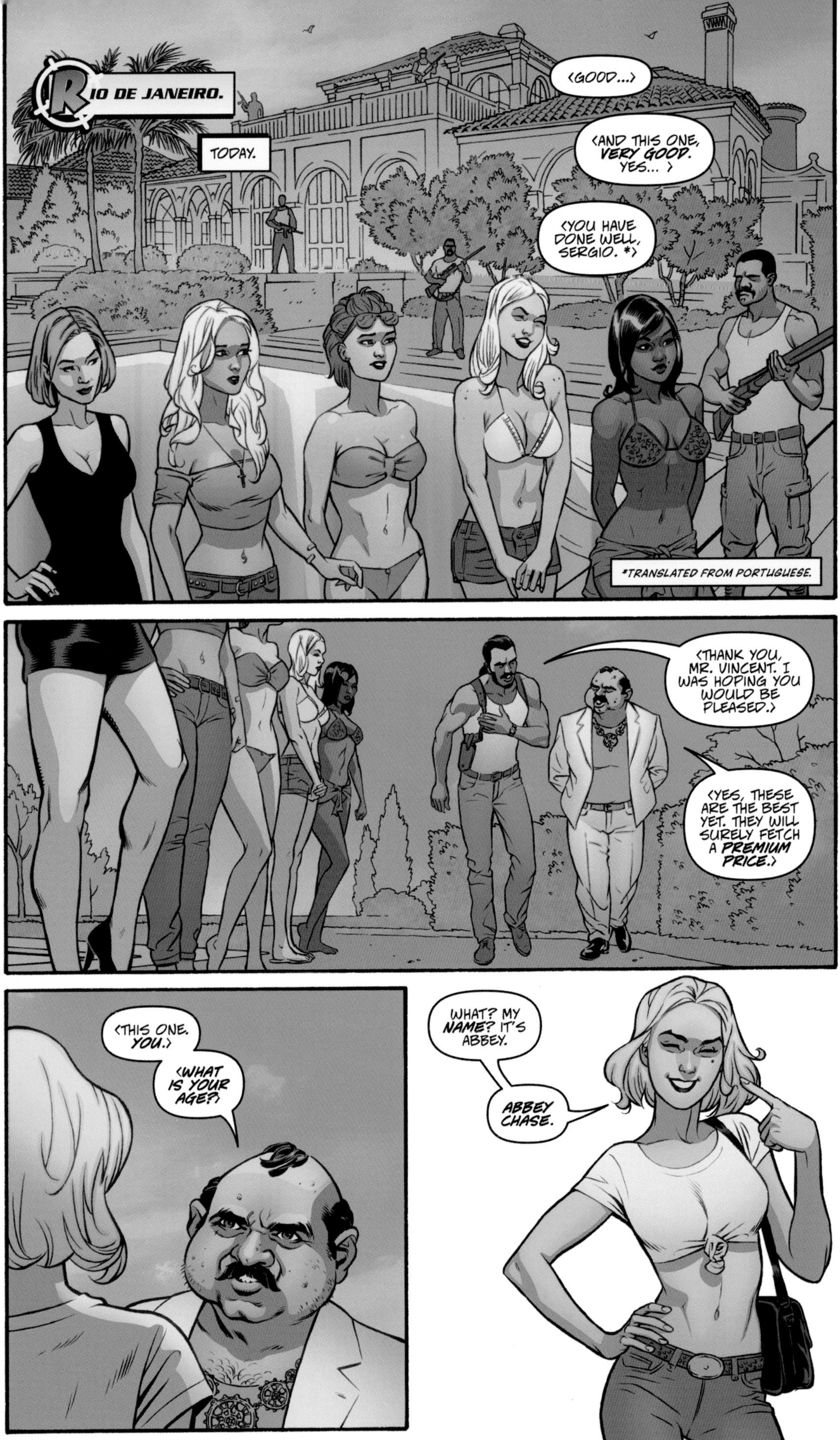
RIO DE JANEIRO.
TODAY.
‹GOOD...›
‹AND THIS ONE, VERY GOOD. YES... ›
‹YOU HAVE DONE WELL, SERGIO. *›
*TRANSLATED FROM PORTUGUESE.
‹THANK YOU, MR. VINCENT. I WAS HOPING YOU WOULD BE PLEASED.›
‹YES, THESE ARE THE BEST YET. THEY WILL SURELY FETCH A PREMIUM PRICE.›
‹THIS ONE. YOU.›
‹WHAT IS YOUR AGE?›
WHAT? MY NAME? IT'S ABBEY.
ABBEY CHASE.

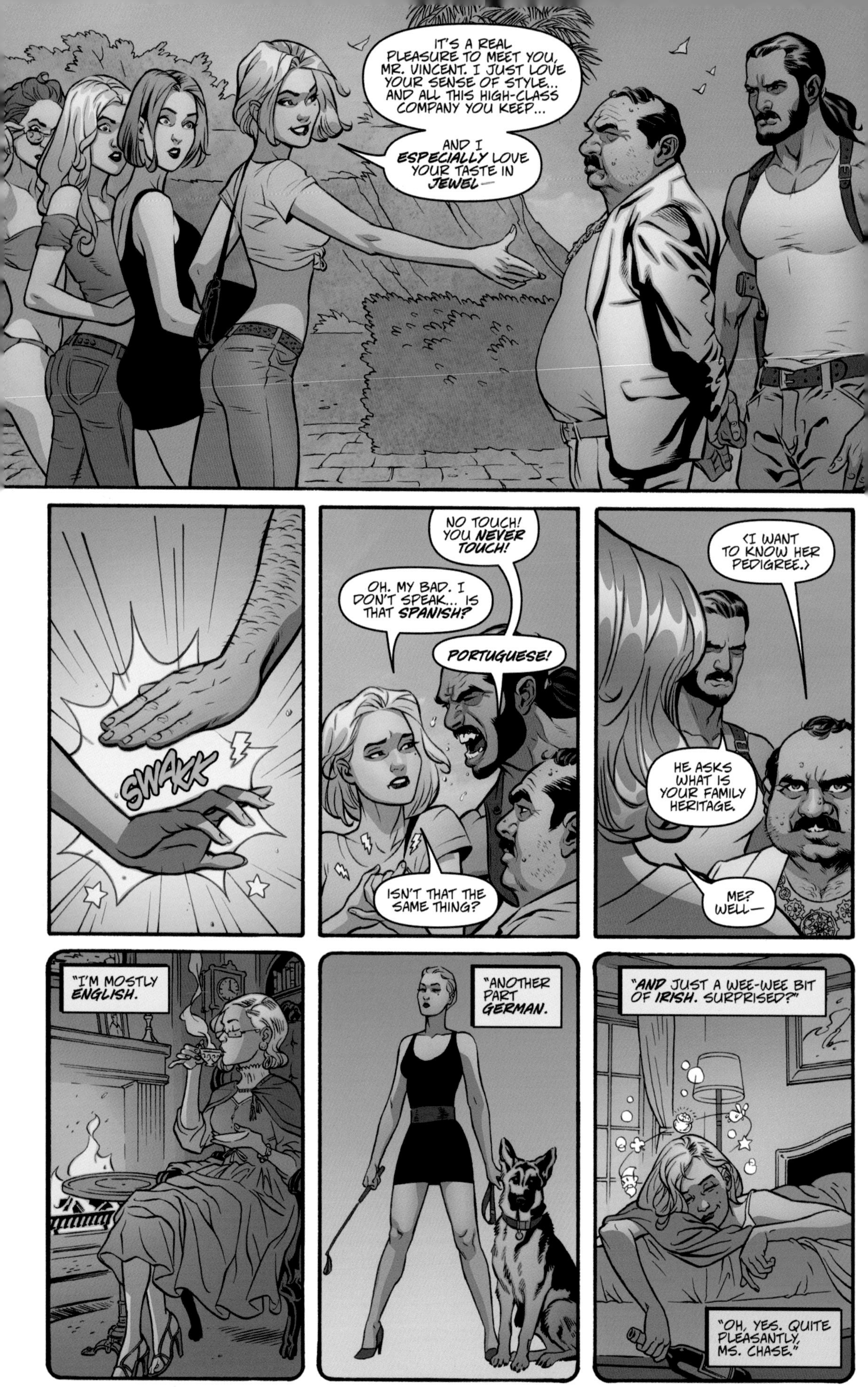

IT'S A REAL PLEASURE TO MEET YOU, MR. VINCENT. I JUST LOVE YOUR SENSE OF STYLE... AND ALL THIS HIGH-CLASS COMPANY YOU KEEP...
AND I ESPECIALLY LOVE YOUR TASTE IN JEWEL—
SWAKK
NO TOUCH! YOU NEVER TOUCH!
OH. MY BAD. I DON'T SPEAK... IS THAT SPANISH?
PORTUGUESE!
ISN'T THAT THE SAME THING?
‹I WANT TO KNOW HER PEDIGREE.›
HE ASKS WHAT IS YOUR FAMILY HERITAGE.
ME? WELL—
"I'M MOSTLY ENGLISH.
"ANOTHER PART GERMAN.
"AND JUST A WEE-WEE BIT OF IRISH. SURPRISED?"
"OH, YES. QUITE PLEASANTLY, MS. CHASE."

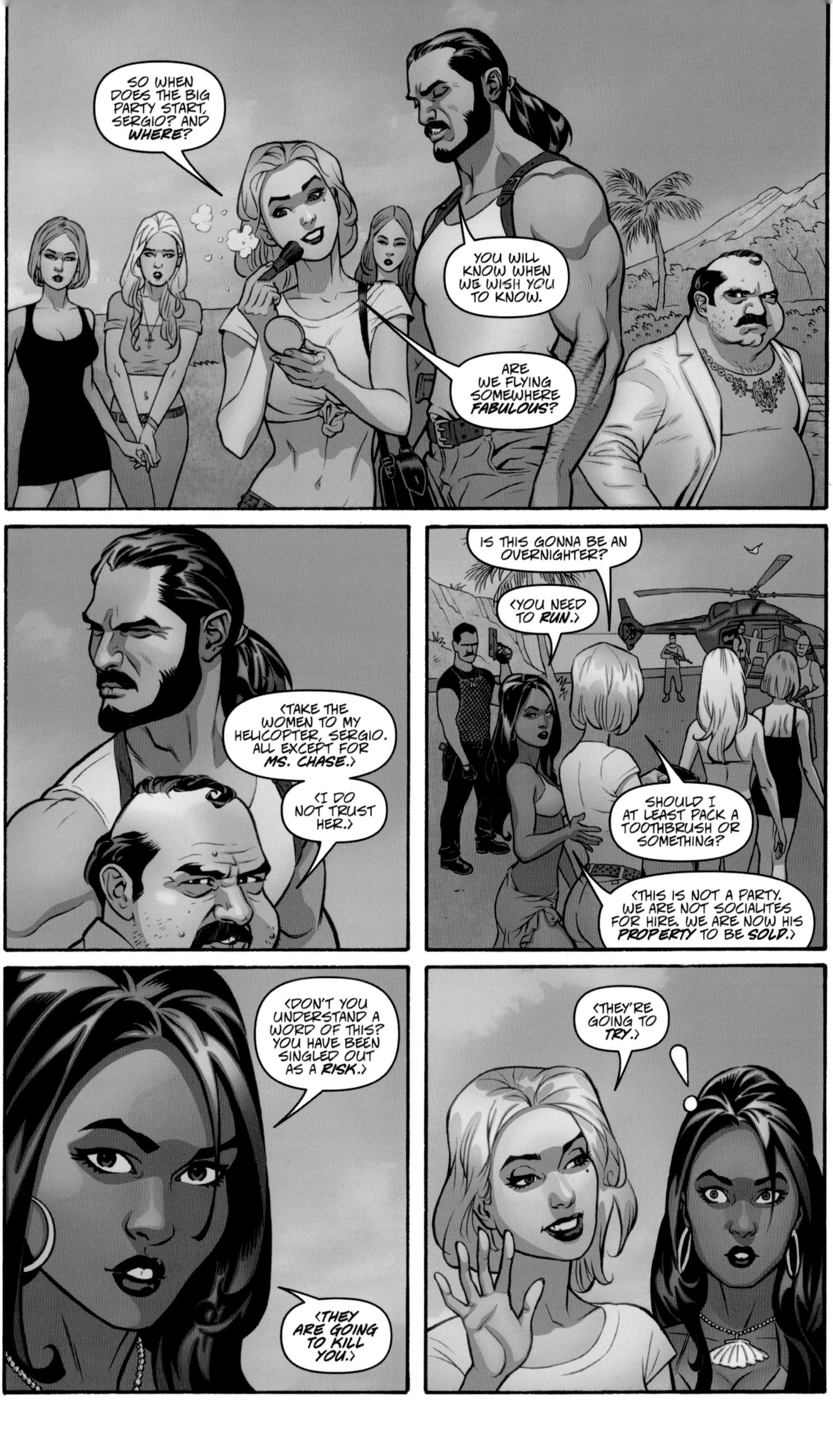
SO WHEN DOES THE BIG PARTY START, SERGIO? AND ***WHERE?***
YOU WILL KNOW WHEN WE WISH YOU TO KNOW.
ARE WE FLYING SOMEWHERE ***FABULOUS?***
<TAKE THE WOMEN TO MY HELICOPTER, SERGIO. ALL EXCEPT FOR ***MS. CHASE.***>
<I DO NOT TRUST HER.>
IS THIS GONNA BE AN OVERNIGHTER?
<YOU NEED TO ***RUN.***>
SHOULD I AT LEAST PACK A TOOTHBRUSH OR SOMETHING?
<THIS IS NOT A PARTY. WE ARE NOT SOCIALITES FOR HIRE. WE ARE NOW HIS ***PROPERTY*** TO BE ***SOLD.***>
<DON'T YOU UNDERSTAND A WORD OF THIS? YOU HAVE BEEN SINGLED OUT AS A ***RISK.***>
<***THEY ARE GOING TO KILL YOU.***>
<THEY'RE GOING TO ***TRY.***>
!

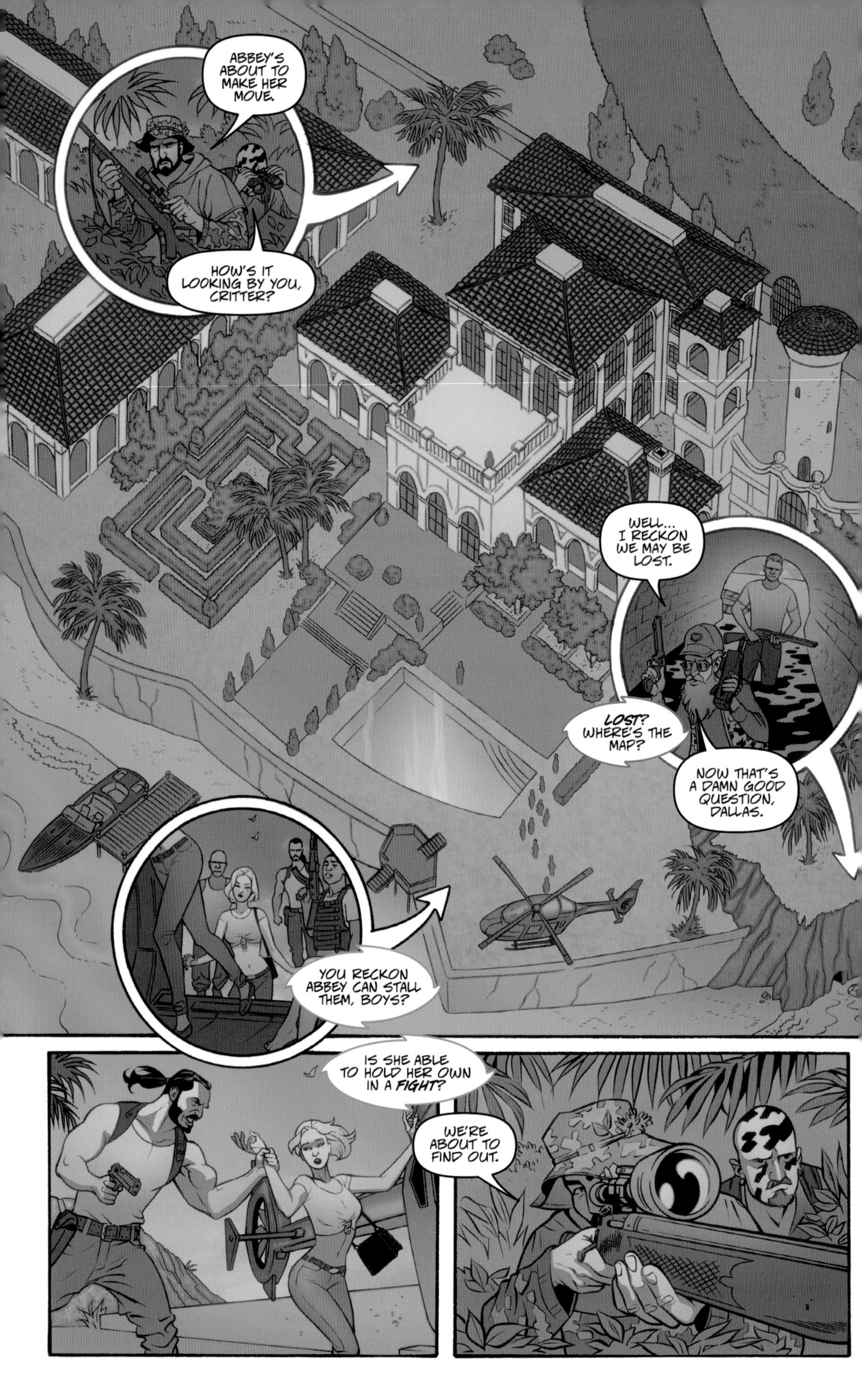
ABBEY'S ABOUT TO MAKE HER MOVE.
HOW'S IT LOOKING BY YOU, CRITTER?
WELL... I RECKON WE MAY BE LOST.
LOST? WHERE'S THE MAP?
NOW THAT'S A DAMN GOOD QUESTION, DALLAS.
YOU RECKON ABBEY CAN STALL THEM, BOYS?
IS SHE ABLE TO HOLD HER OWN IN A FIGHT?
WE'RE ABOUT TO FIND OUT.

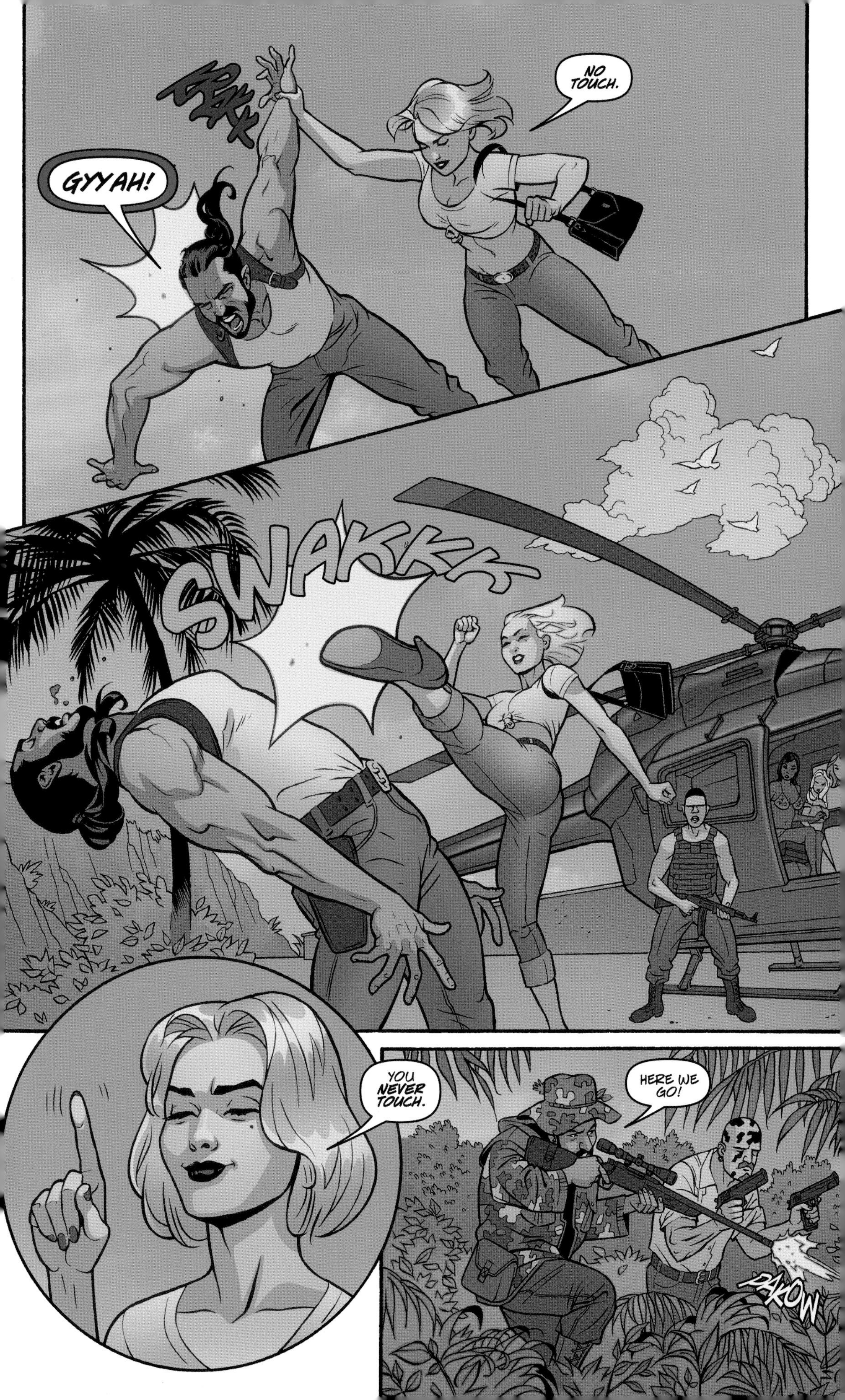

KRAKK
NO TOUCH.
GYYAH!
SWAKKK
YOU NEVER TOUCH.
HERE WE GO!
BLAM

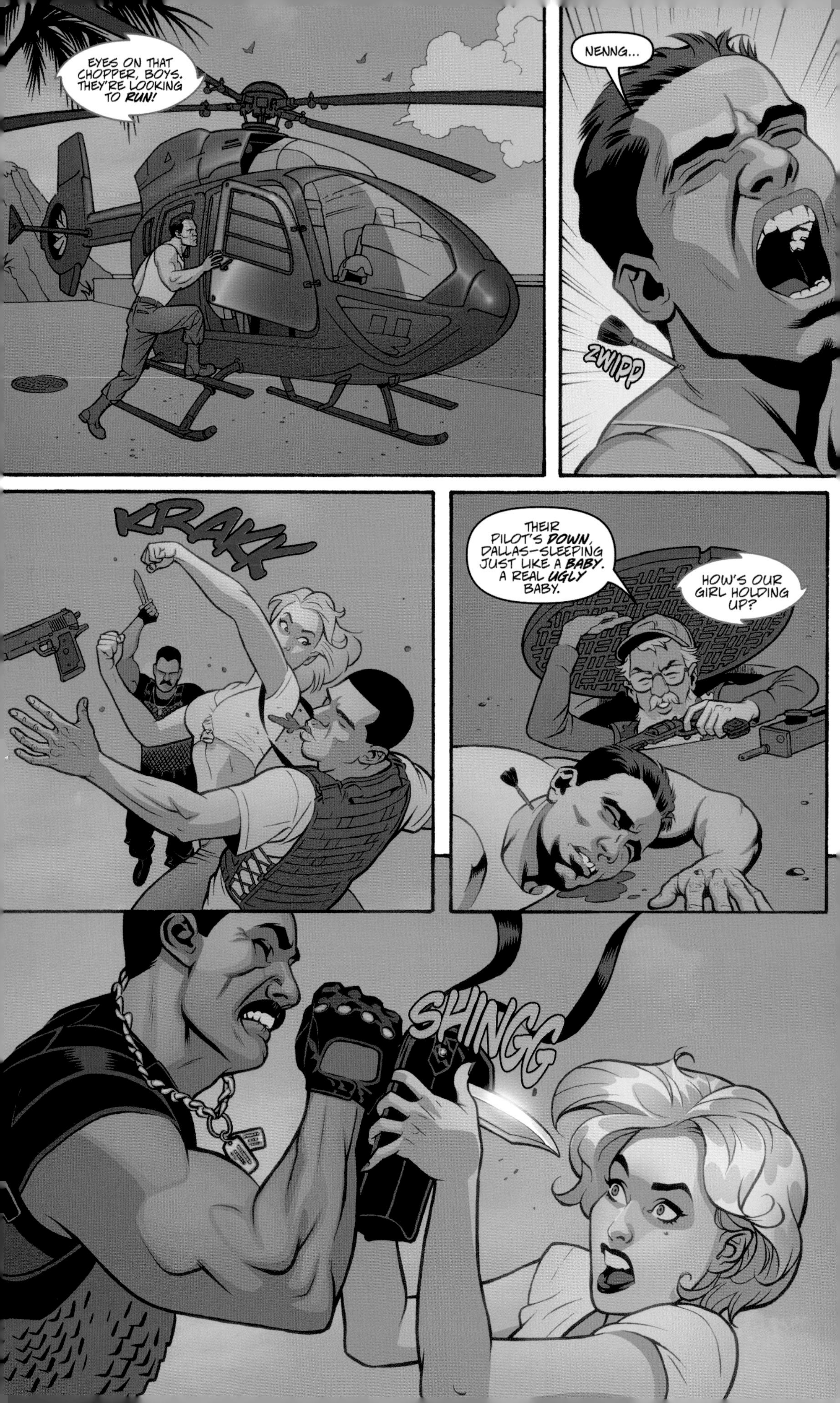
EYES ON THAT CHOPPER, BOYS. THEY'RE LOOKING TO RUN!
NENNG...
ZWIPP
KRAKK
THEIR PILOT'S DOWN, DALLAS—SLEEPING JUST LIKE A BABY. A REAL UGLY BABY.
HOW'S OUR GIRL HOLDING UP?
SHINGG

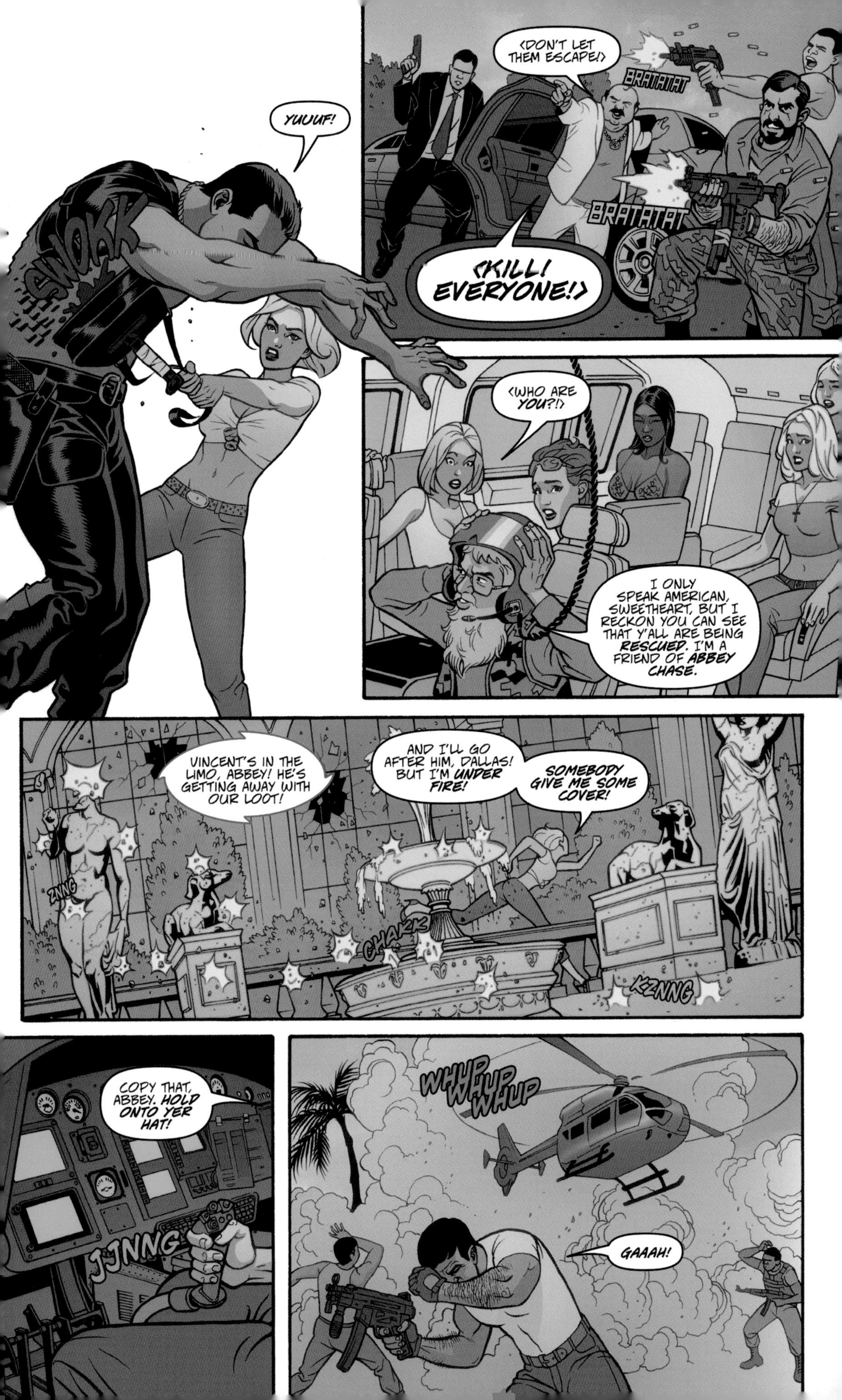
YUUUF!
SWOKK
<DON'T LET THEM ESCAPE!>
BRATATAT
BRATATAT
<KILL! EVERYONE!>
<WHO ARE YOU?!>
I ONLY SPEAK AMERICAN, SWEETHEART, BUT I RECKON YOU CAN SEE THAT Y'ALL ARE BEING RESCUED. I'M A FRIEND OF ABBEY CHASE.
VINCENT'S IN THE LIMO, ABBEY! HE'S GETTING AWAY WITH OUR LOOT!
AND I'LL GO AFTER HIM, DALLAS! BUT I'M UNDER FIRE!
SOMEBODY GIVE ME SOME COVER!
ZNNG
CHAKK
KZNNG
COPY THAT, ABBEY. HOLD ONTO YER HAT!
JJNNG
WHUP WHUP WHUP
GAAAH!

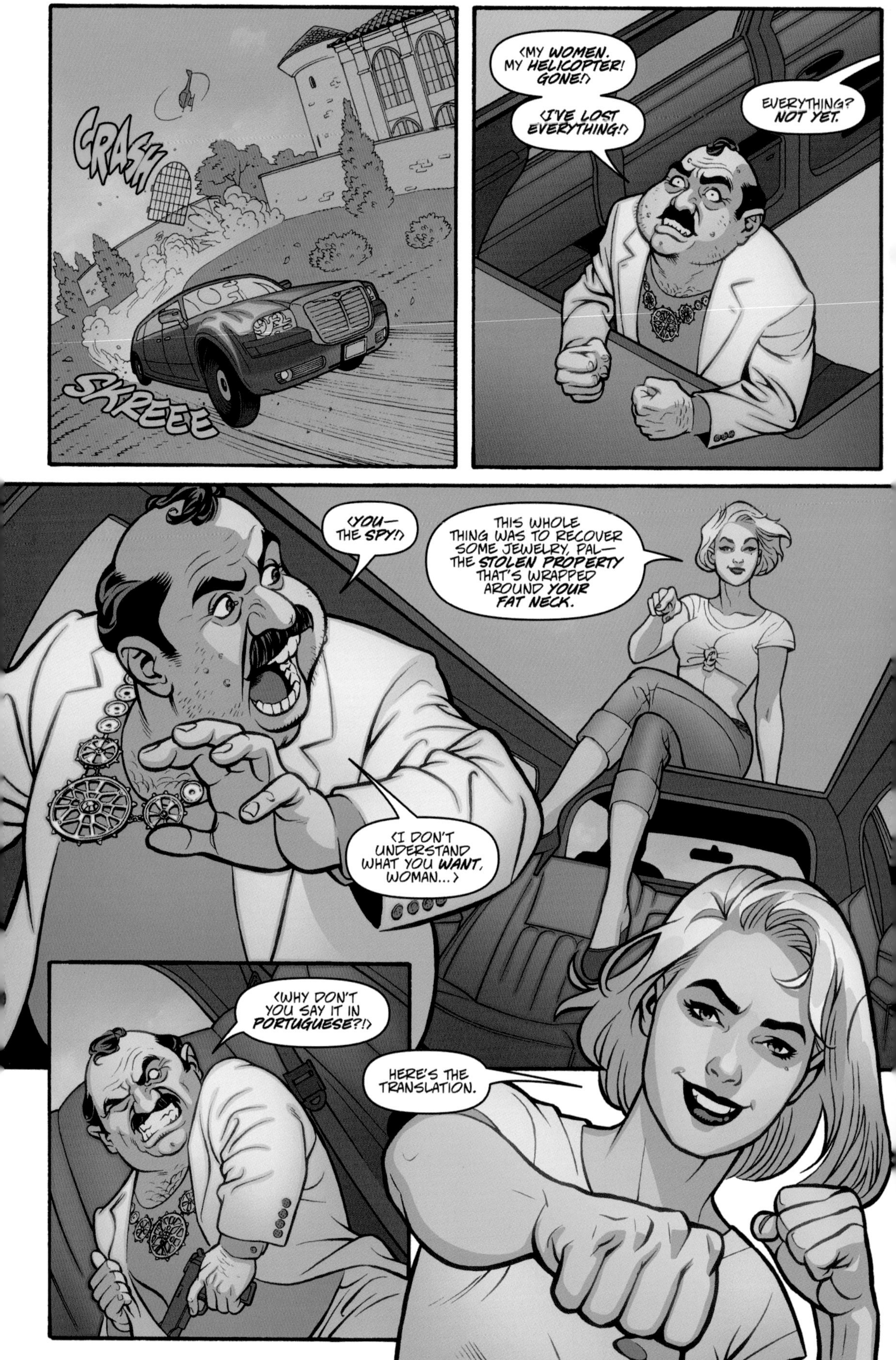
CRASH
SKREEEE
<MY WOMEN. MY HELICOPTER! GONE!>
<I'VE LOST EVERYTHING!>
EVERYTHING? NOT YET.
<YOU— THE SPY!>
THIS WHOLE THING WAS TO RECOVER SOME JEWELRY, PAL— THE STOLEN PROPERTY THAT'S WRAPPED AROUND YOUR FAT NECK.
<I DON'T UNDERSTAND WHAT YOU WANT, WOMAN...>
<WHY DON'T YOU SAY IT IN PORTUGUESE?!>
HERE'S THE TRANSLATION.

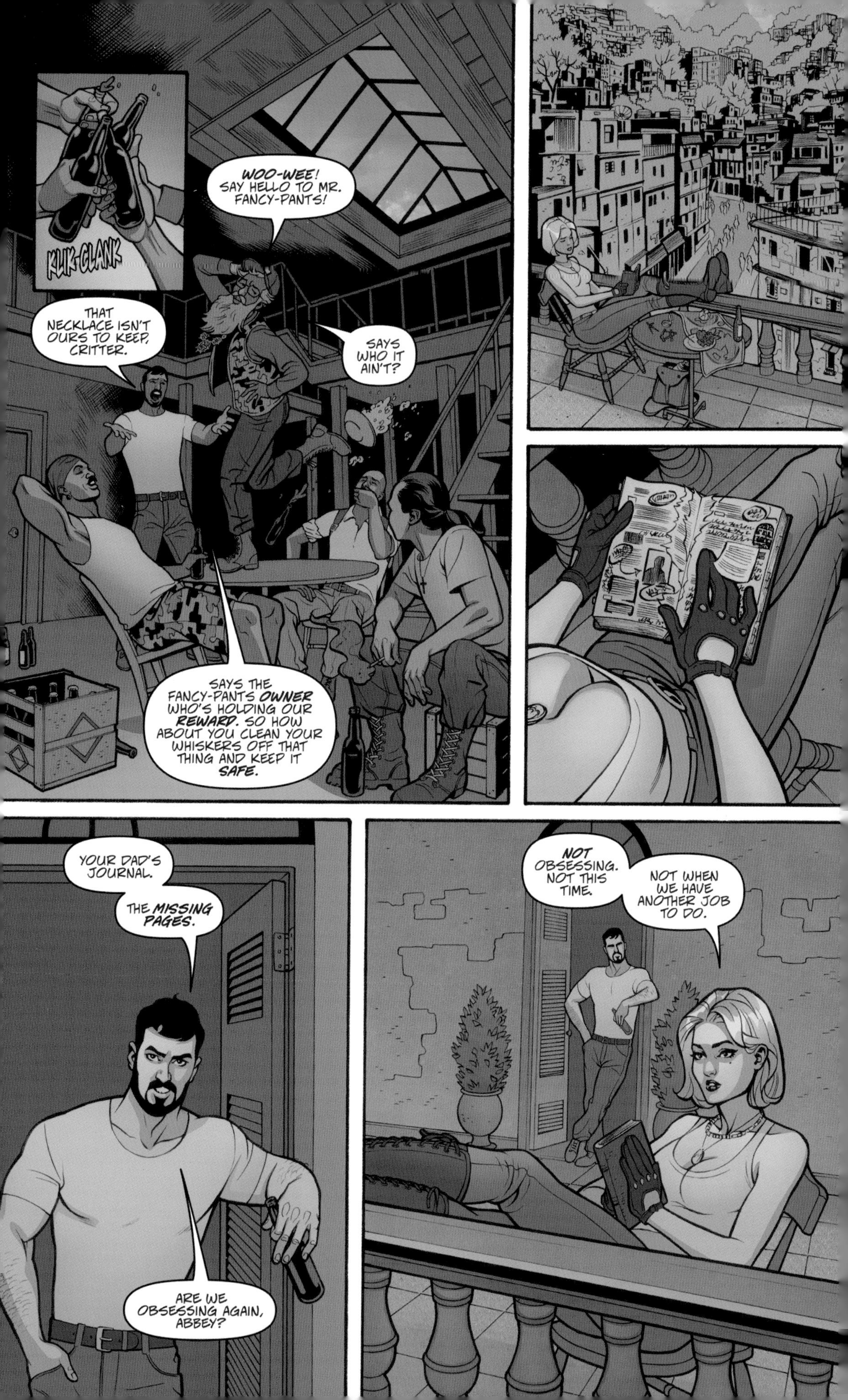

KLIK-CLANK
WOO-WEE! SAY HELLO TO MR. FANCY-PANTS!
THAT NECKLACE ISN'T OURS TO KEEP, CRITTER.
SAYS WHO IT AIN'T?
SAYS THE FANCY-PANTS OWNER WHO'S HOLDING OUR REWARD. SO HOW ABOUT YOU CLEAN YOUR WHISKERS OFF THAT THING AND KEEP IT SAFE.
YOUR DAD'S JOURNAL.
THE MISSING PAGES.
ARE WE OBSESSING AGAIN, ABBEY?
NOT OBSESSING. NOT THIS TIME.
NOT WHEN WE HAVE ANOTHER JOB TO DO.

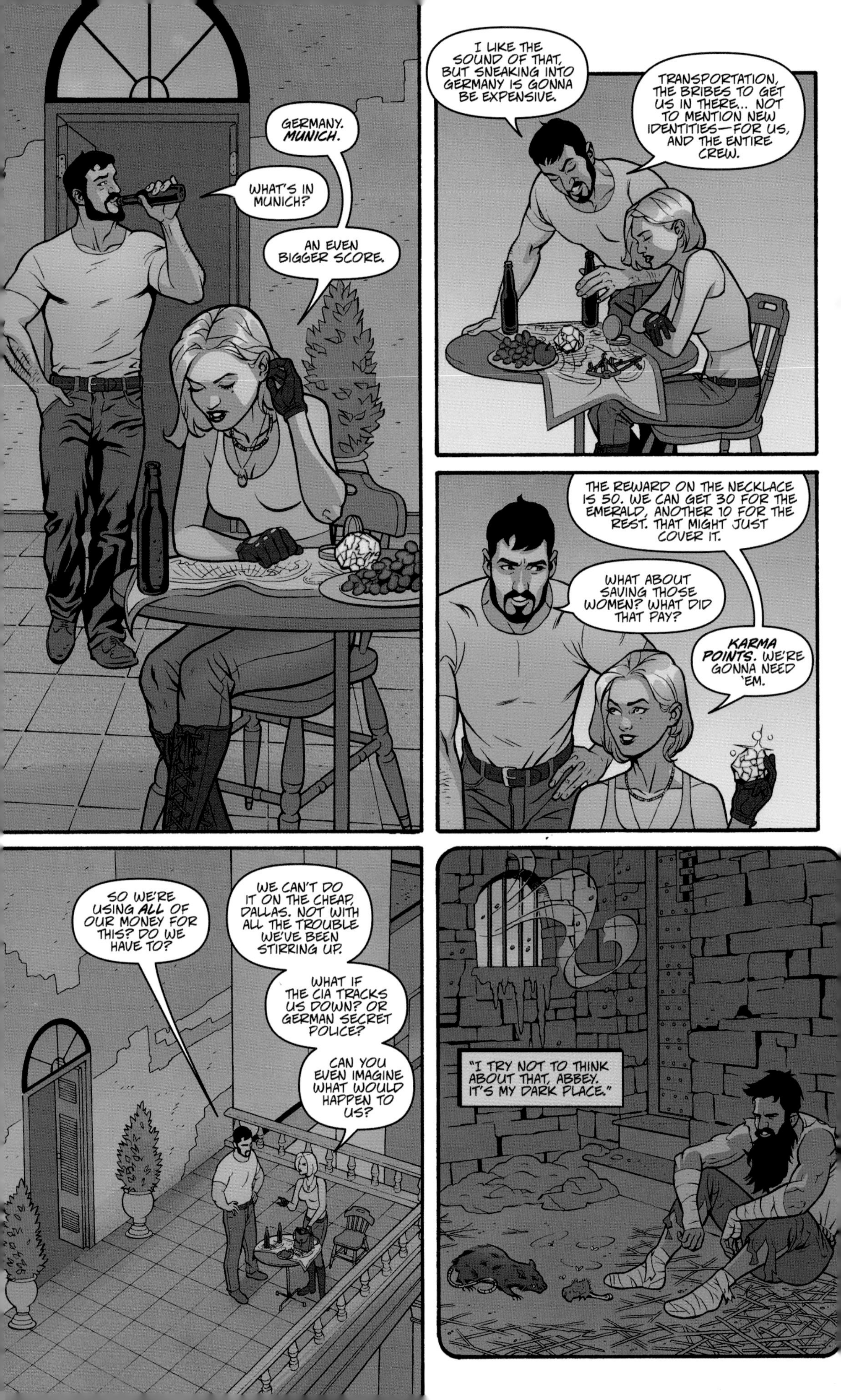
GERMANY. MUNICH.
WHAT'S IN MUNICH?
AN EVEN BIGGER SCORE.
I LIKE THE SOUND OF THAT, BUT SNEAKING INTO GERMANY IS GONNA BE EXPENSIVE.
TRANSPORTATION, THE BRIBES TO GET US IN THERE... NOT TO MENTION NEW IDENTITIES—FOR US, AND THE ENTIRE CREW.
THE REWARD ON THE NECKLACE IS 50. WE CAN GET 30 FOR THE EMERALD, ANOTHER 10 FOR THE REST. THAT MIGHT JUST COVER IT.
WHAT ABOUT SAVING THOSE WOMEN? WHAT DID THAT PAY?
KARMA POINTS. WE'RE GONNA NEED 'EM.
SO WE'RE USING ALL OF OUR MONEY FOR THIS? DO WE HAVE TO?
WE CAN'T DO IT ON THE CHEAP, DALLAS. NOT WITH ALL THE TROUBLE WE'VE BEEN STIRRING UP.
WHAT IF THE CIA TRACKS US DOWN? OR GERMAN SECRET POLICE?
CAN YOU EVEN IMAGINE WHAT WOULD HAPPEN TO US?
"I TRY NOT TO THINK ABOUT THAT, ABBEY. IT'S MY DARK PLACE."

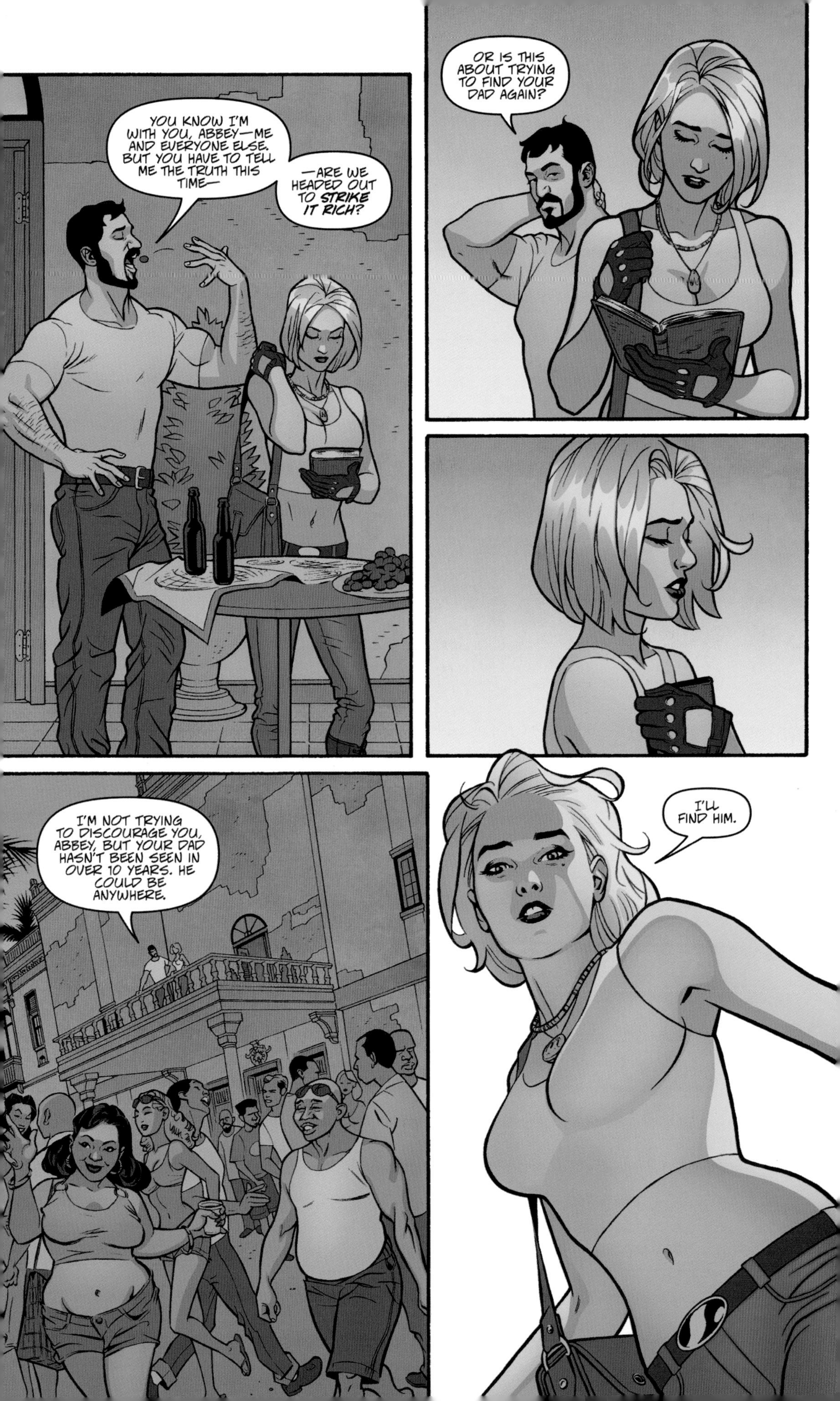
YOU KNOW I'M WITH YOU, ABBEY—ME AND EVERYONE ELSE. BUT YOU HAVE TO TELL ME THE TRUTH THIS TIME—
—ARE WE HEADED OUT TO **STRIKE IT RICH?**
OR IS THIS ABOUT TRYING TO FIND YOUR DAD AGAIN?
I'M NOT TRYING TO DISCOURAGE YOU, ABBEY, BUT YOUR DAD HASN'T BEEN SEEN IN OVER 10 YEARS. HE COULD BE ANYWHERE.
I'LL FIND HIM.

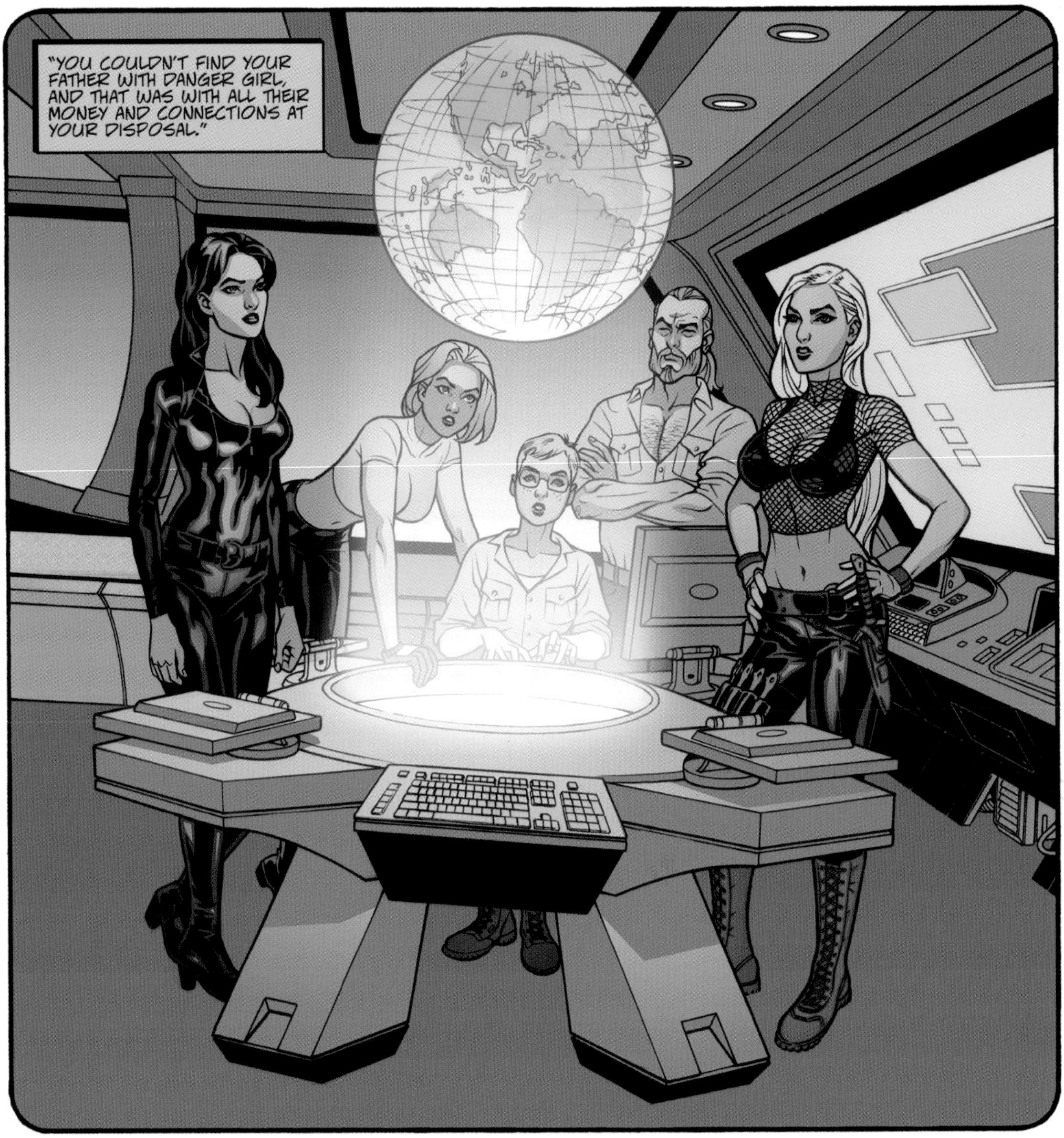
"YOU COULDN'T FIND YOUR FATHER WITH DANGER GIRL, AND THAT WAS WITH ALL THEIR MONEY AND CONNECTIONS AT YOUR DISPOSAL."

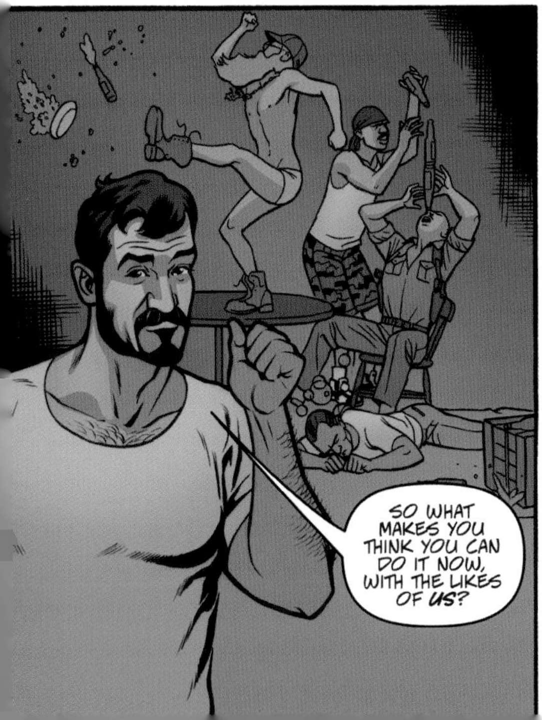
SO WHAT MAKES YOU THINK YOU CAN DO IT NOW, WITH THE LIKES OF US?

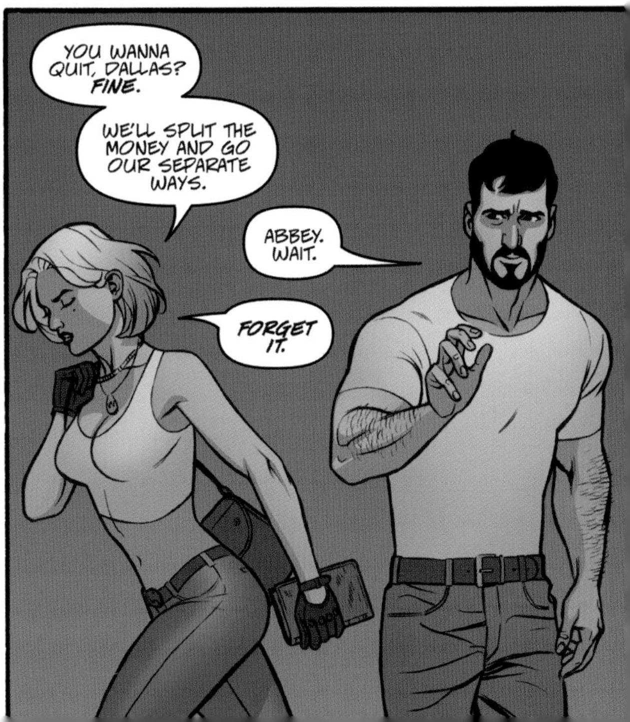
YOU WANNA QUIT, DALLAS? FINE.
WE'LL SPLIT THE MONEY AND GO OUR SEPARATE WAYS.
ABBEY. WAIT.
FORGET IT.

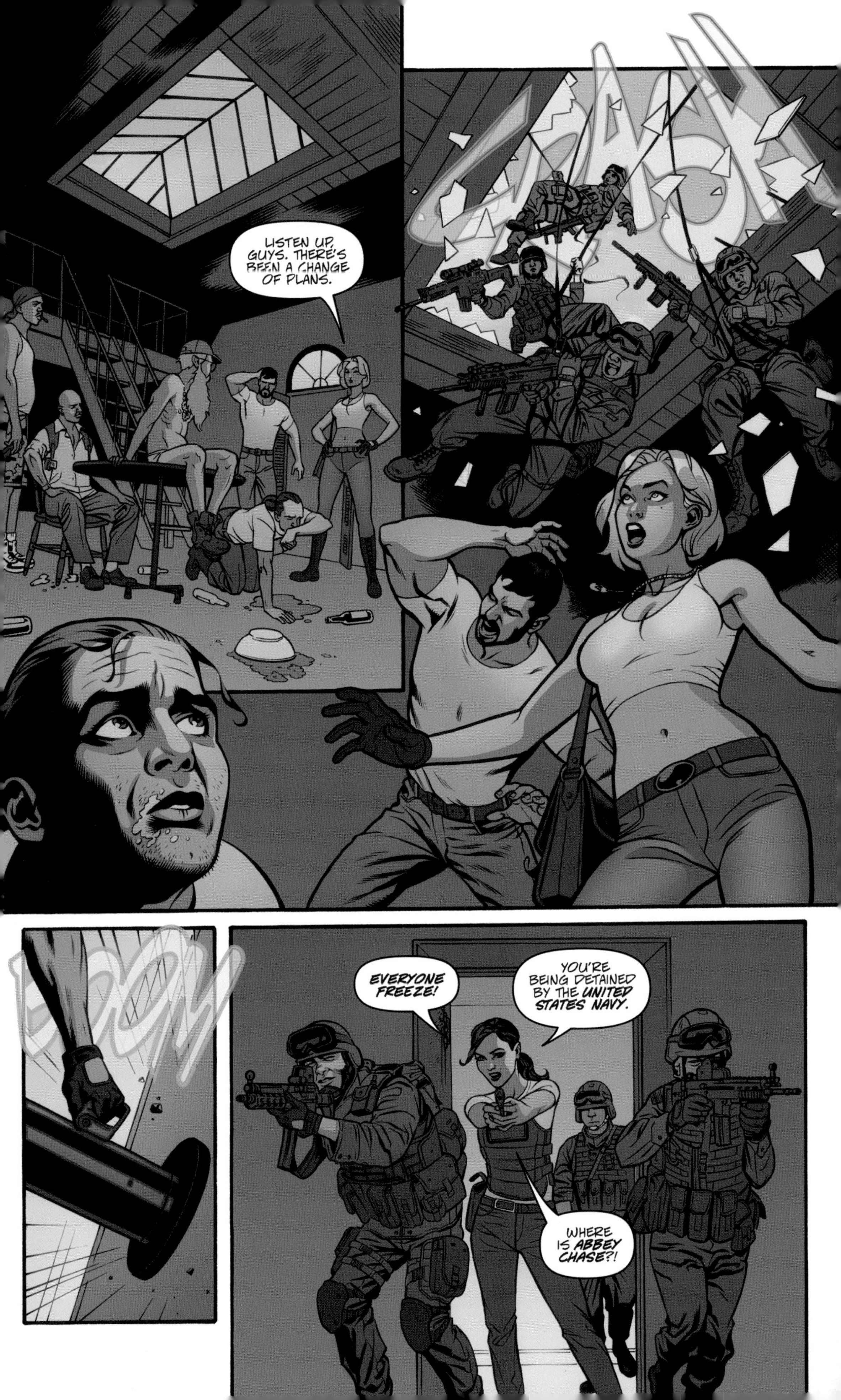
LISTEN UP, GUYS. THERE'S BEEN A CHANGE OF PLANS.
CRASH
BOOM
EVERYONE FREEZE!
YOU'RE BEING DETAINED BY THE UNITED STATES NAVY.
WHERE IS ABBEY CHASE?!

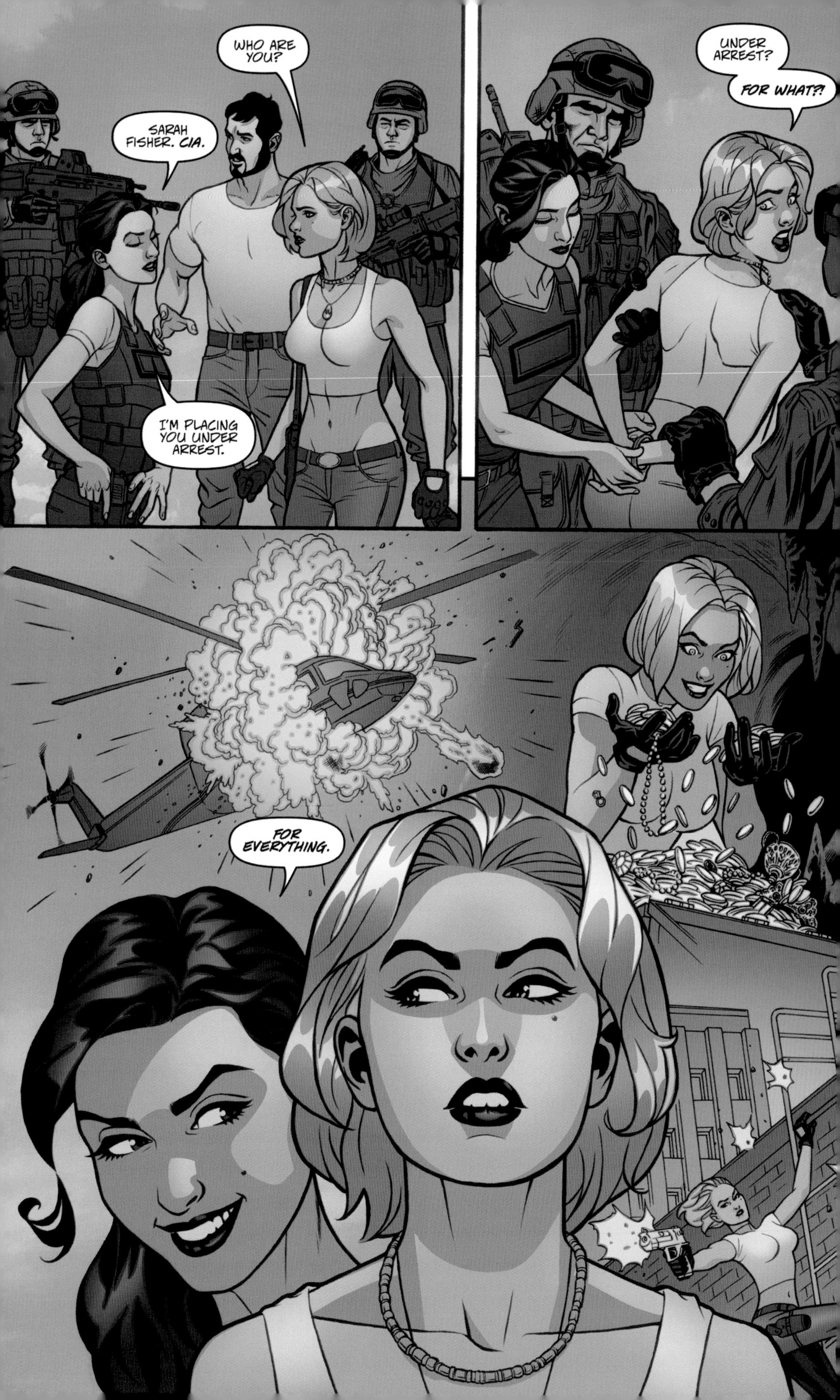
WHO ARE YOU?
SARAH FISHER. CIA.
I'M PLACING YOU UNDER ARREST.
UNDER ARREST?
FOR WHAT?!
FOR EVERYTHING.

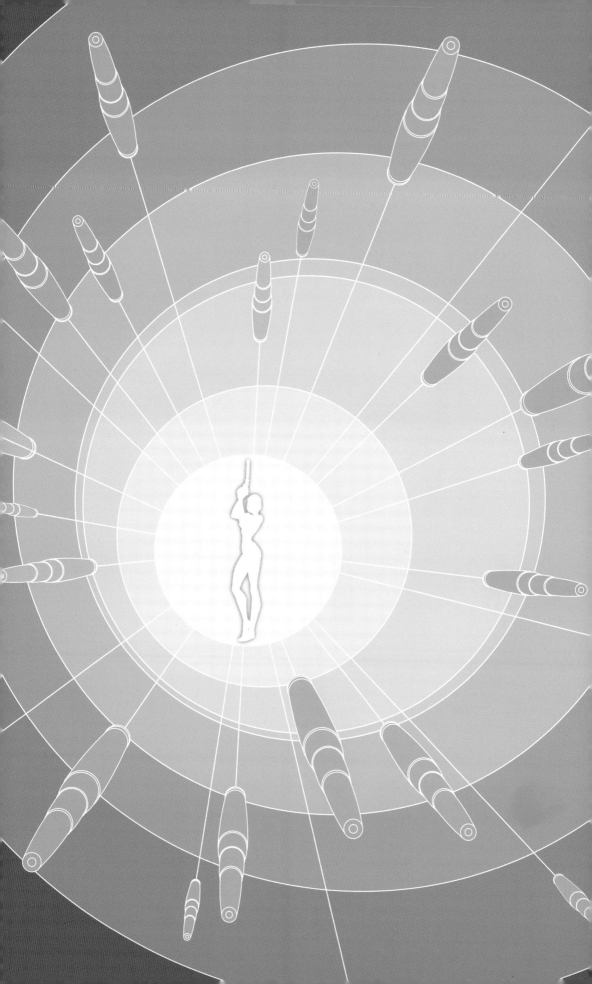

CHAPTER 3

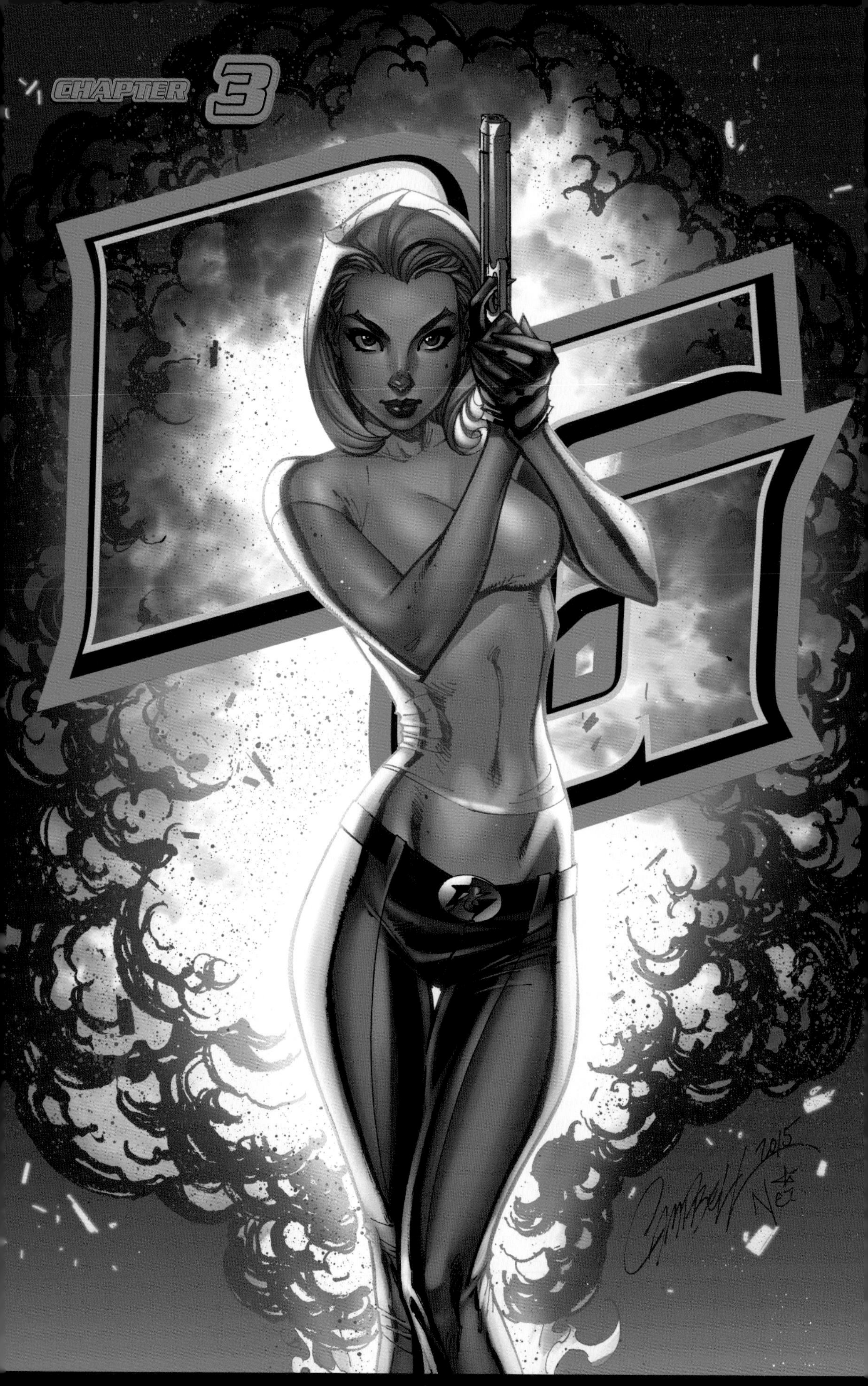

Campbell 2015
Nei

Art by J. Scott Campbell • Colors by Nei Ruffino

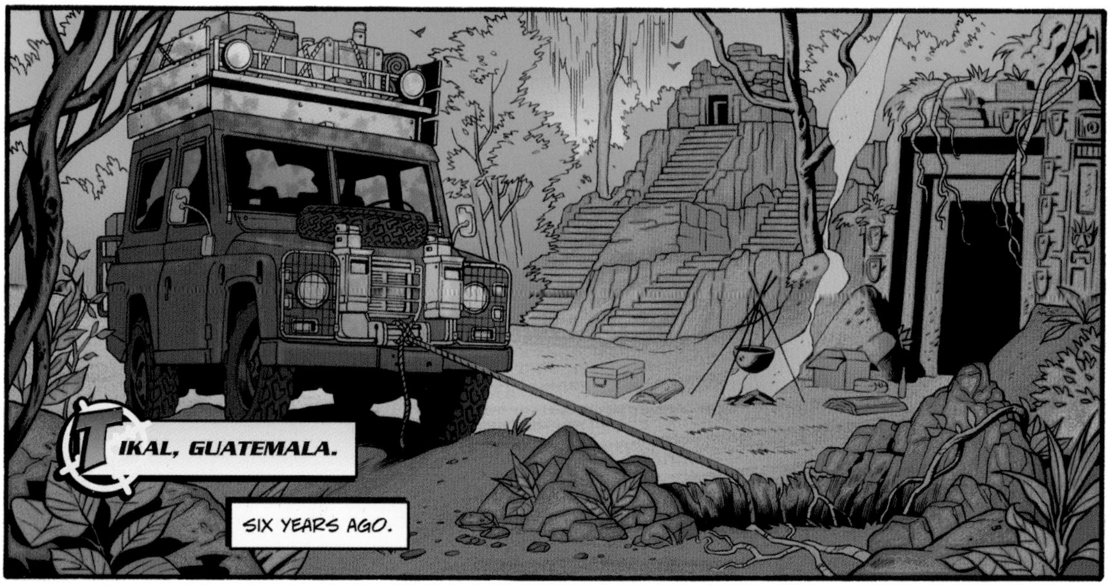
TIKAL, GUATEMALA.
SIX YEARS AGO.

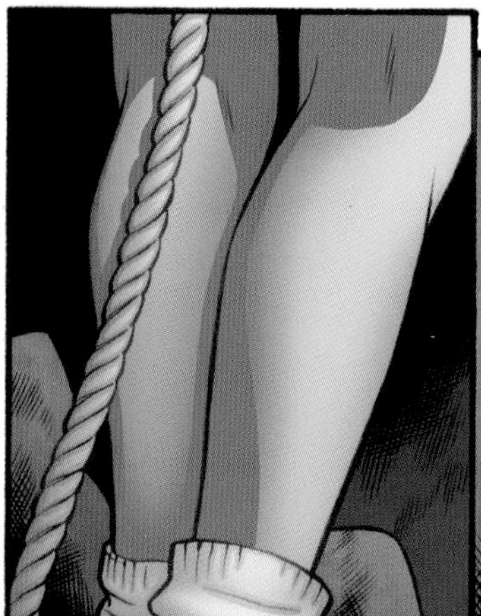
SSSSSS

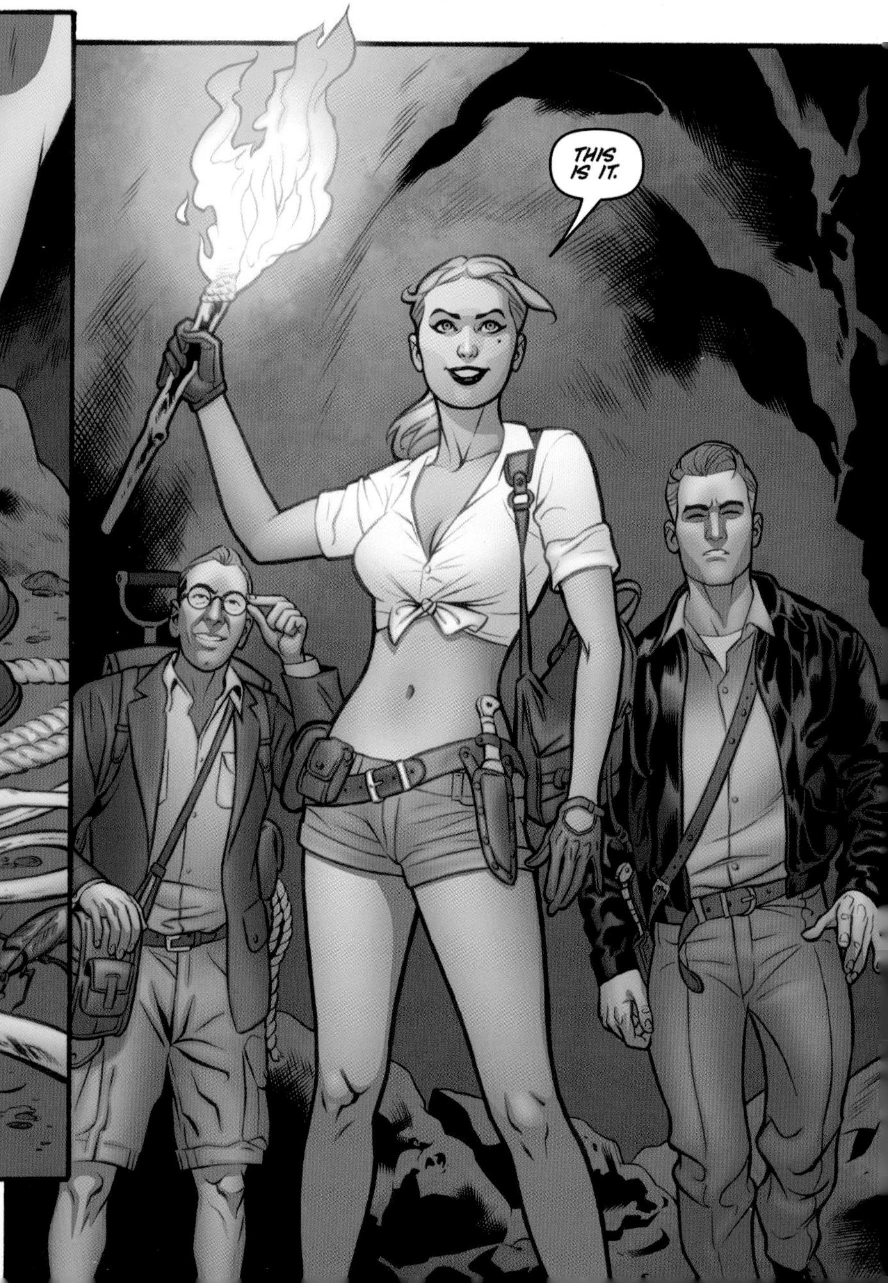
THIS IS IT.

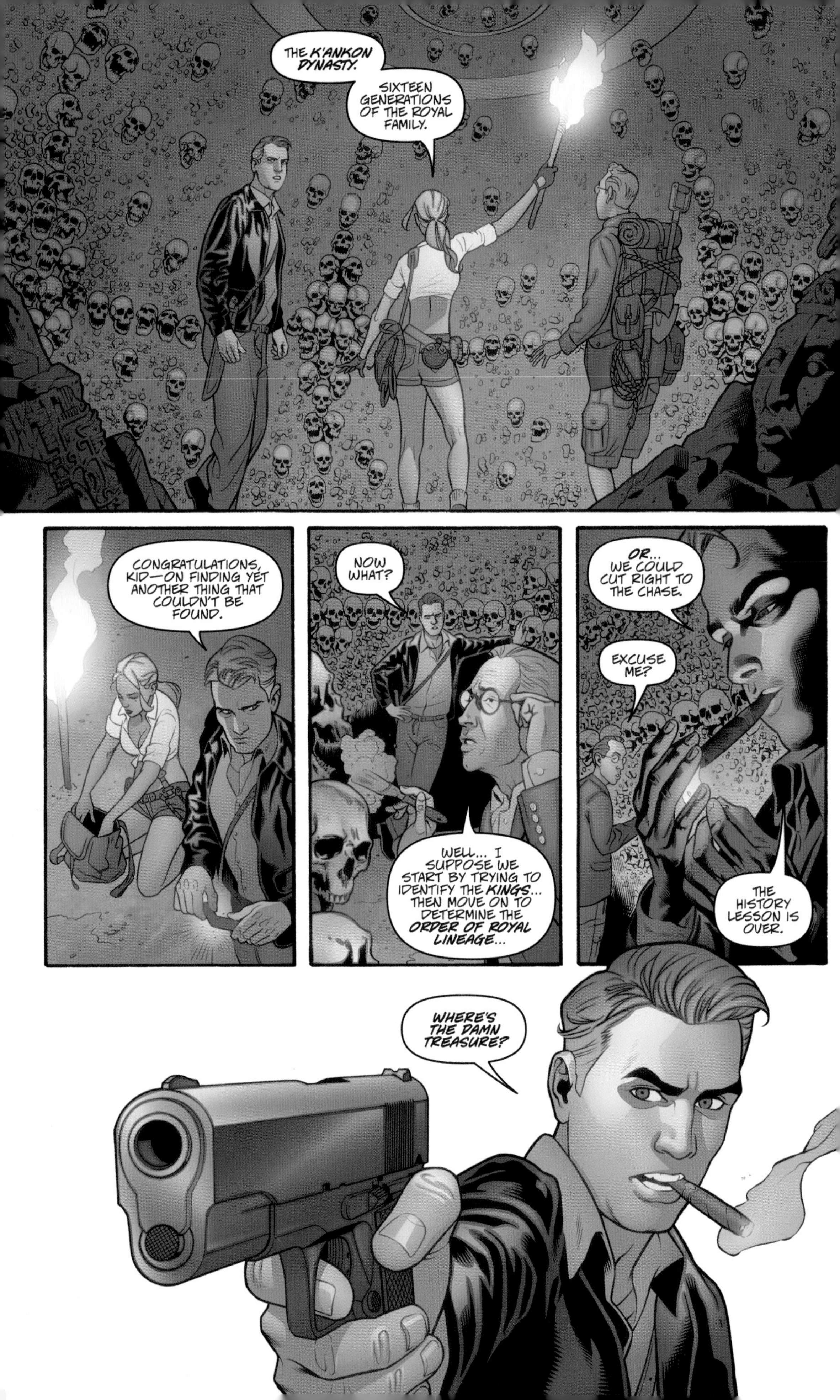
THE K'ANKON DYNASTY.
SIXTEEN GENERATIONS OF THE ROYAL FAMILY.
CONGRATULATIONS, KID—ON FINDING YET ANOTHER THING THAT COULDN'T BE FOUND.
NOW WHAT?
WELL... I SUPPOSE WE START BY TRYING TO IDENTIFY THE KINGS... THEN MOVE ON TO DETERMINE THE ORDER OF ROYAL LINEAGE...
OR... WE COULD CUT RIGHT TO THE CHASE.
EXCUSE ME?
THE HISTORY LESSON IS OVER.
WHERE'S THE DAMN TREASURE?

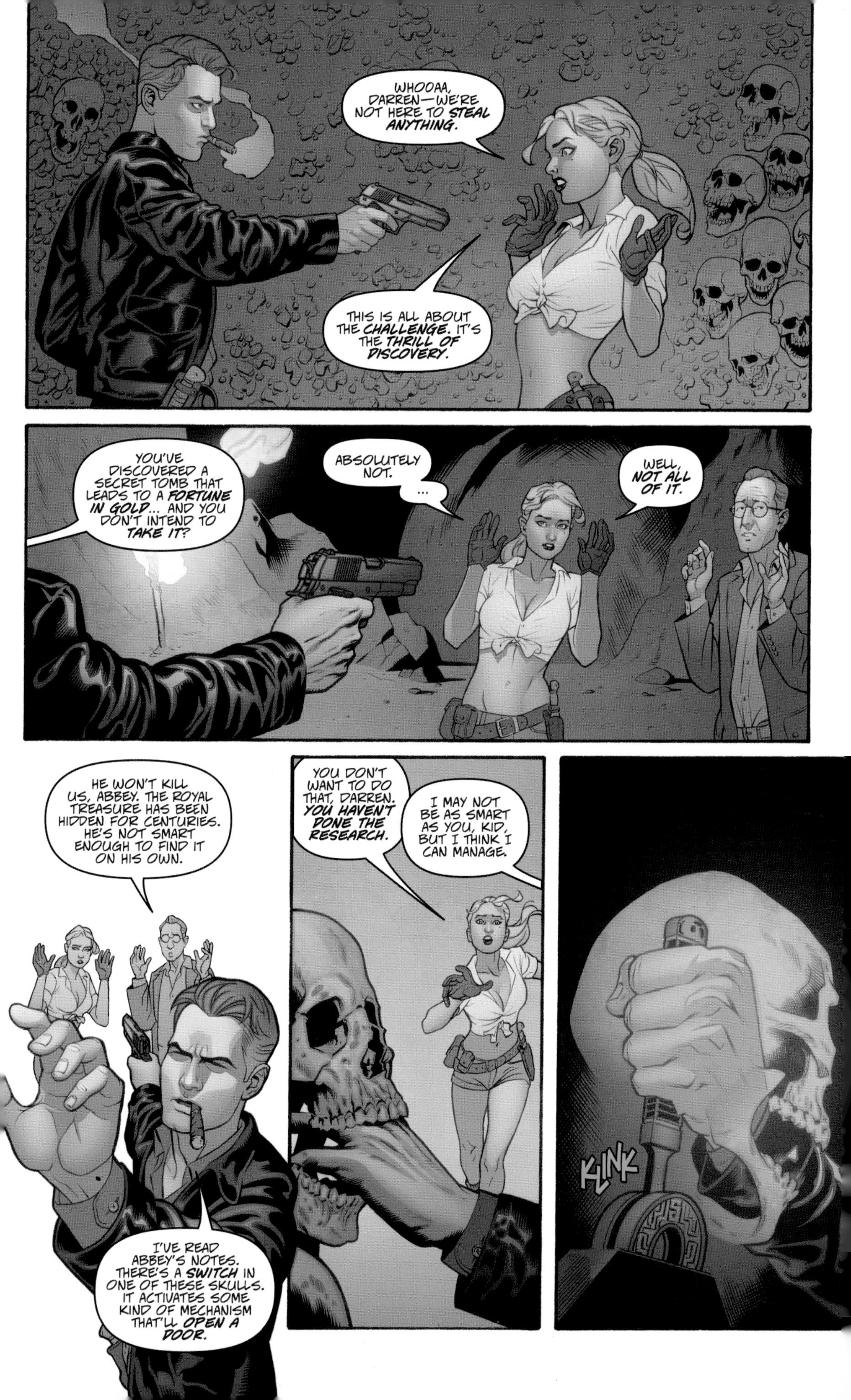
WHOOAA, DARREN—WE'RE NOT HERE TO STEAL ANYTHING.
THIS IS ALL ABOUT THE CHALLENGE. IT'S THE THRILL OF DISCOVERY.
YOU'VE DISCOVERED A SECRET TOMB THAT LEADS TO A FORTUNE IN GOLD... AND YOU DON'T INTEND TO TAKE IT?
ABSOLUTELY NOT.
...
WELL, NOT ALL OF IT.
HE WON'T KILL US, ABBEY. THE ROYAL TREASURE HAS BEEN HIDDEN FOR CENTURIES. HE'S NOT SMART ENOUGH TO FIND IT ON HIS OWN.
I'VE READ ABBEY'S NOTES. THERE'S A SWITCH IN ONE OF THESE SKULLS. IT ACTIVATES SOME KIND OF MECHANISM THAT'LL OPEN A DOOR.
YOU DON'T WANT TO DO THAT, DARREN. YOU HAVEN'T DONE THE RESEARCH.
I MAY NOT BE AS SMART AS YOU, KID, BUT I THINK I CAN MANAGE.
KLINK

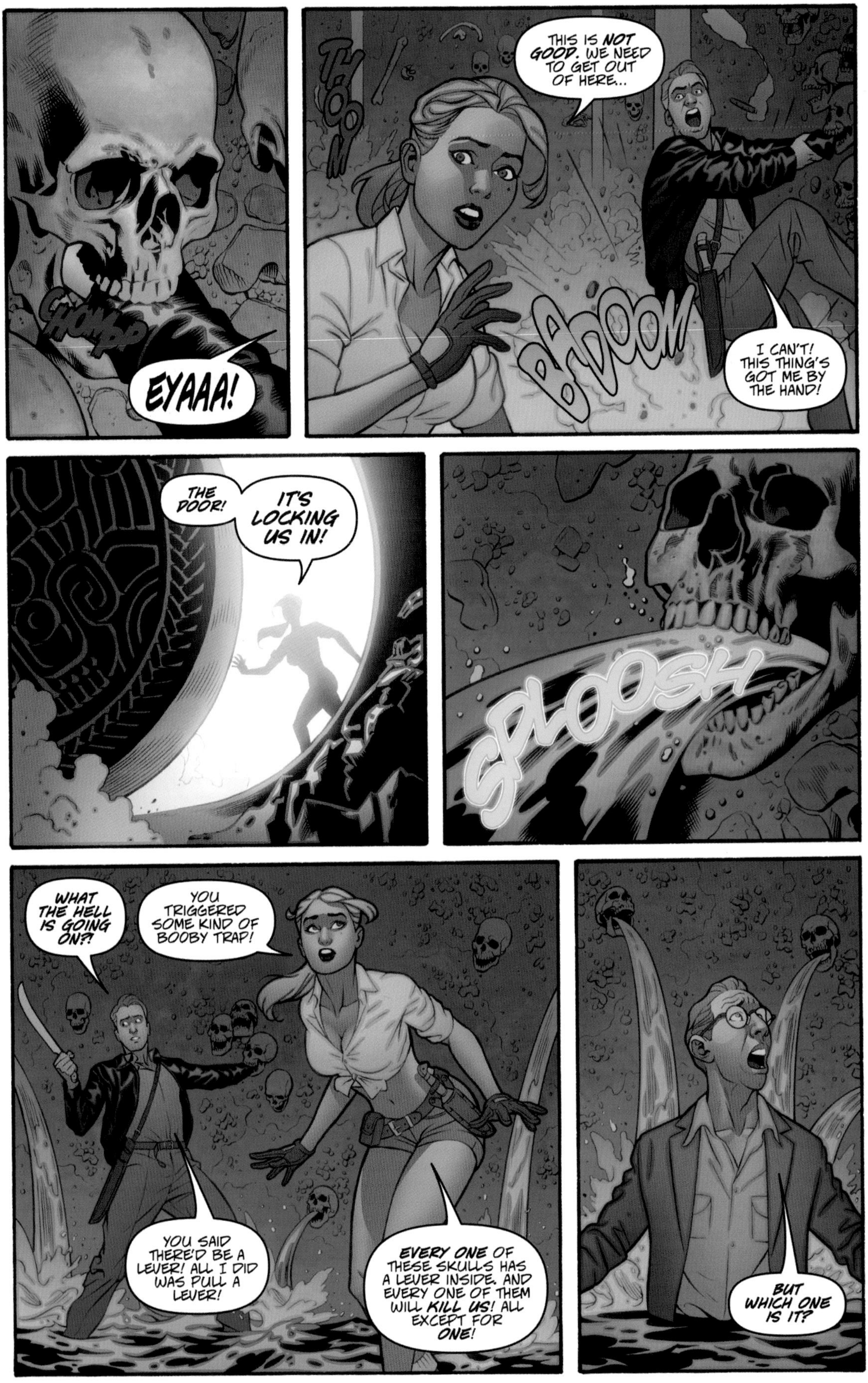
CHOMP
EYAAA!
THOOM
THIS IS NOT GOOD. WE NEED TO GET OUT OF HERE...
BADOOM
I CAN'T! THIS THING'S GOT ME BY THE HAND!
THE DOOR!
IT'S LOCKING US IN!
SPLOOSH
WHAT THE HELL IS GOING ON?!
YOU TRIGGERED SOME KIND OF BOOBY TRAP!
YOU SAID THERE'D BE A LEVER! ALL I DID WAS PULL A LEVER!
EVERY ONE OF THESE SKULLS HAS A LEVER INSIDE. AND EVERY ONE OF THEM WILL KILL US! ALL EXCEPT FOR ONE!
BUT WHICH ONE IS IT?

IS THIS SOME KIND OF TEST? DO YOU ALREADY KNOW WHICH ONE OF THESE SKULLS WILL SAVE US?

I HAVEN'T A CLUE... BUT I DO BELIEVE THAT THOSE WHO ONCE WISHED TO PROTECT THE ROYAL WEALTH MUST HAVE TRIGGERED THIS TRAP...

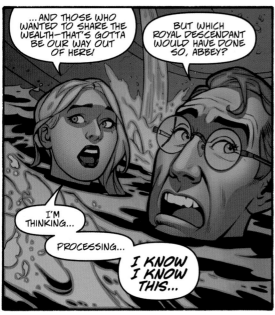

...AND THOSE WHO WANTED TO SHARE THE WEALTH—THAT'S GOTTA BE OUR WAY OUT OF HERE!

BUT WHICH ROYAL DESCENDANT WOULD HAVE DONE SO, ABBEY?

I'M THINKING...

PROCESSING...

I KNOW I KNOW THIS...

IT WAS THE FOURTH KING!

HE WAS HORRIBLE! A TYRANT!

BUT HE HAD A BROTHER!

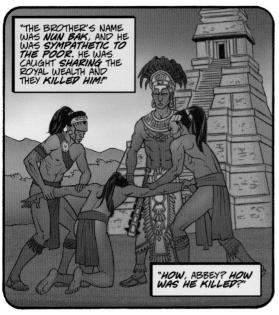

"THE BROTHER'S NAME WAS NUN BAK, AND HE WAS SYMPATHETIC TO THE POOR. HE WAS CAUGHT SHARING THE ROYAL WEALTH AND THEY KILLED HIM!"

"HOW, ABBEY? HOW WAS HE KILLED?"

"HIS HEAD! HE TOOK A FATAL BLOW TO THE HEAD!

"I CAN FIND HIM!"

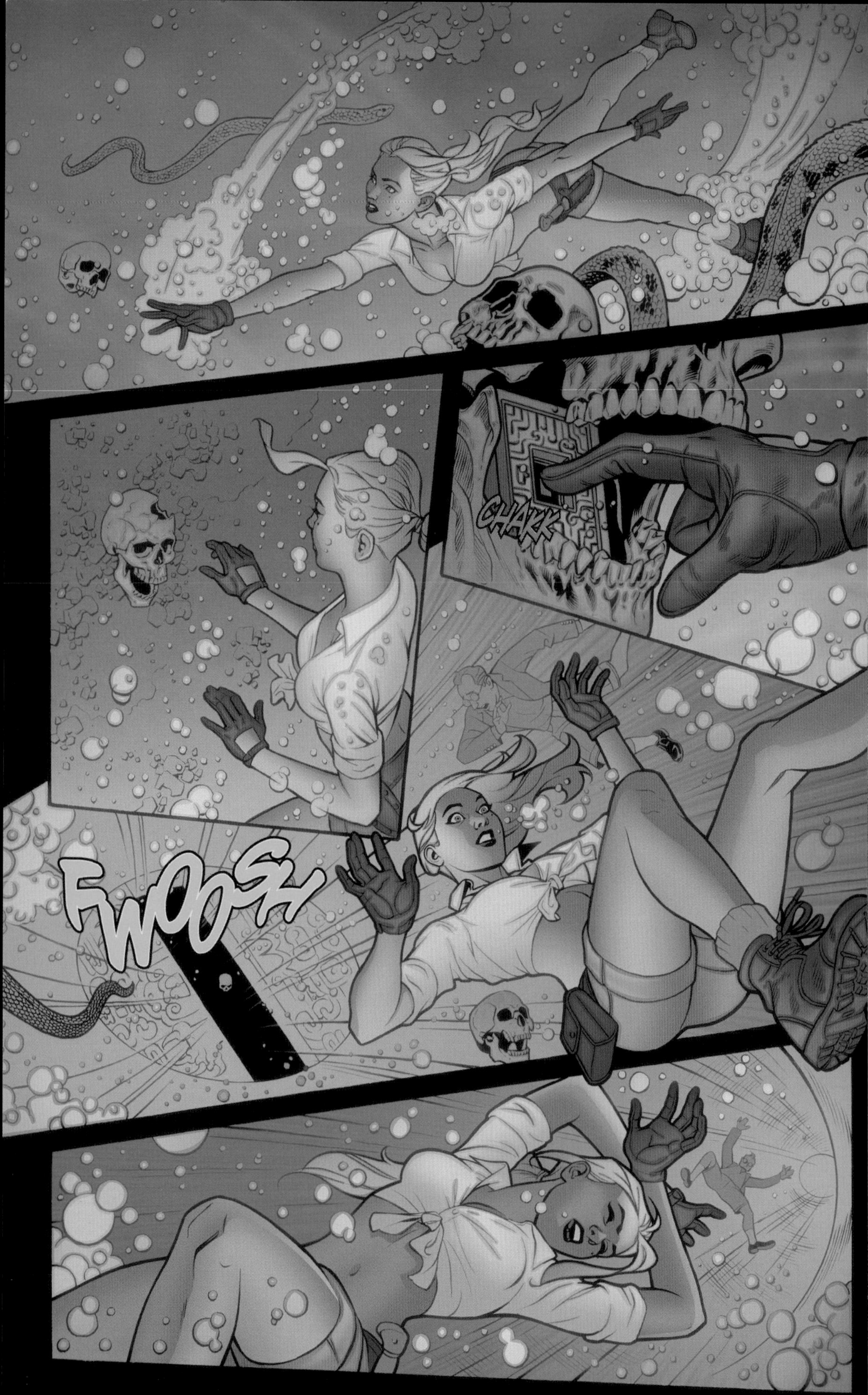
CHAKK
FWOOSH

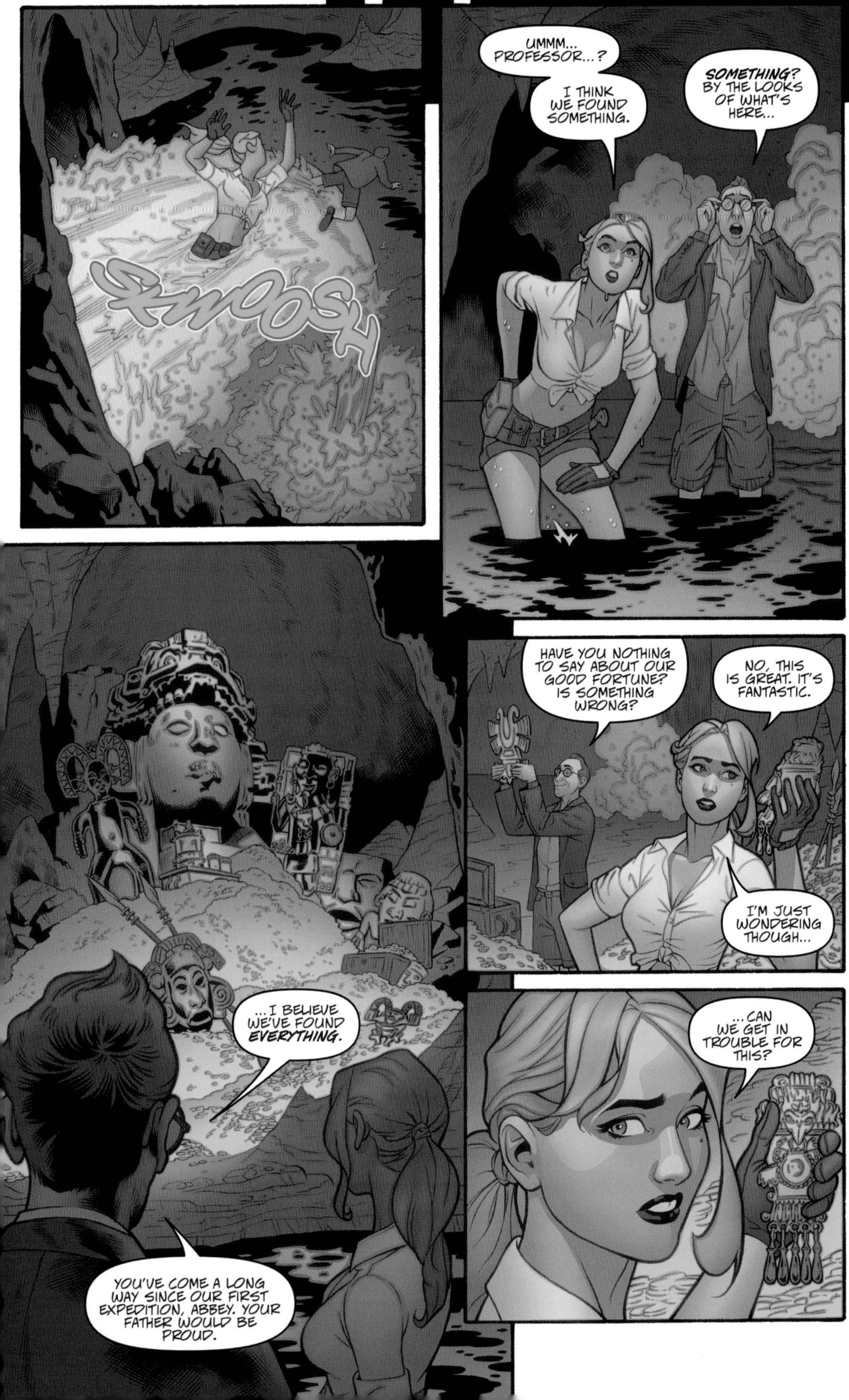
SWOOSH
UMMM... PROFESSOR...?
I THINK WE FOUND SOMETHING.
SOMETHING? BY THE LOOKS OF WHAT'S HERE...
...I BELIEVE WE'VE FOUND EVERYTHING.
YOU'VE COME A LONG WAY SINCE OUR FIRST EXPEDITION, ABBEY. YOUR FATHER WOULD BE PROUD.
HAVE YOU NOTHING TO SAY ABOUT OUR GOOD FORTUNE? IS SOMETHING WRONG?
NO, THIS IS GREAT. IT'S FANTASTIC.
I'M JUST WONDERING THOUGH...
...CAN WE GET IN TROUBLE FOR THIS?

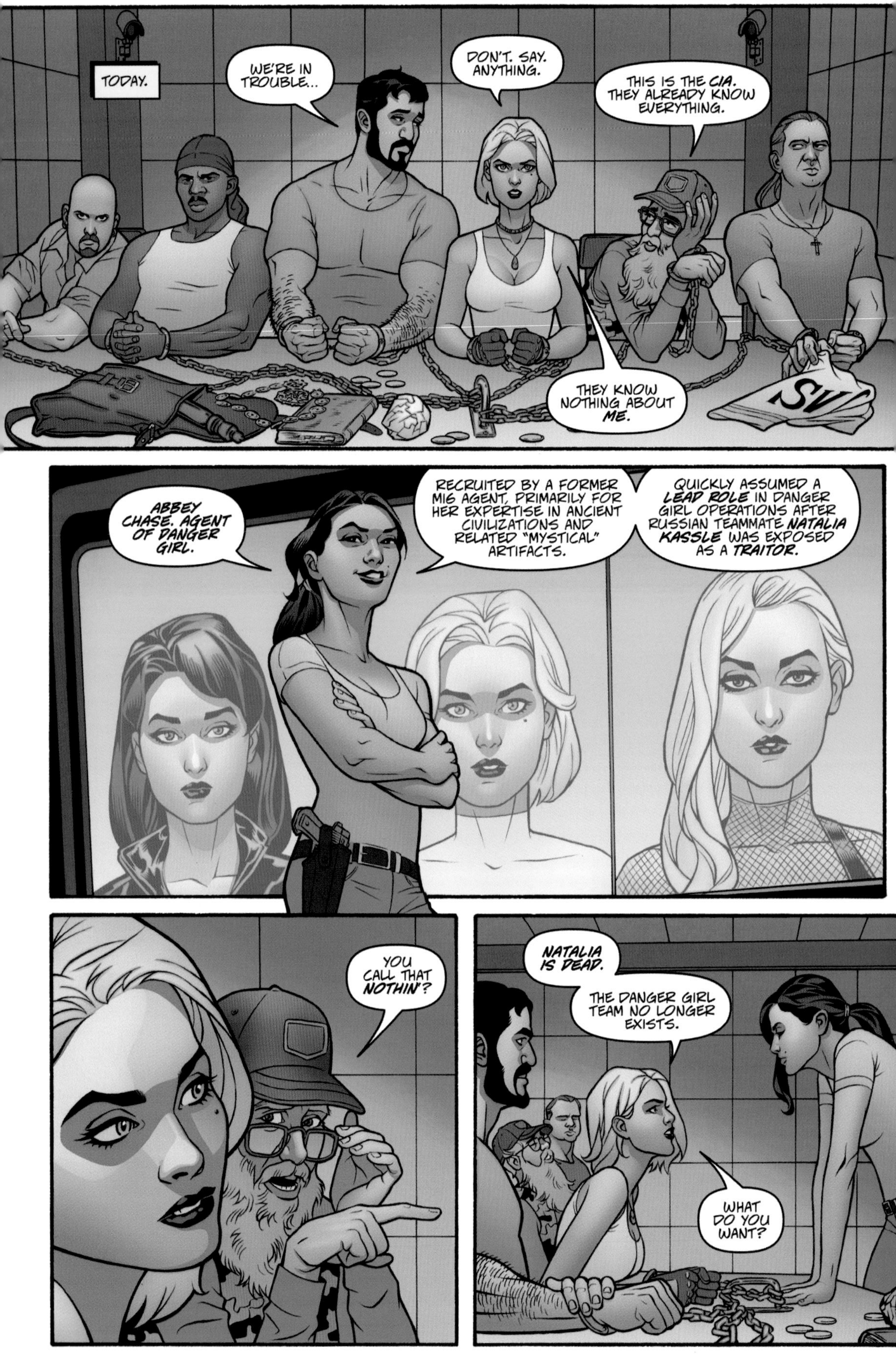
TODAY.
WE'RE IN TROUBLE...
DON'T. SAY. ANYTHING.
THIS IS THE CIA. THEY ALREADY KNOW EVERYTHING.
THEY KNOW NOTHING ABOUT ME.
ABBEY CHASE. AGENT OF DANGER GIRL.
RECRUITED BY A FORMER MI6 AGENT, PRIMARILY FOR HER EXPERTISE IN ANCIENT CIVILIZATIONS AND RELATED "MYSTICAL" ARTIFACTS.
QUICKLY ASSUMED A LEAD ROLE IN DANGER GIRL OPERATIONS AFTER RUSSIAN TEAMMATE NATALIA KASSLE WAS EXPOSED AS A TRAITOR.
YOU CALL THAT NOTHIN'?
NATALIA IS DEAD.
THE DANGER GIRL TEAM NO LONGER EXISTS.
WHAT DO YOU WANT?

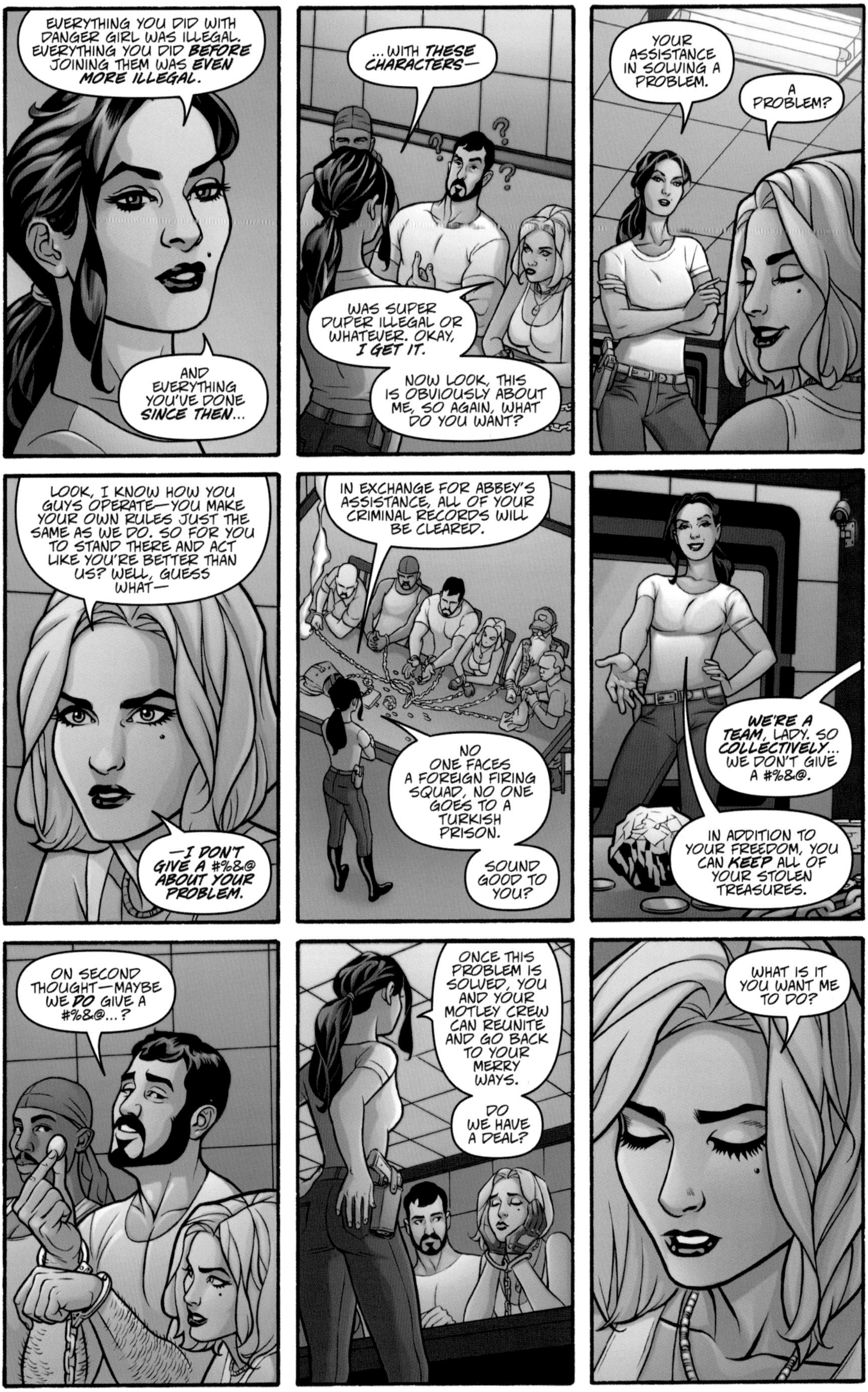
EVERYTHING YOU DID WITH DANGER GIRL WAS ILLEGAL. EVERYTHING YOU DID BEFORE JOINING THEM WAS EVEN MORE ILLEGAL.
AND EVERYTHING YOU'VE DONE SINCE THEN...
...WITH THESE CHARACTERS—
WAS SUPER DUPER ILLEGAL OR WHATEVER. OKAY, I GET IT.
NOW LOOK, THIS IS OBVIOUSLY ABOUT ME, SO AGAIN, WHAT DO YOU WANT?
YOUR ASSISTANCE IN SOLVING A PROBLEM.
A PROBLEM?
LOOK, I KNOW HOW YOU GUYS OPERATE—YOU MAKE YOUR OWN RULES JUST THE SAME AS WE DO. SO FOR YOU TO STAND THERE AND ACT LIKE YOU'RE BETTER THAN US? WELL, GUESS WHAT—
—I DON'T GIVE A #%&@ ABOUT YOUR PROBLEM.
IN EXCHANGE FOR ABBEY'S ASSISTANCE, ALL OF YOUR CRIMINAL RECORDS WILL BE CLEARED.
NO ONE FACES A FOREIGN FIRING SQUAD, NO ONE GOES TO A TURKISH PRISON.
SOUND GOOD TO YOU?
WE'RE A TEAM, LADY. SO COLLECTIVELY... WE DON'T GIVE A #%&@.
IN ADDITION TO YOUR FREEDOM, YOU CAN KEEP ALL OF YOUR STOLEN TREASURES.
ON SECOND THOUGHT—MAYBE WE DO GIVE A #%&@...?
ONCE THIS PROBLEM IS SOLVED, YOU AND YOUR MOTLEY CREW CAN REUNITE AND GO BACK TO YOUR MERRY WAYS.
DO WE HAVE A DEAL?
WHAT IS IT YOU WANT ME TO DO?

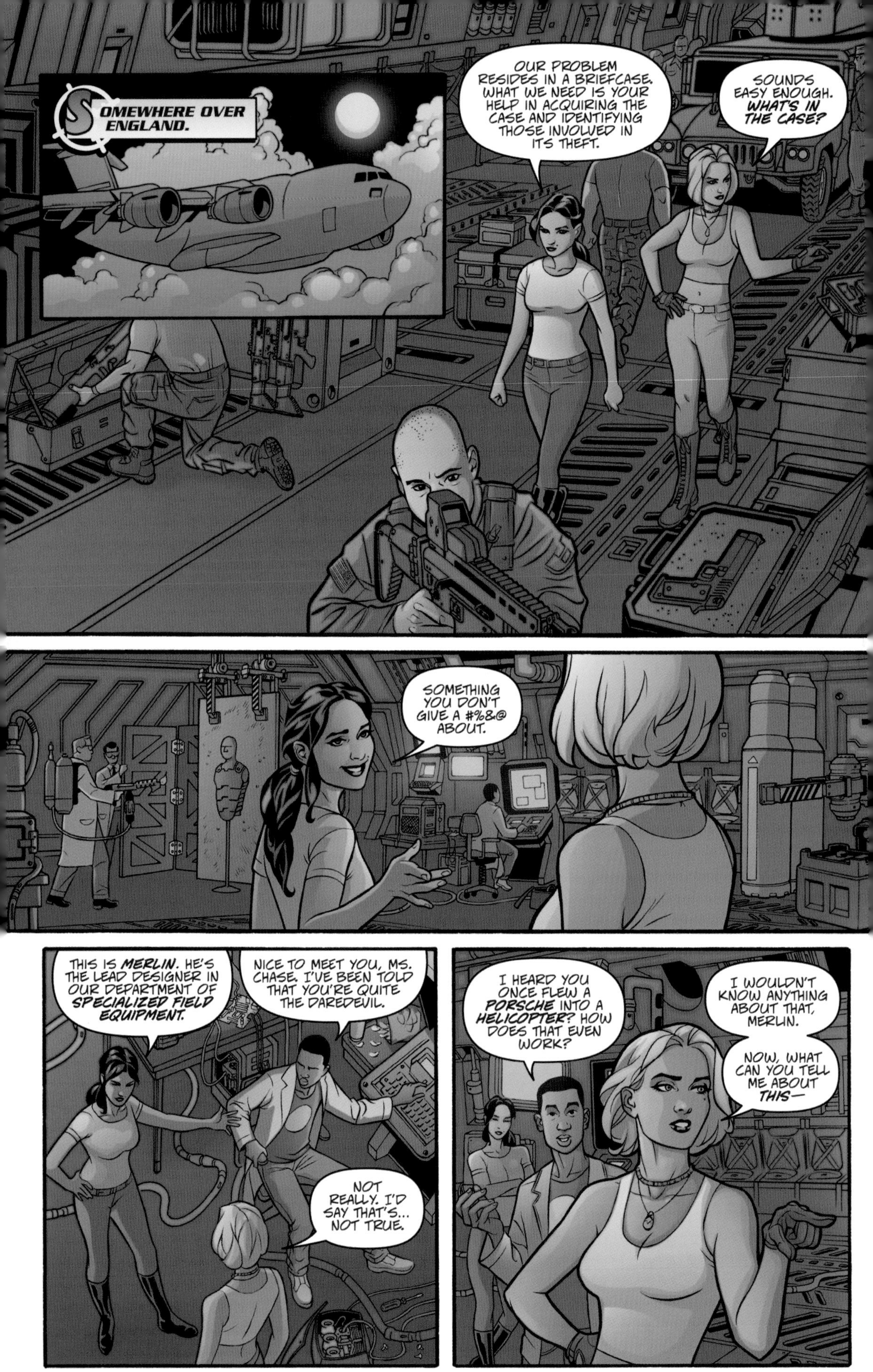
SOMEWHERE OVER ENGLAND.
OUR PROBLEM RESIDES IN A BRIEFCASE. WHAT WE NEED IS YOUR HELP IN ACQUIRING THE CASE AND IDENTIFYING THOSE INVOLVED IN ITS THEFT.
SOUNDS EASY ENOUGH. WHAT'S IN THE CASE?
SOMETHING YOU DON'T GIVE A #%&@ ABOUT.
THIS IS MERLIN. HE'S THE LEAD DESIGNER IN OUR DEPARTMENT OF SPECIALIZED FIELD EQUIPMENT.
NICE TO MEET YOU, MS. CHASE. I'VE BEEN TOLD THAT YOU'RE QUITE THE DAREDEVIL.
NOT REALLY. I'D SAY THAT'S... NOT TRUE.
I HEARD YOU ONCE FLEW A PORSCHE INTO A HELICOPTER? HOW DOES THAT EVEN WORK?
I WOULDN'T KNOW ANYTHING ABOUT THAT, MERLIN.
NOW, WHAT CAN YOU TELL ME ABOUT THIS—

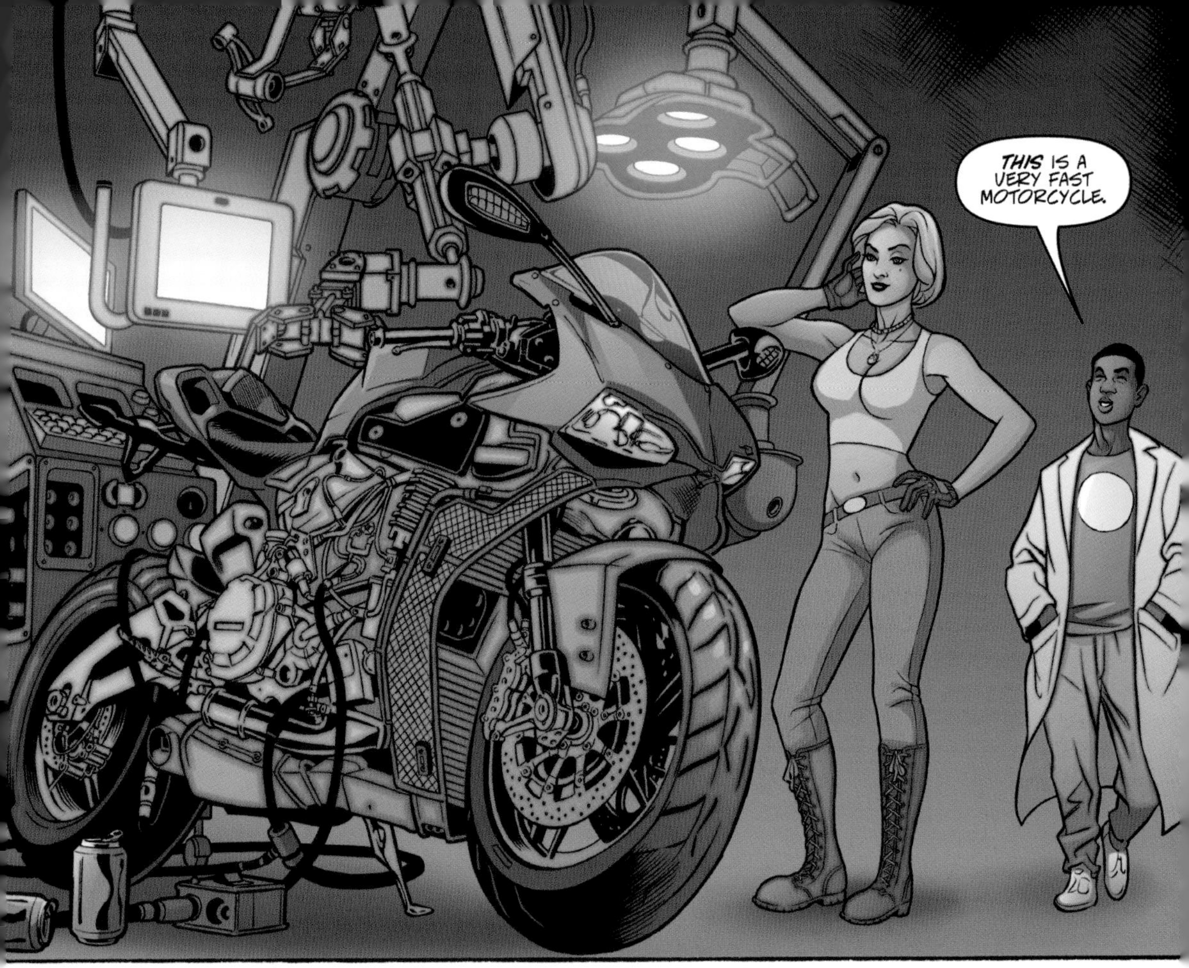
THIS IS A VERY FAST MOTORCYCLE.

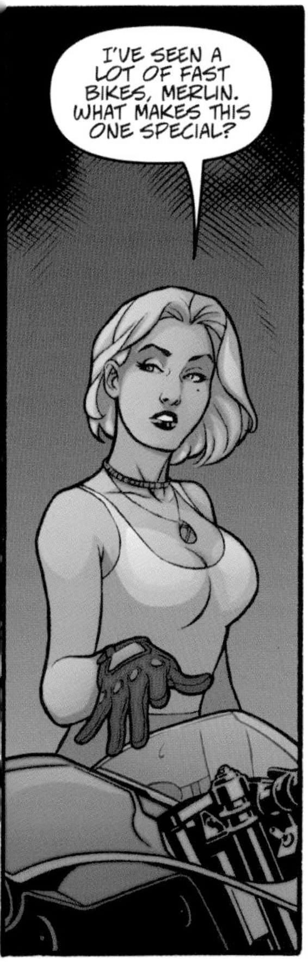
I'VE SEEN A LOT OF FAST BIKES, MERLIN. WHAT MAKES THIS ONE SPECIAL?

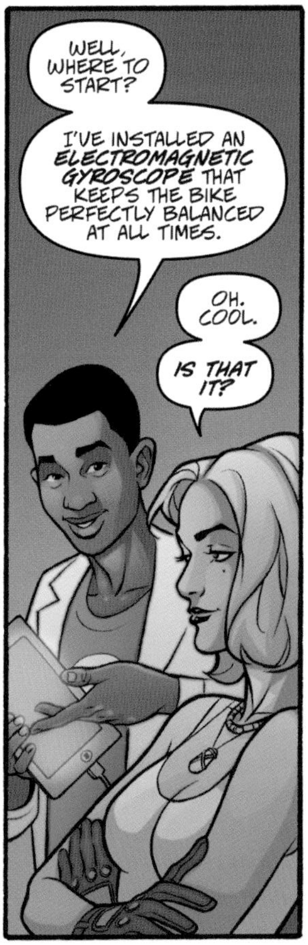
WELL, WHERE TO START?
I'VE INSTALLED AN ELECTROMAGNETIC GYROSCOPE THAT KEEPS THE BIKE PERFECTLY BALANCED AT ALL TIMES.
OH. COOL.
IS THAT IT?

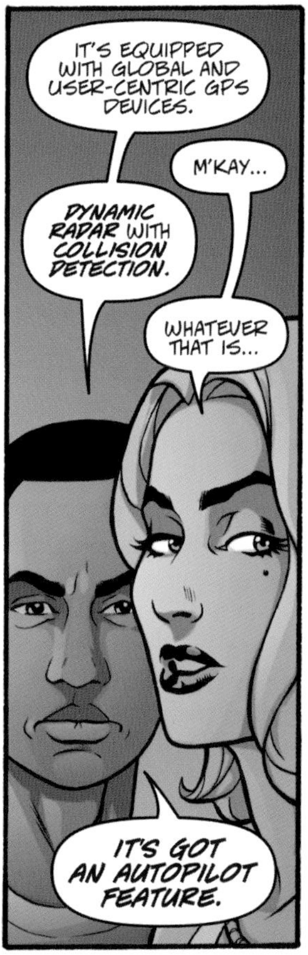
IT'S EQUIPPED WITH GLOBAL AND USER-CENTRIC GPS DEVICES.
M'KAY...
DYNAMIC RADAR WITH COLLISION DETECTION.
WHATEVER THAT IS...
IT'S GOT AN AUTOPILOT FEATURE.

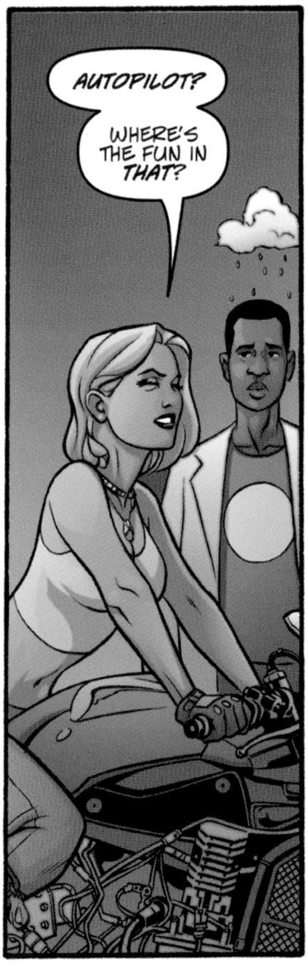
AUTOPILOT?
WHERE'S THE FUN IN THAT?

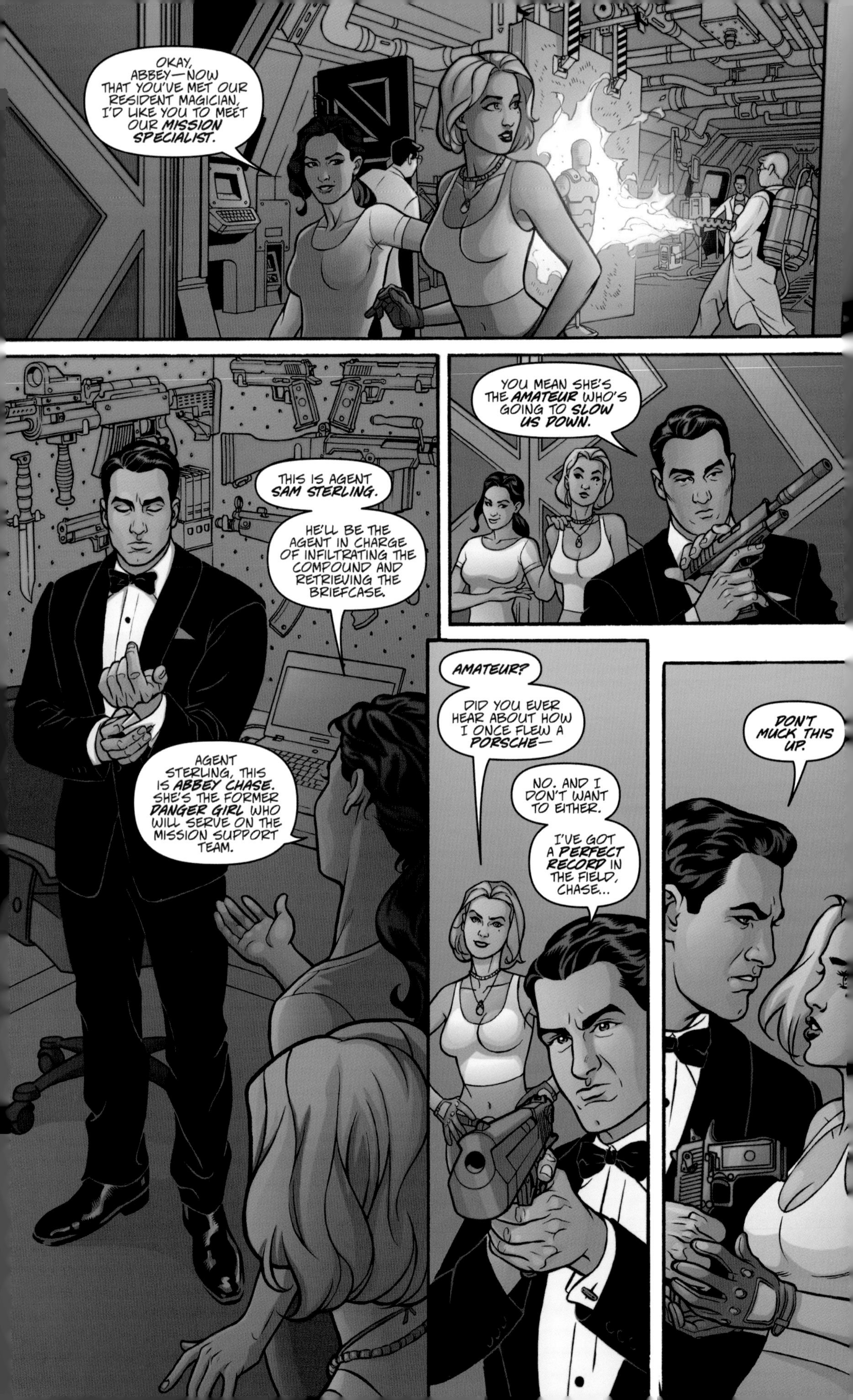

OKAY, ABBEY—NOW THAT YOU'VE MET OUR RESIDENT MAGICIAN, I'D LIKE YOU TO MEET OUR MISSION SPECIALIST.
THIS IS AGENT SAM STERLING.
HE'LL BE THE AGENT IN CHARGE OF INFILTRATING THE COMPOUND AND RETRIEVING THE BRIEFCASE.
AGENT STERLING, THIS IS ABBEY CHASE. SHE'S THE FORMER DANGER GIRL WHO WILL SERVE ON THE MISSION SUPPORT TEAM.
YOU MEAN SHE'S THE AMATEUR WHO'S GOING TO SLOW US DOWN.
AMATEUR?
DID YOU EVER HEAR ABOUT HOW I ONCE FLEW A PORSCHE—
NO. AND I DON'T WANT TO EITHER.
I'VE GOT A PERFECT RECORD IN THE FIELD, CHASE...
DON'T MUCK THIS UP.

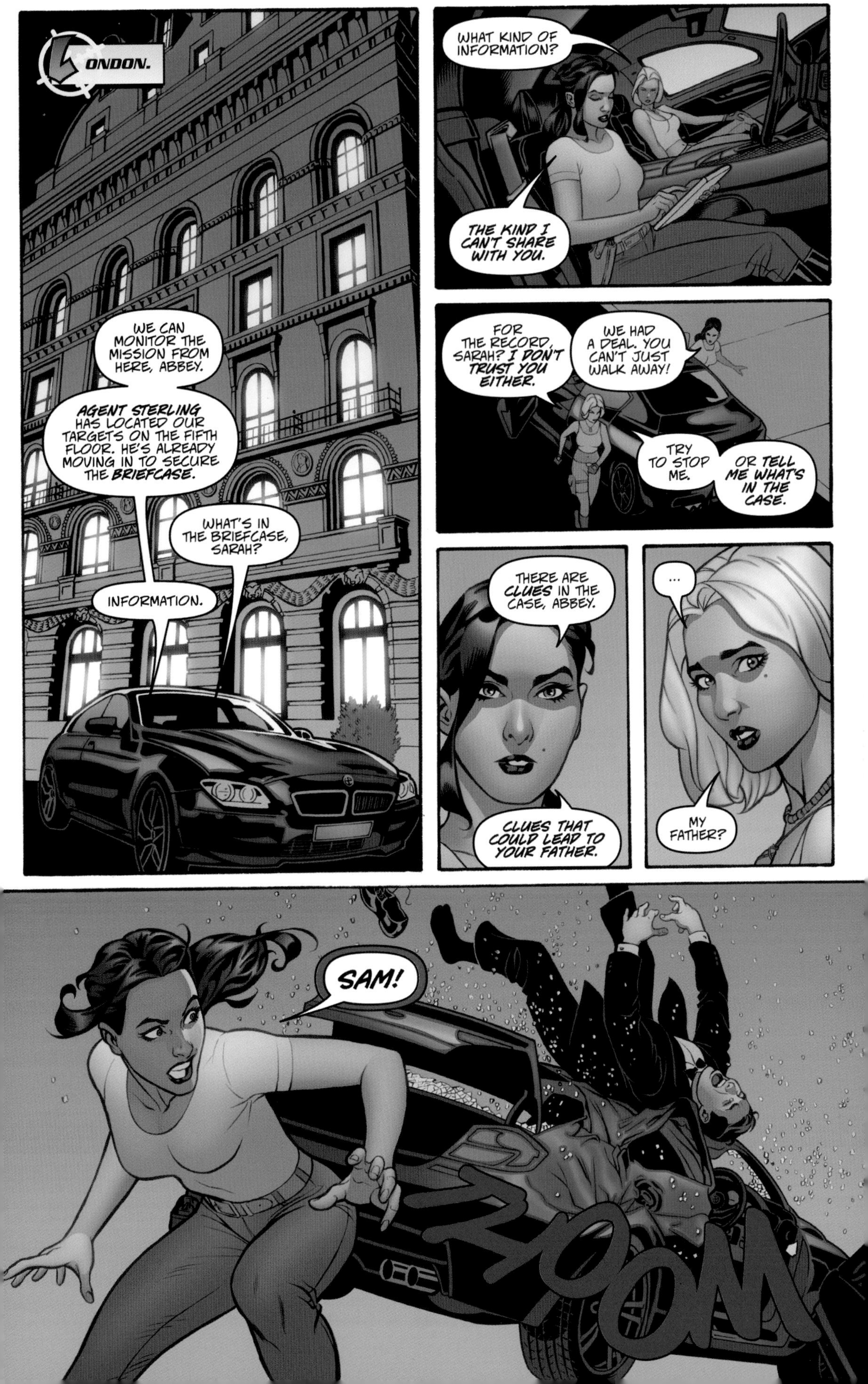
LONDON.
WE CAN MONITOR THE MISSION FROM HERE, ABBEY.
AGENT STERLING HAS LOCATED OUR TARGETS ON THE FIFTH FLOOR. HE'S ALREADY MOVING IN TO SECURE THE BRIEFCASE.
WHAT'S IN THE BRIEFCASE, SARAH?
INFORMATION.
WHAT KIND OF INFORMATION?
THE KIND I CAN'T SHARE WITH YOU.
WE HAD A DEAL. YOU CAN'T JUST WALK AWAY!
FOR THE RECORD, SARAH? I DON'T TRUST YOU EITHER.
TRY TO STOP ME.
OR TELL ME WHAT'S IN THE CASE.
THERE ARE CLUES IN THE CASE, ABBEY.
CLUES THAT COULD LEAD TO YOUR FATHER.
...
MY FATHER?
SAM!
BOOM

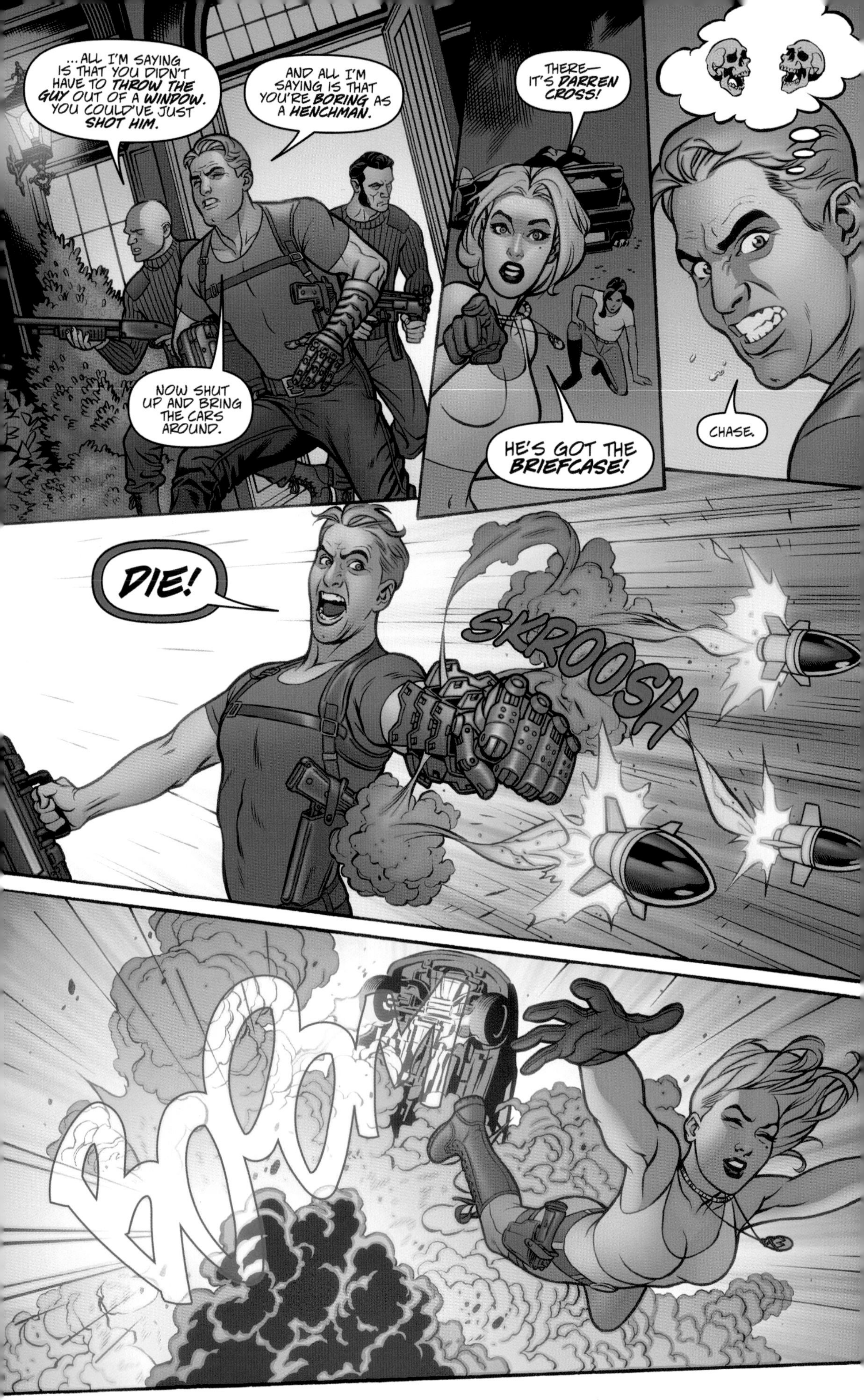
...ALL I'M SAYING IS THAT YOU DIDN'T HAVE TO THROW THE GUY OUT OF A WINDOW. YOU COULD'VE JUST SHOT HIM.
AND ALL I'M SAYING IS THAT YOU'RE BORING AS A HENCHMAN.
NOW SHUT UP AND BRING THE CARS AROUND.
THERE— IT'S DARREN CROSS!
HE'S GOT THE BRIEFCASE!
CHASE.
DIE!
SKROOSH

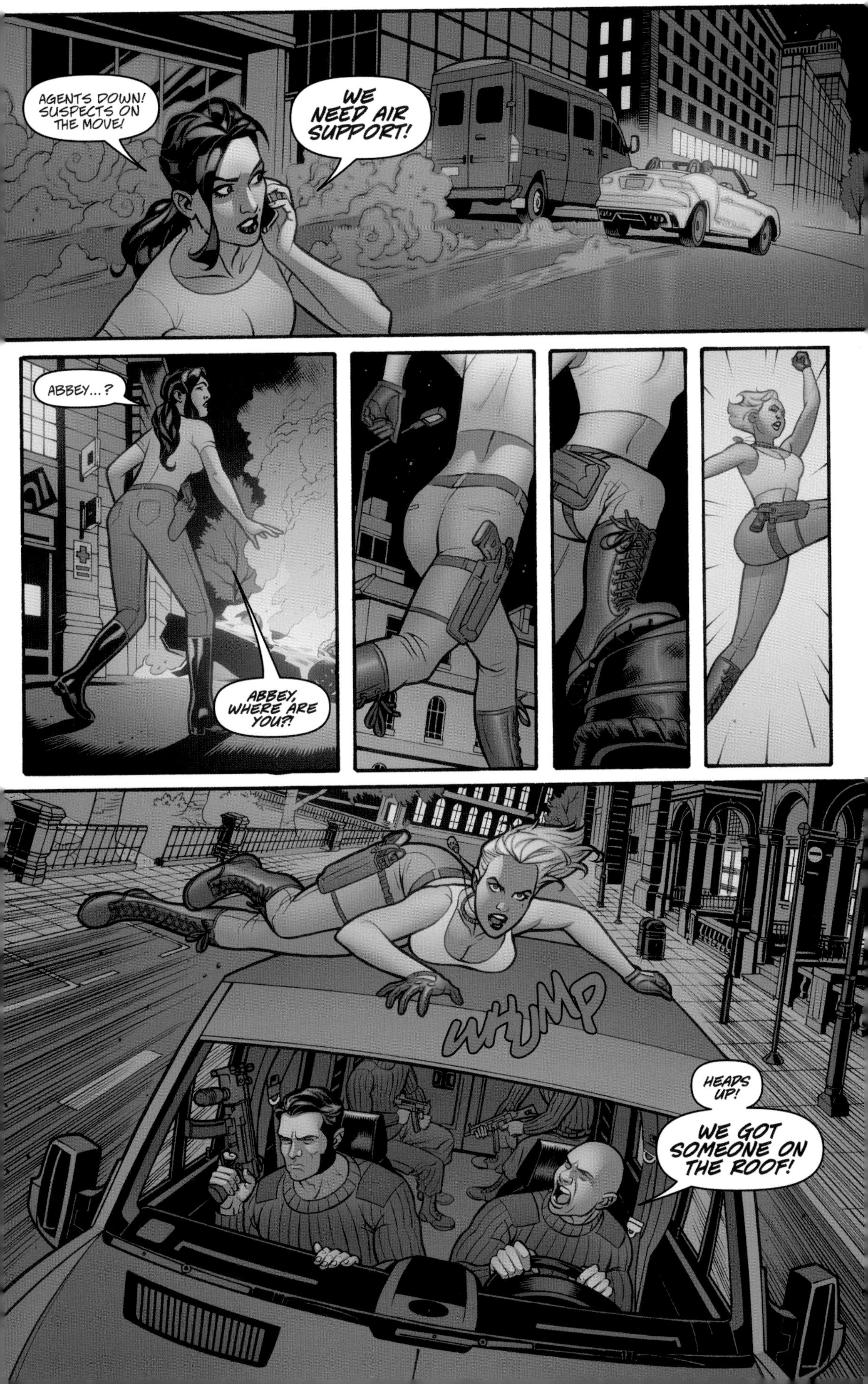
AGENTS DOWN! SUSPECTS ON THE MOVE!
WE NEED AIR SUPPORT!
ABBEY...?
ABBEY, WHERE ARE YOU?!
WHUMP
HEADS UP!
WE GOT SOMEONE ON THE ROOF!

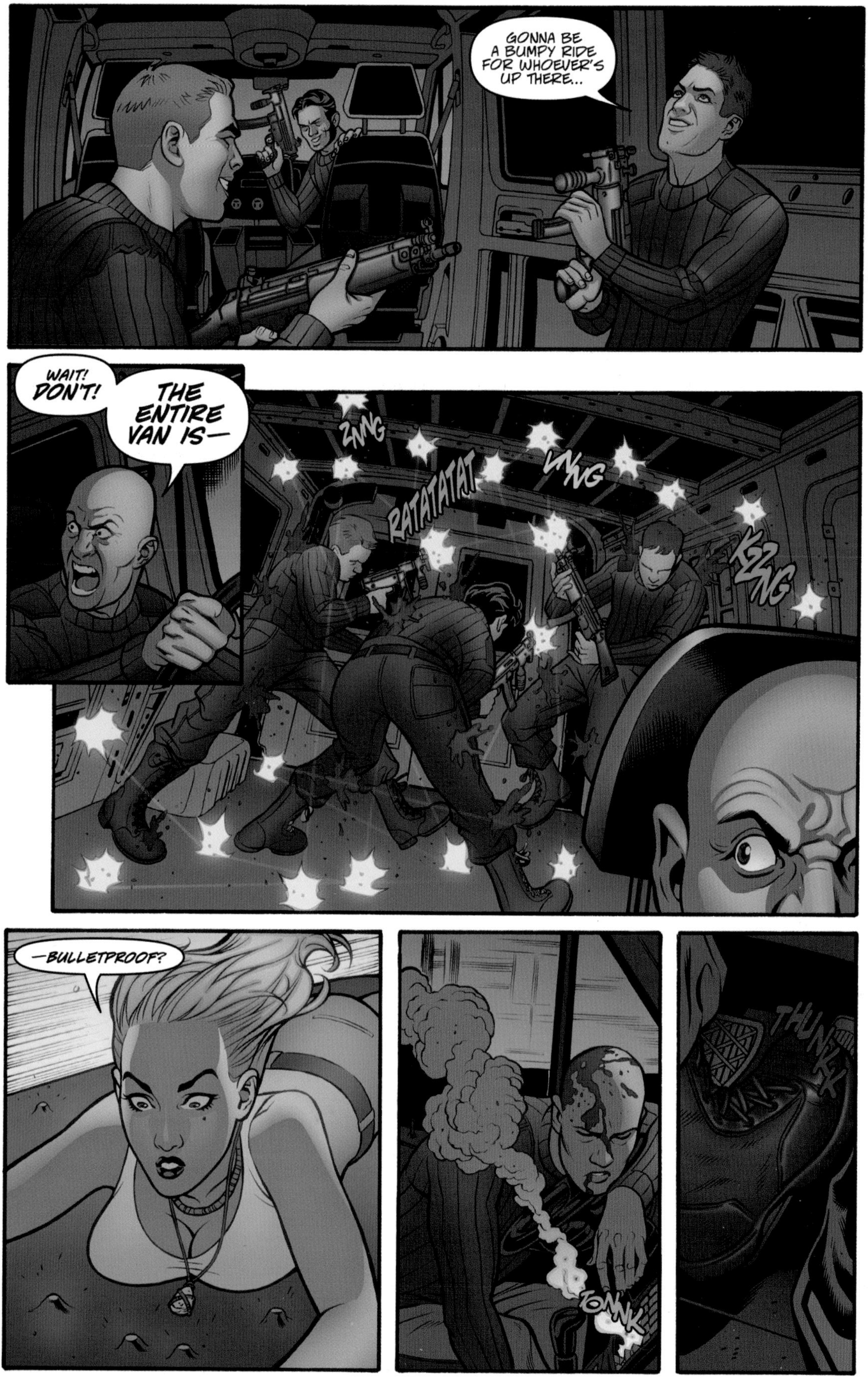
GONNA BE A BUMPY RIDE FOR WHOEVER'S UP THERE...
WAIT! DON'T!
THE ENTIRE VAN IS—
ZNNG
RATATATAT
VNNG
KZZNG
—BULLETPROOF?
TONNK
THUNKK

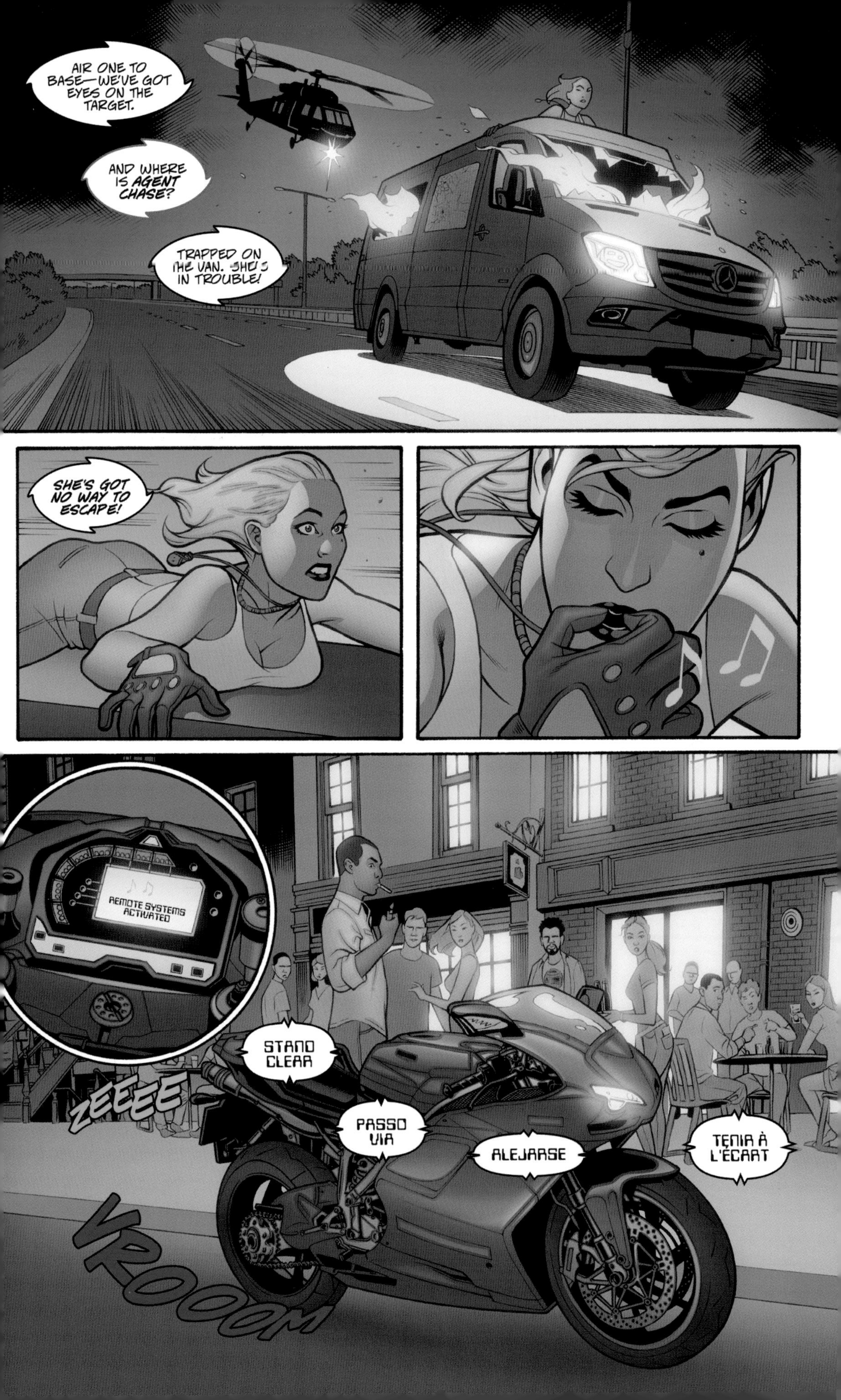
AIR ONE TO BASE—WE'VE GOT EYES ON THE TARGET.
AND WHERE IS AGENT CHASE?
TRAPPED ON THE VAN. SHE'S IN TROUBLE!
SHE'S GOT NO WAY TO ESCAPE!
REMOTE SYSTEMS ACTIVATED
ZEEEE
STAND CLEAR
PASSO VIA
ALEJARSE
TENIR À L'ÉCART
VROOOM

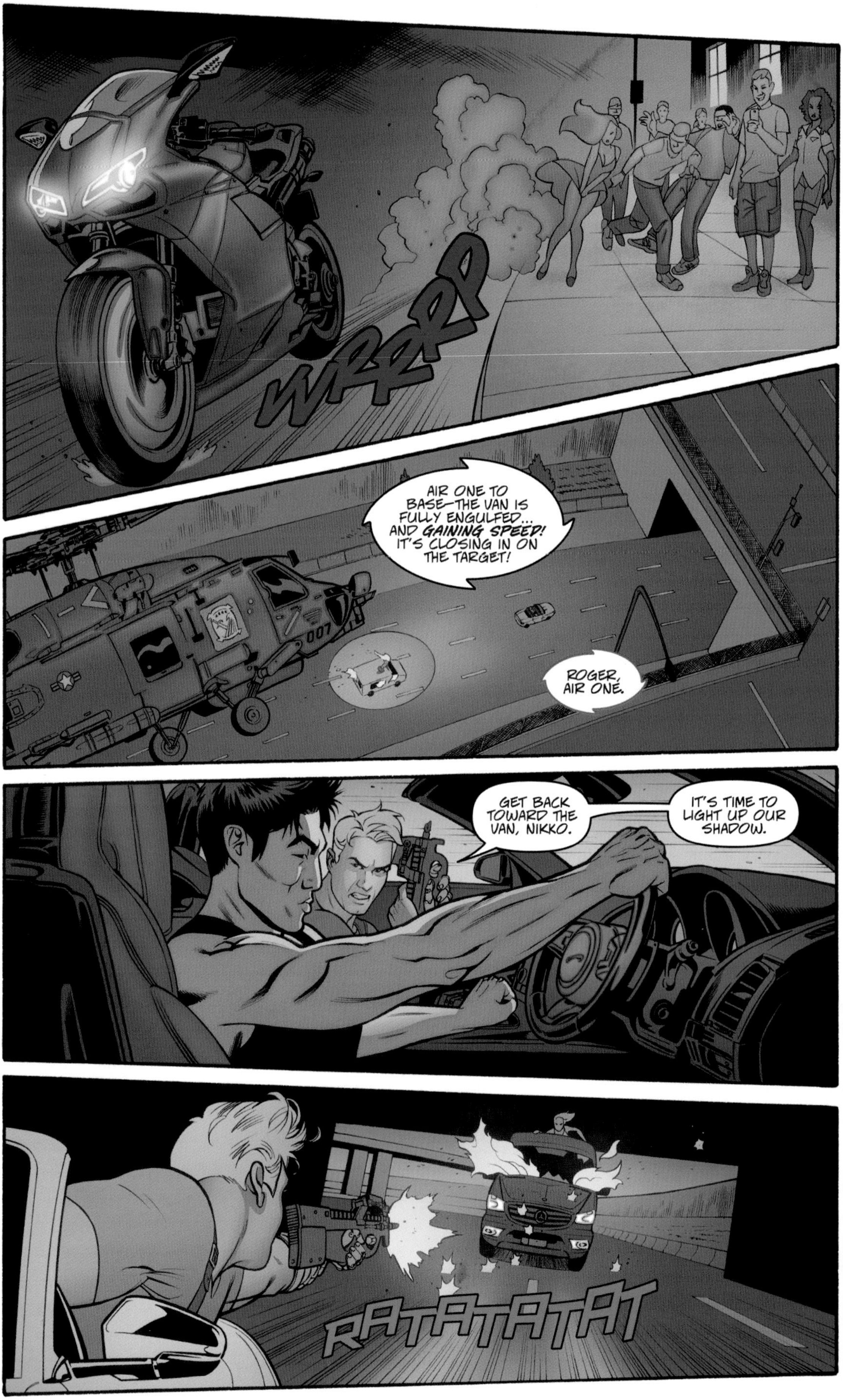
WRRRP
AIR ONE TO BASE—THE VAN IS FULLY ENGULFED... AND GAINING SPEED! IT'S CLOSING IN ON THE TARGET!
ROGER, AIR ONE.
GET BACK TOWARD THE VAN, NIKKO.
IT'S TIME TO LIGHT UP OUR SHADOW.
RATATATAT

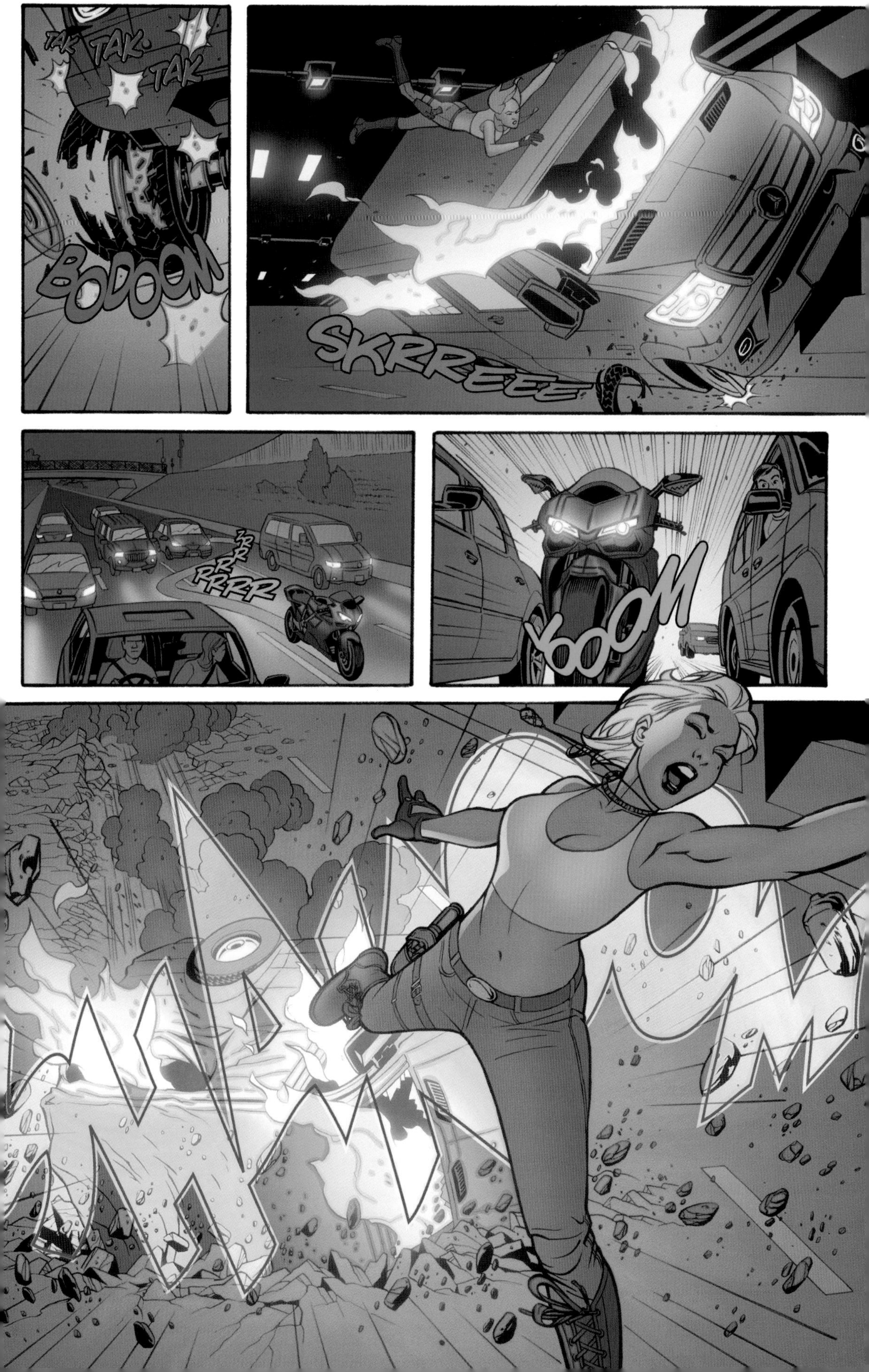
TAK TAK TAK
BODOOM
SKRREEEE
VOOOM

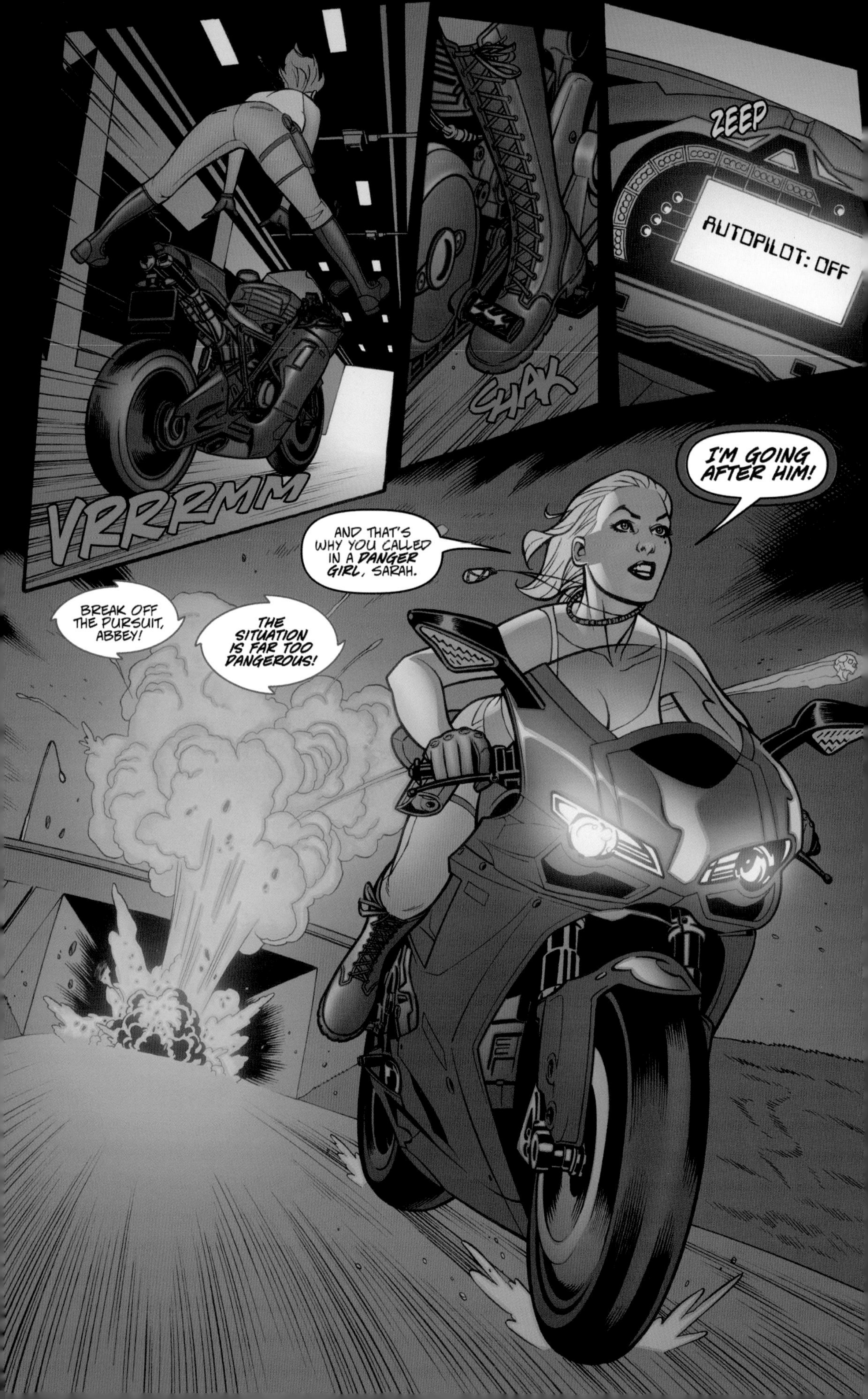
VRRRMM
SHAK
ZEEP
AUTOPILOT: OFF
I'M GOING AFTER HIM!
AND THAT'S WHY YOU CALLED IN A DANGER GIRL, SARAH.
BREAK OFF THE PURSUIT, ABBEY!
THE SITUATION IS FAR TOO DANGEROUS!

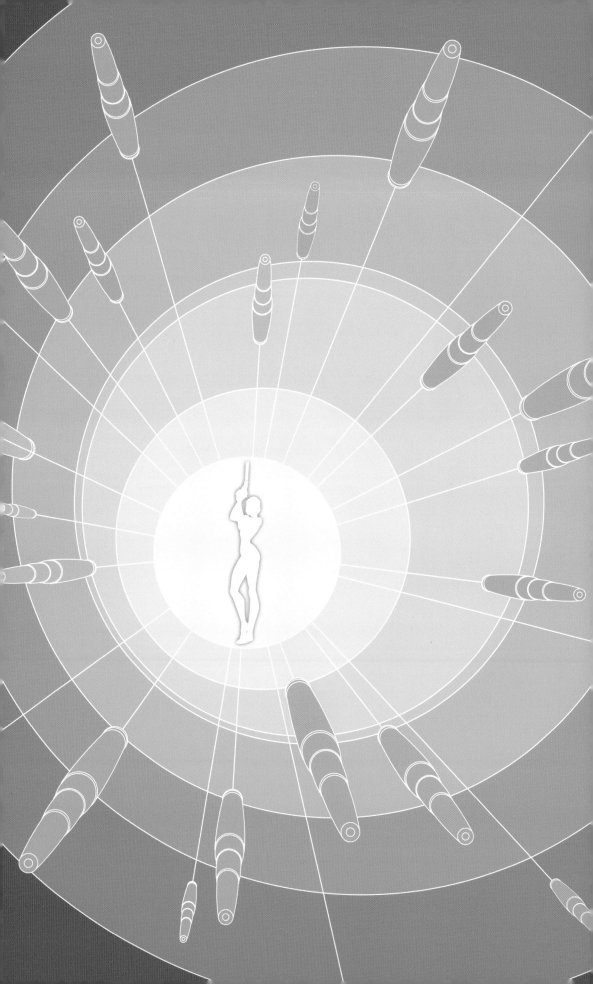

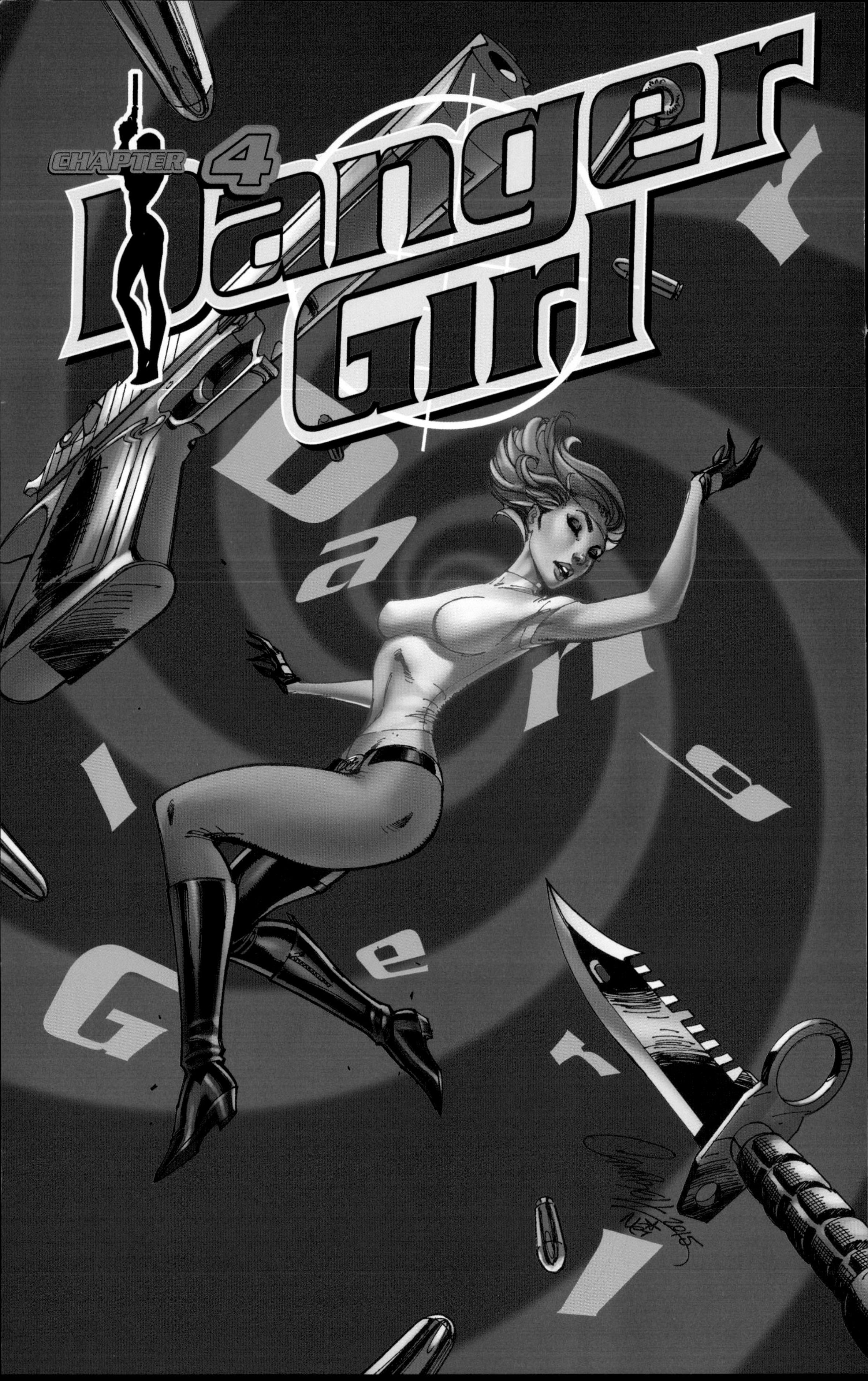
CHAPTER 4
Danger Girl

Art by J. Scott Campbell • Colors by Nei Ruffino

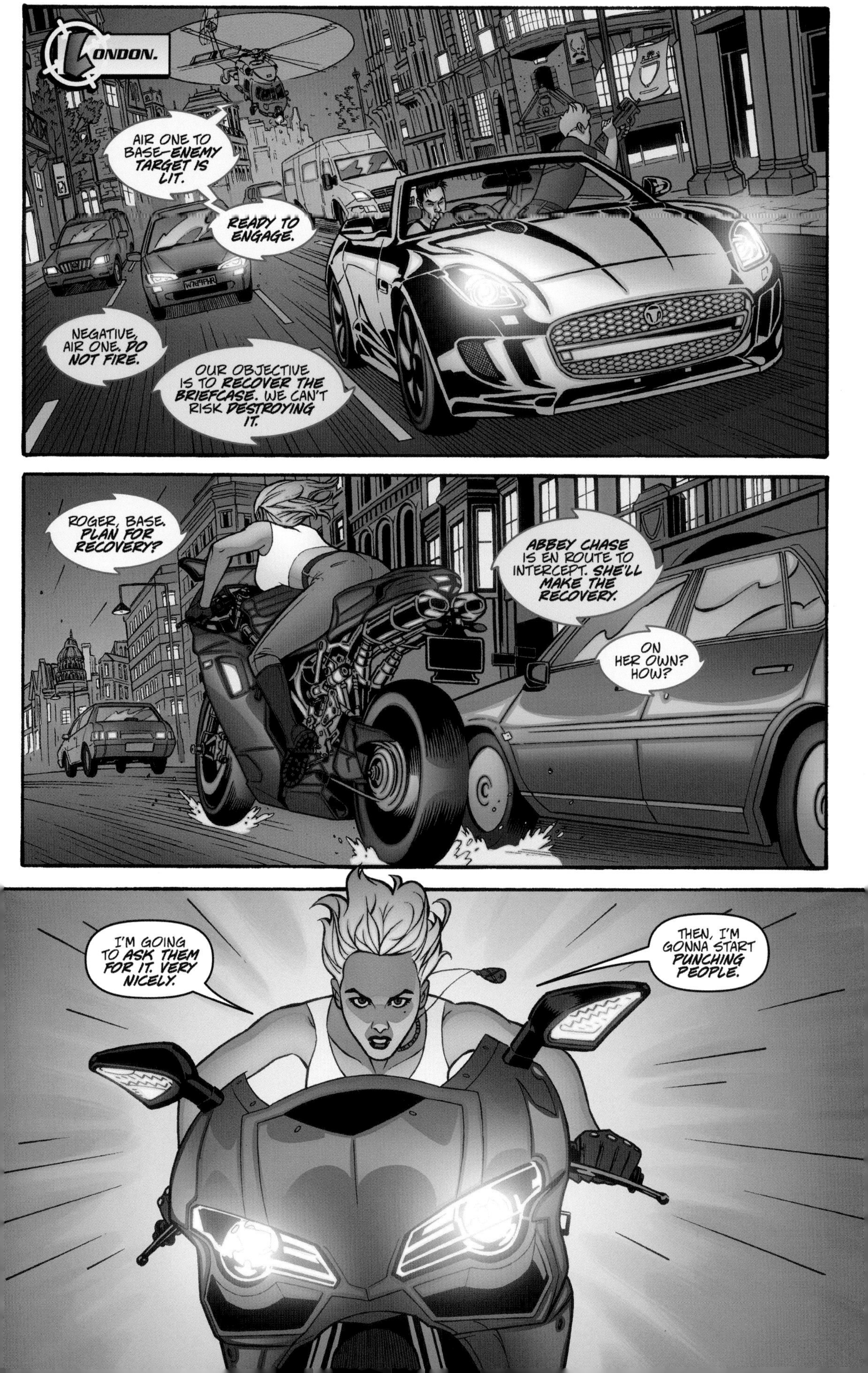
LONDON.
AIR ONE TO BASE—ENEMY TARGET IS LIT.
READY TO ENGAGE.
NEGATIVE, AIR ONE. DO NOT FIRE.
OUR OBJECTIVE IS TO RECOVER THE BRIEFCASE. WE CAN'T RISK DESTROYING IT.
ROGER, BASE. PLAN FOR RECOVERY?
ABBEY CHASE IS EN ROUTE TO INTERCEPT. SHE'LL MAKE THE RECOVERY.
ON HER OWN? HOW?
I'M GOING TO ASK THEM FOR IT. VERY NICELY.
THEN, I'M GONNA START PUNCHING PEOPLE.

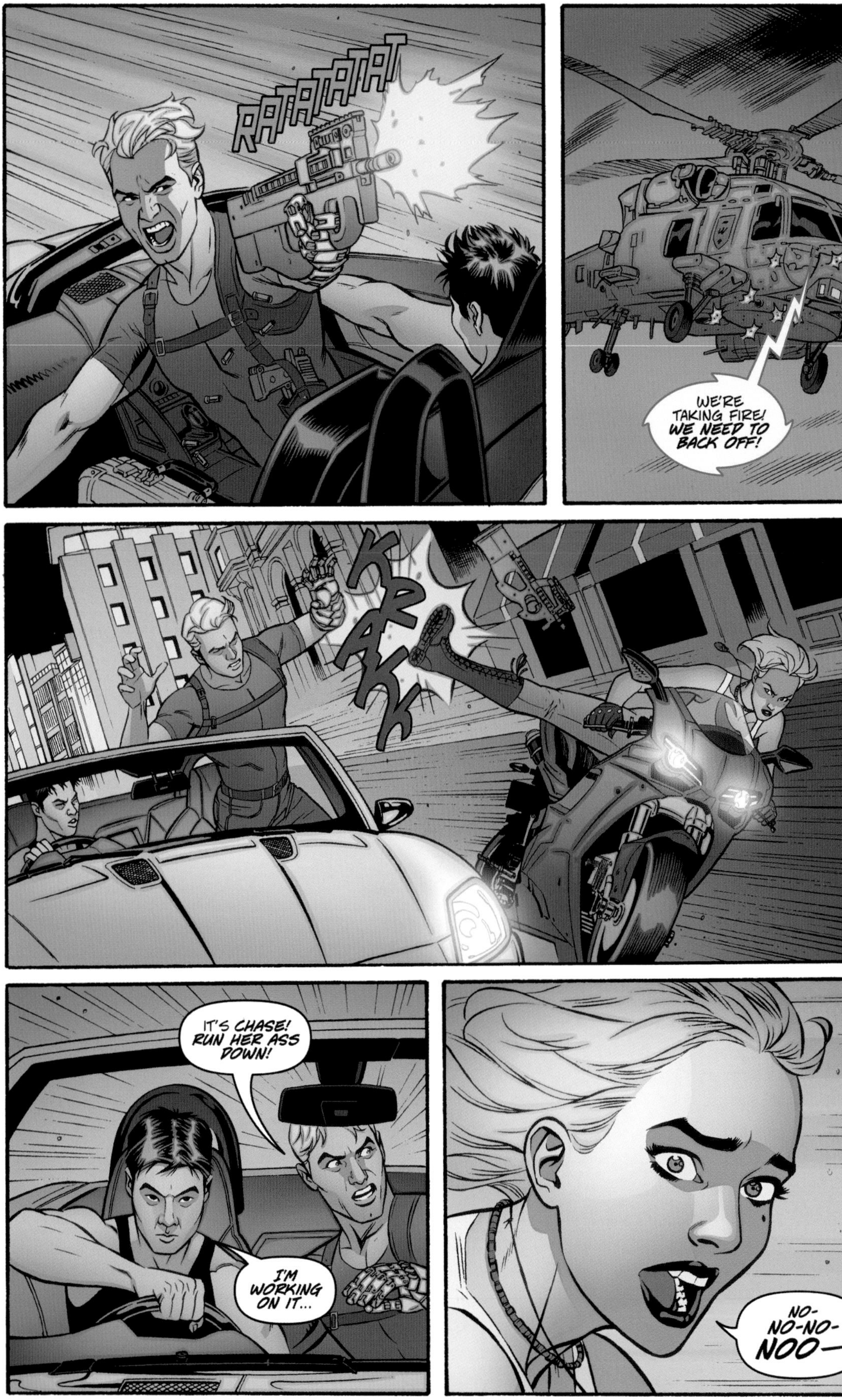
RATATATAT
WE'RE TAKING FIRE! WE NEED TO BACK OFF!
KRAKK
IT'S CHASE! RUN HER ASS DOWN!
I'M WORKING ON IT...
NO-NO-NO-NOO—

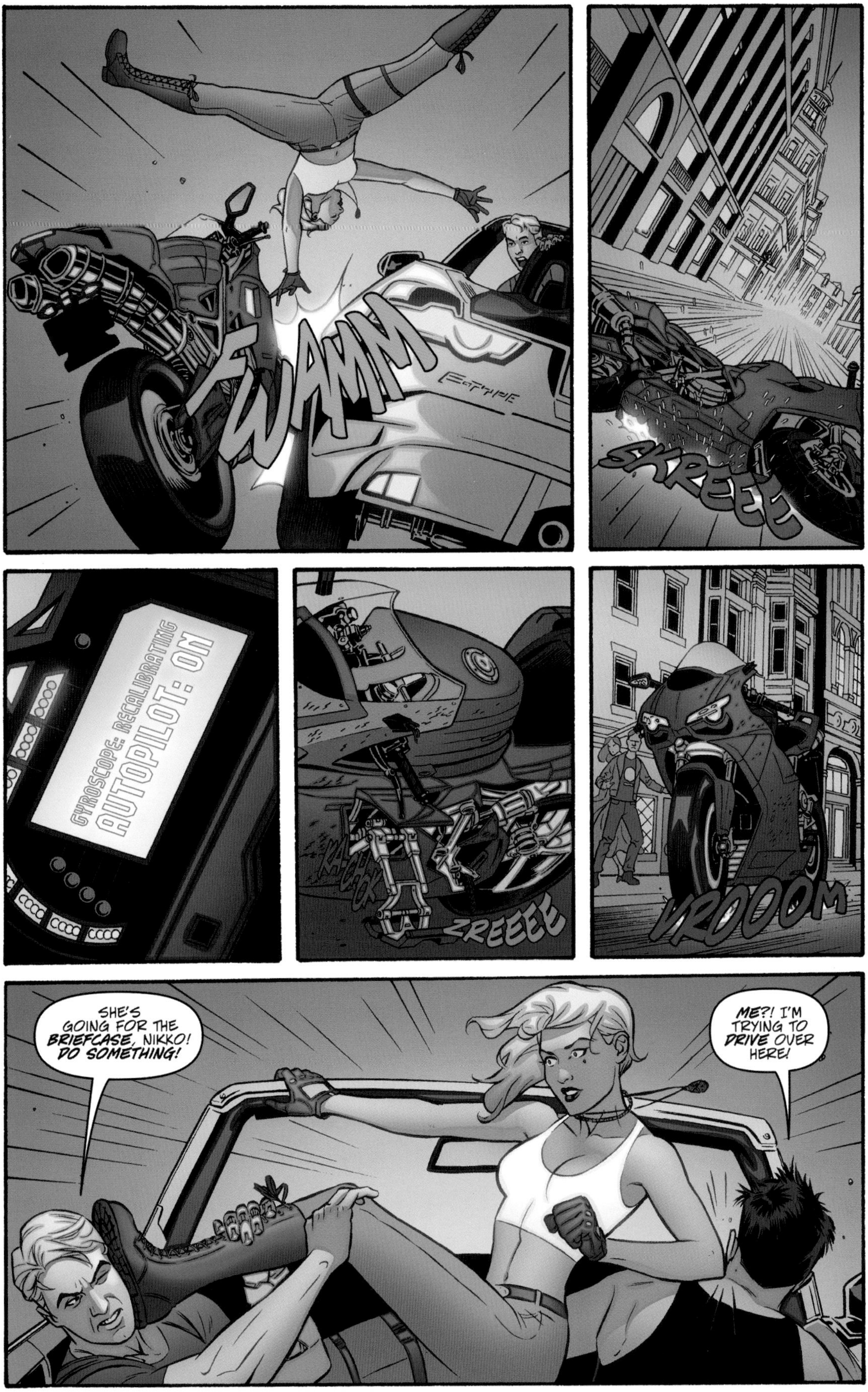
FWAMM
SKREEE
GYROSCOPE: RECALIBRATING
AUTOPILOT: ON
ZREEEE
VROOOM
SHE'S GOING FOR THE *BRIEFCASE*, NIKKO! *DO SOMETHING!*
ME?! I'M TRYING TO *DRIVE* OVER HERE!

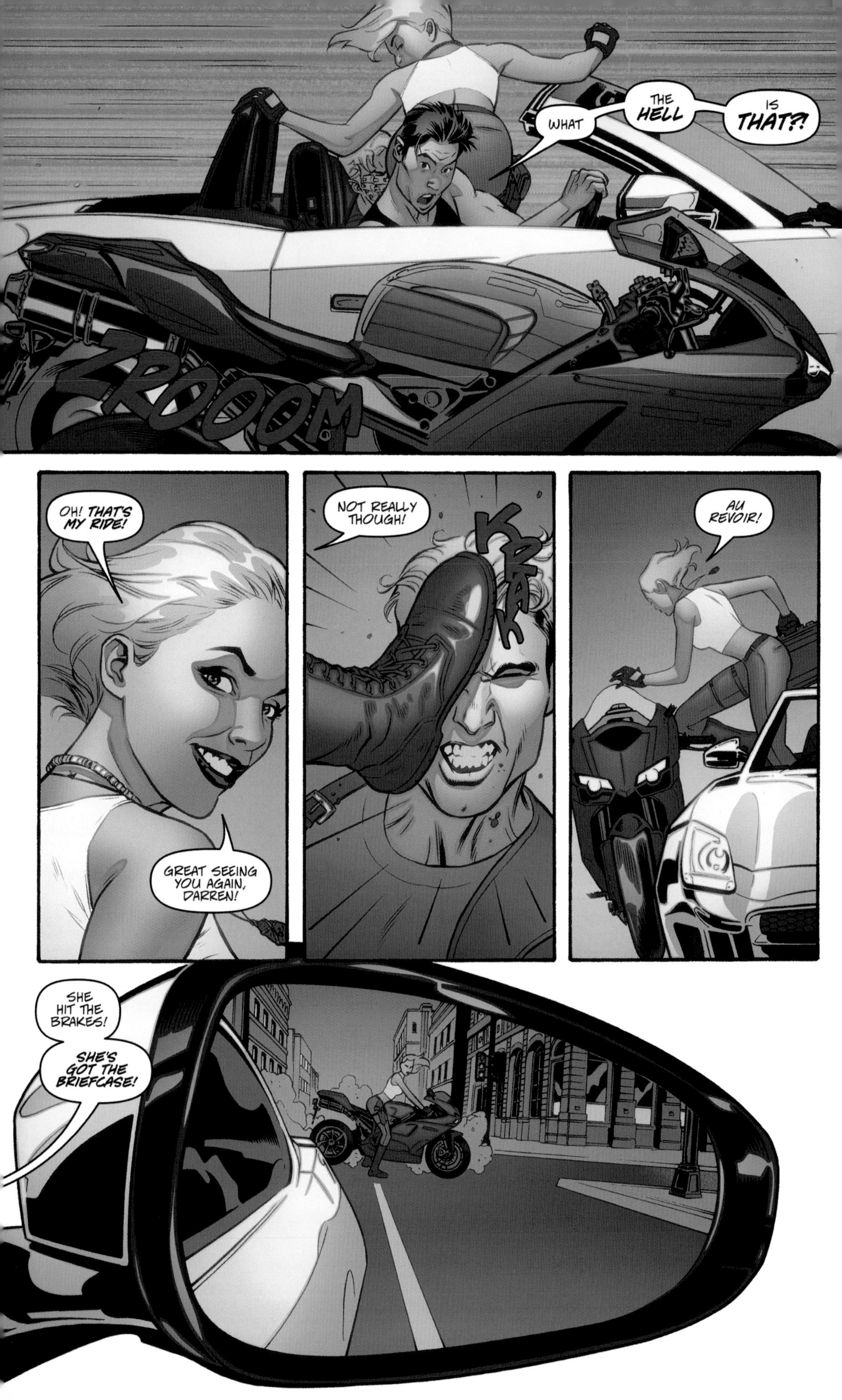
WHAT
THE HELL
IS THAT?!
ZROOOM
OH! THAT'S MY RIDE!
GREAT SEEING YOU AGAIN, DARREN!
NOT REALLY THOUGH!
KRAK
AU REVOIR!
SHE HIT THE BRAKES!
SHE'S GOT THE BRIEFCASE!

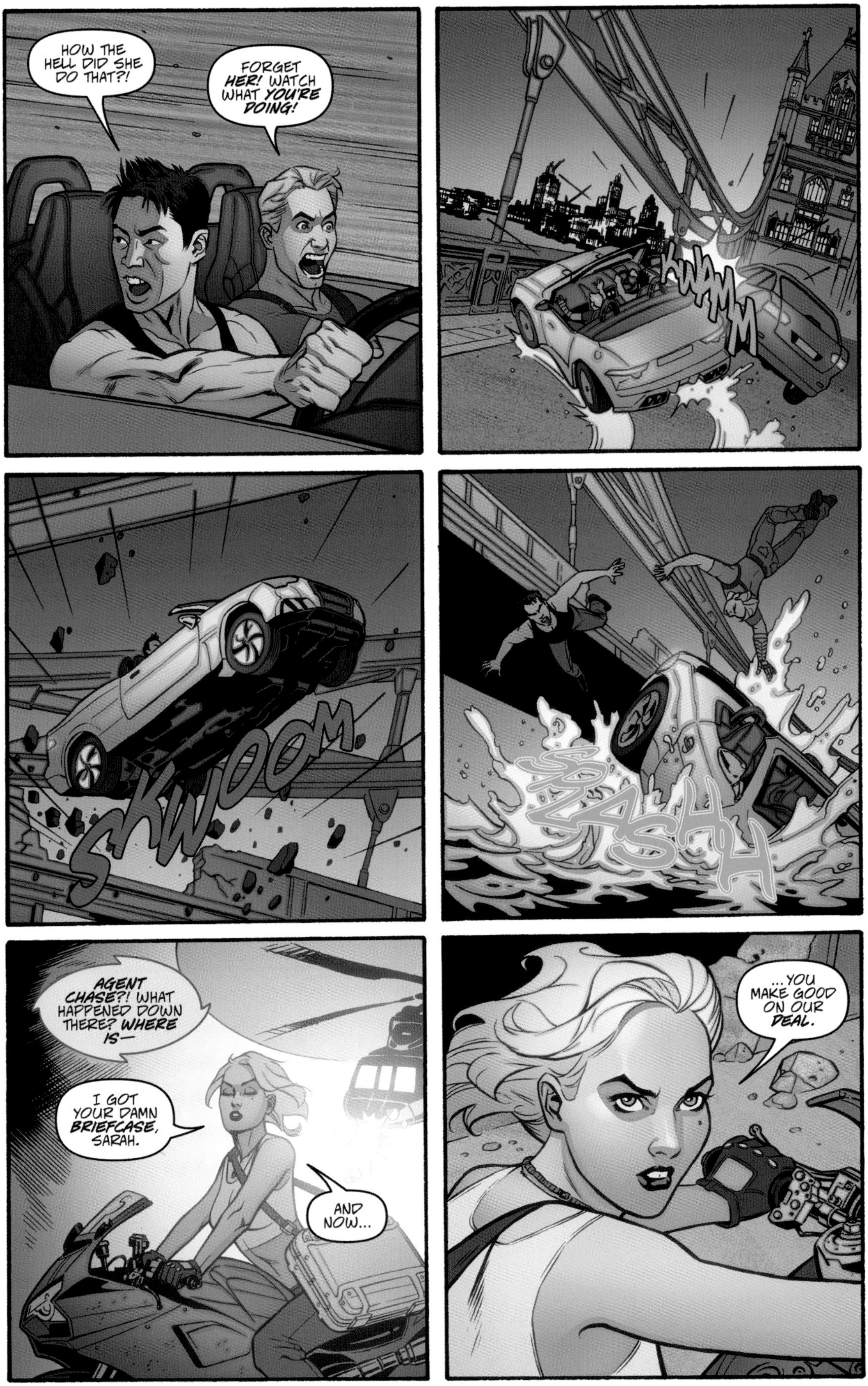

HOW THE HELL DID SHE DO THAT?!
FORGET HER! WATCH WHAT YOU'RE DOING!
KWAMM
SKWOOOM
SPLASHH
AGENT CHASE?! WHAT HAPPENED DOWN THERE? WHERE IS—
I GOT YOUR DAMN BRIEFCASE, SARAH.
AND NOW...
...YOU MAKE GOOD ON OUR DEAL.

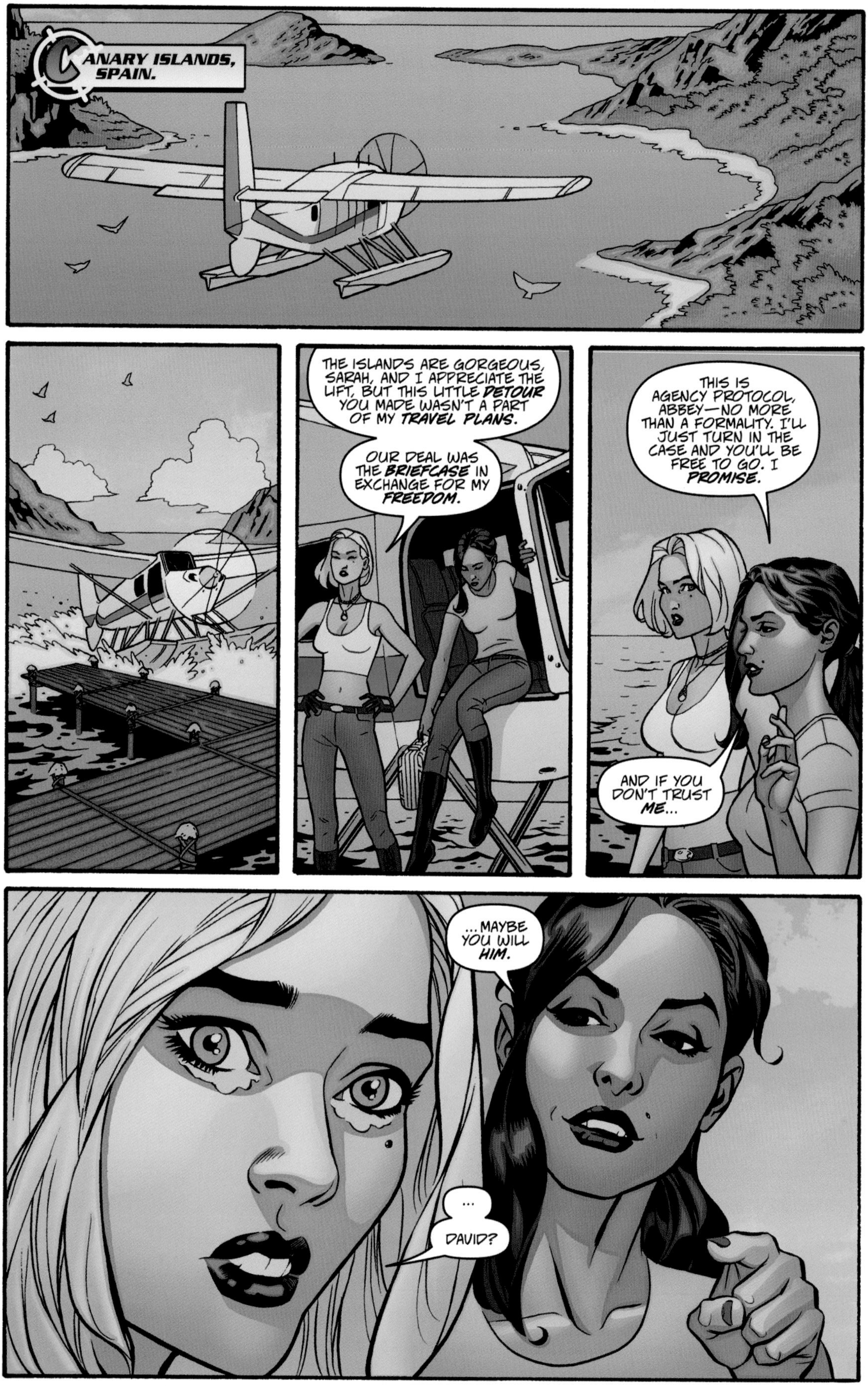
CANARY ISLANDS, SPAIN.
THE ISLANDS ARE GORGEOUS, SARAH, AND I APPRECIATE THE LIFT, BUT THIS LITTLE DETOUR YOU MADE WASN'T A PART OF MY TRAVEL PLANS.
OUR DEAL WAS THE BRIEFCASE IN EXCHANGE FOR MY FREEDOM.
THIS IS AGENCY PROTOCOL, ABBEY—NO MORE THAN A FORMALITY. I'LL JUST TURN IN THE CASE AND YOU'LL BE FREE TO GO. I PROMISE.
AND IF YOU DON'T TRUST ME...
...MAYBE YOU WILL HIM.
...
DAVID?

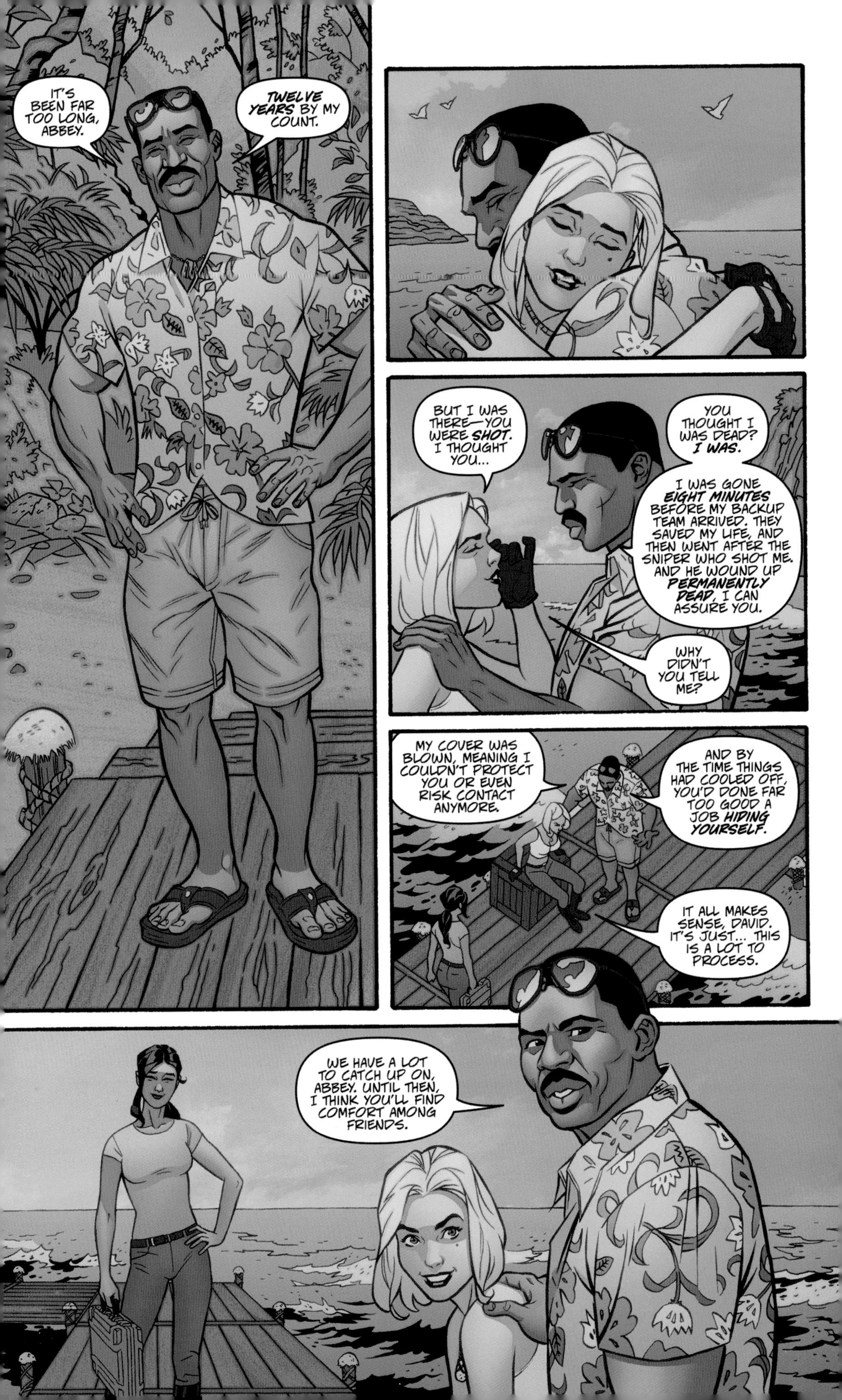
IT'S BEEN FAR TOO LONG, ABBEY.
TWELVE YEARS BY MY COUNT.
BUT I WAS THERE—YOU WERE SHOT. I THOUGHT YOU...
YOU THOUGHT I WAS DEAD? I WAS.
I WAS GONE EIGHT MINUTES BEFORE MY BACKUP TEAM ARRIVED. THEY SAVED MY LIFE, AND THEN WENT AFTER THE SNIPER WHO SHOT ME. AND HE WOUND UP PERMANENTLY DEAD, I CAN ASSURE YOU.
WHY DIDN'T YOU TELL ME?
MY COVER WAS BLOWN, MEANING I COULDN'T PROTECT YOU OR EVEN RISK CONTACT ANYMORE.
AND BY THE TIME THINGS HAD COOLED OFF, YOU'D DONE FAR TOO GOOD A JOB HIDING YOURSELF.
IT ALL MAKES SENSE, DAVID. IT'S JUST... THIS IS A LOT TO PROCESS.
WE HAVE A LOT TO CATCH UP ON, ABBEY. UNTIL THEN, I THINK YOU'LL FIND COMFORT AMONG FRIENDS.

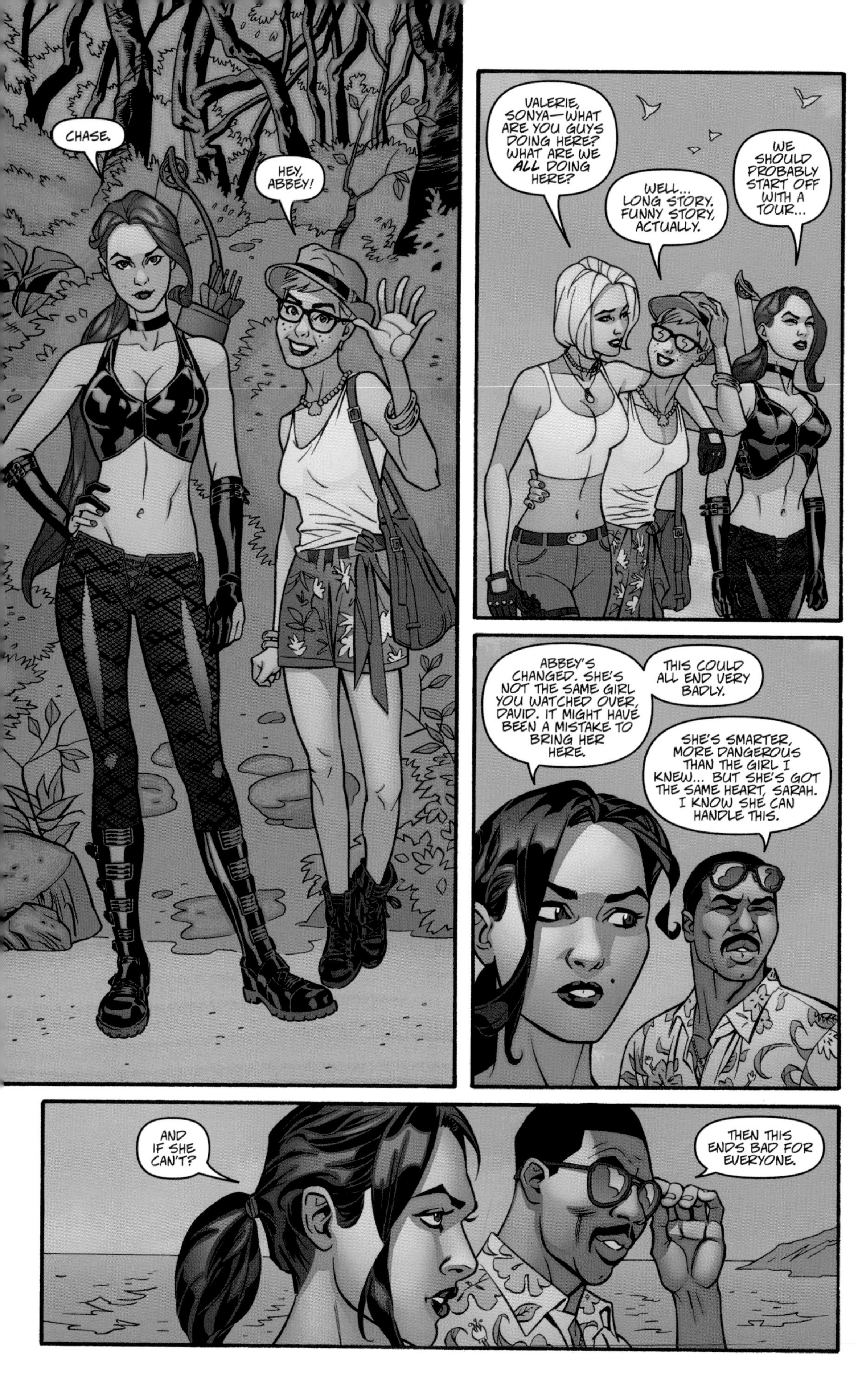
CHASE.
HEY, ABBEY!
VALERIE, SONYA—WHAT ARE YOU GUYS DOING HERE? WHAT ARE WE ALL DOING HERE?
WELL... LONG STORY. FUNNY STORY, ACTUALLY.
WE SHOULD PROBABLY START OFF WITH A TOUR...
ABBEY'S CHANGED. SHE'S NOT THE SAME GIRL YOU WATCHED OVER, DAVID. IT MIGHT HAVE BEEN A MISTAKE TO BRING HER HERE.
THIS COULD ALL END VERY BADLY.
SHE'S SMARTER, MORE DANGEROUS THAN THE GIRL I KNEW... BUT SHE'S GOT THE SAME HEART, SARAH. I KNOW SHE CAN HANDLE THIS.
AND IF SHE CAN'T?
THEN THIS ENDS BAD FOR EVERYONE.

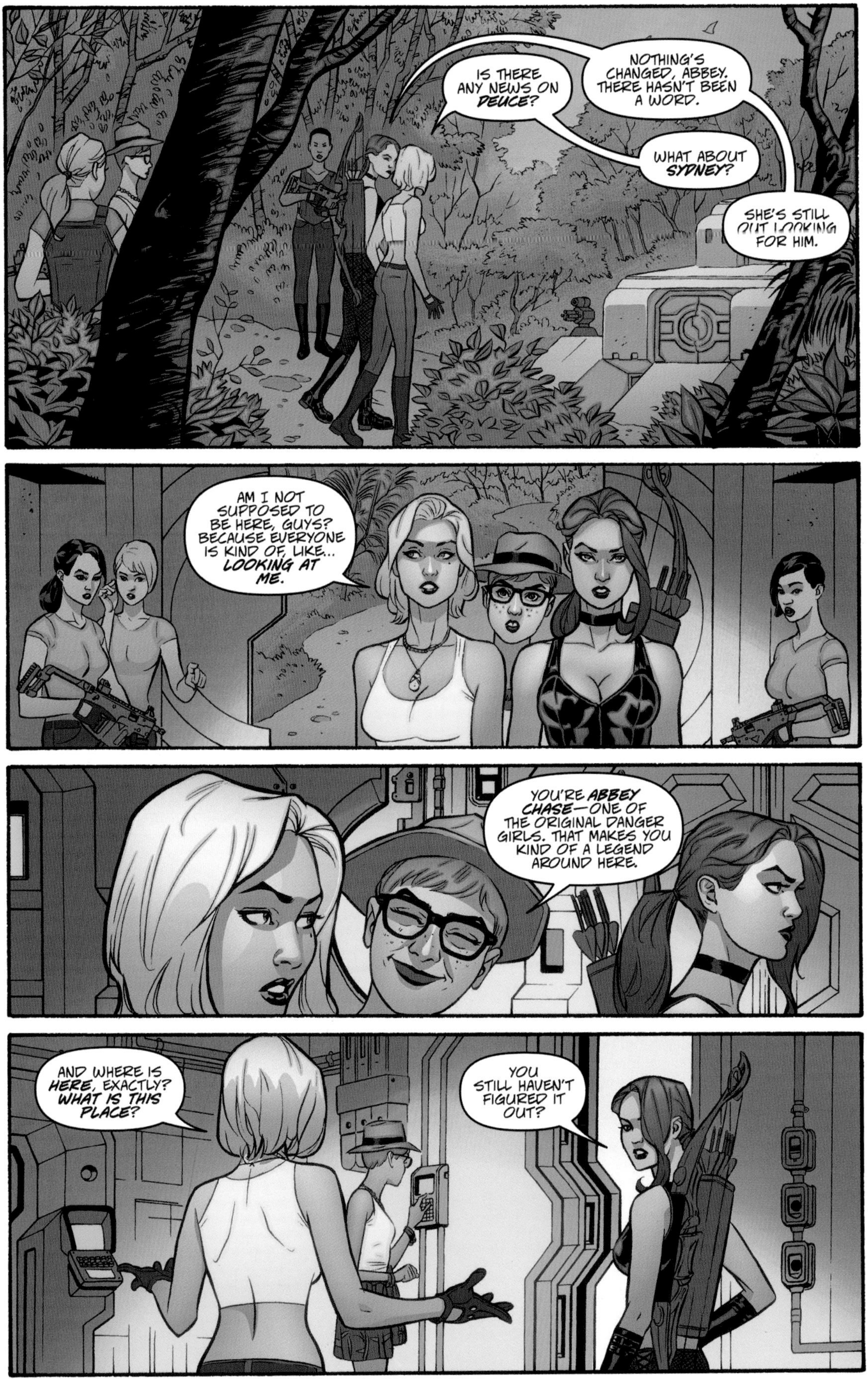
IS THERE ANY NEWS ON DEUCE?
NOTHING'S CHANGED, ABBEY. THERE HASN'T BEEN A WORD.
WHAT ABOUT SYDNEY?
SHE'S STILL OUT LOOKING FOR HIM.
AM I NOT SUPPOSED TO BE HERE, GUYS? BECAUSE EVERYONE IS KIND OF, LIKE... LOOKING AT ME.
YOU'RE ABBEY CHASE—ONE OF THE ORIGINAL DANGER GIRLS. THAT MAKES YOU KIND OF A LEGEND AROUND HERE.
AND WHERE IS HERE, EXACTLY? WHAT IS THIS PLACE?
YOU STILL HAVEN'T FIGURED IT OUT?

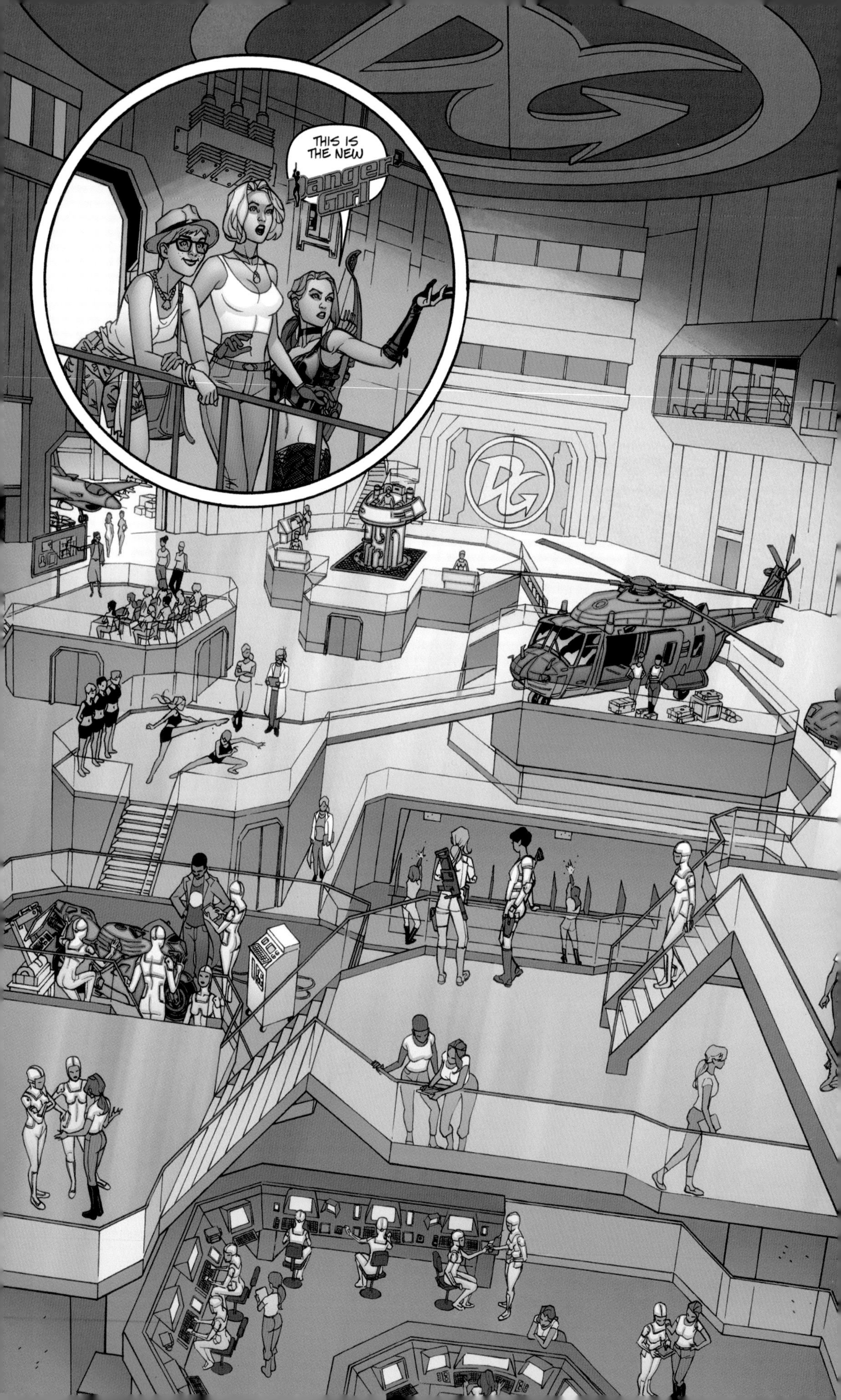
THIS IS THE NEW
Danger Girl

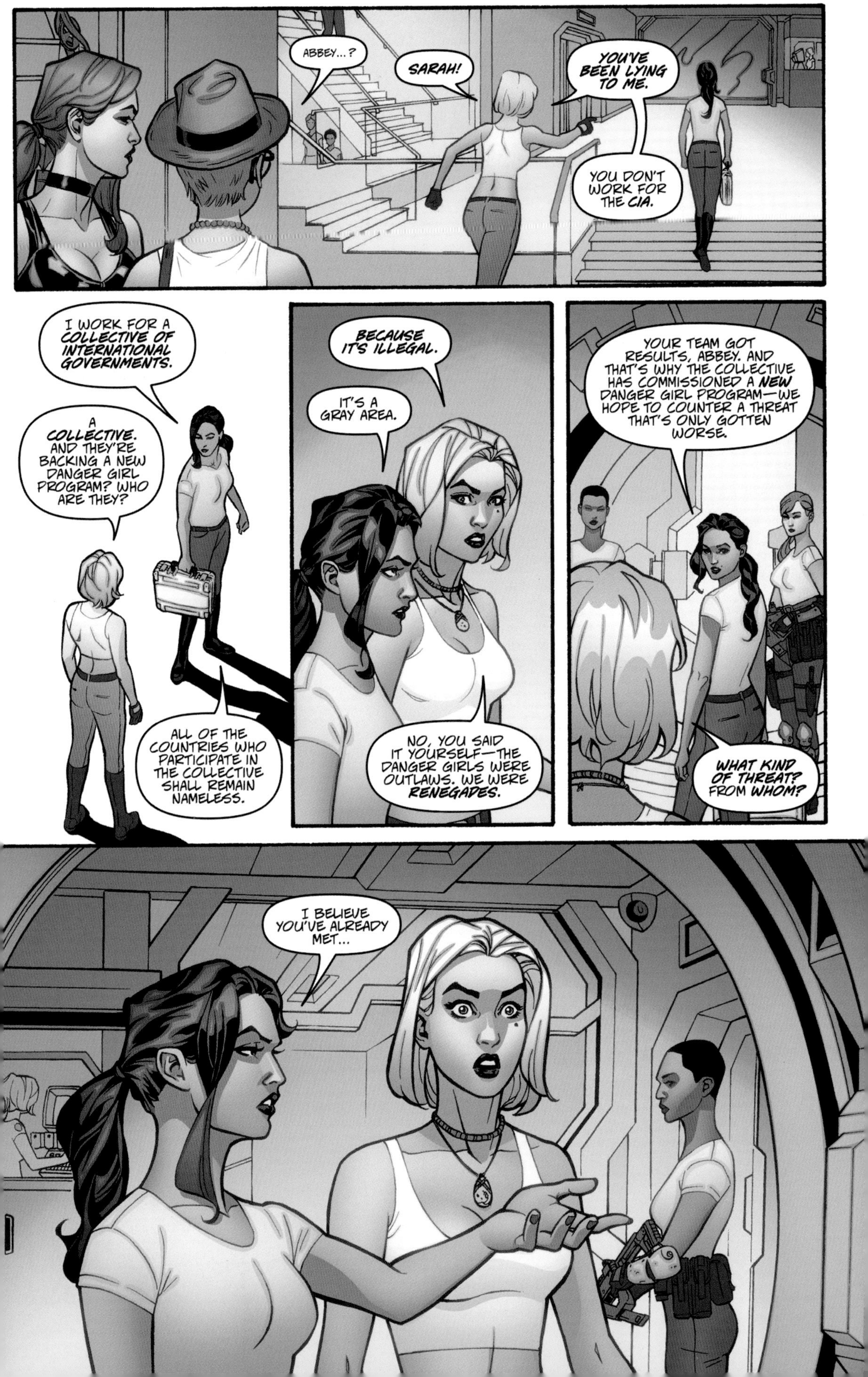
ABBEY...?
SARAH!
YOU'VE BEEN LYING TO ME.
YOU DON'T WORK FOR THE CIA.
I WORK FOR A COLLECTIVE OF INTERNATIONAL GOVERNMENTS.
A COLLECTIVE. AND THEY'RE BACKING A NEW DANGER GIRL PROGRAM? WHO ARE THEY?
ALL OF THE COUNTRIES WHO PARTICIPATE IN THE COLLECTIVE SHALL REMAIN NAMELESS.
BECAUSE IT'S ILLEGAL.
IT'S A GRAY AREA.
NO, YOU SAID IT YOURSELF—THE DANGER GIRLS WERE OUTLAWS. WE WERE RENEGADES.
YOUR TEAM GOT RESULTS, ABBEY. AND THAT'S WHY THE COLLECTIVE HAS COMMISSIONED A NEW DANGER GIRL PROGRAM—WE HOPE TO COUNTER A THREAT THAT'S ONLY GOTTEN WORSE.
WHAT KIND OF THREAT? FROM WHOM?
I BELIEVE YOU'VE ALREADY MET...

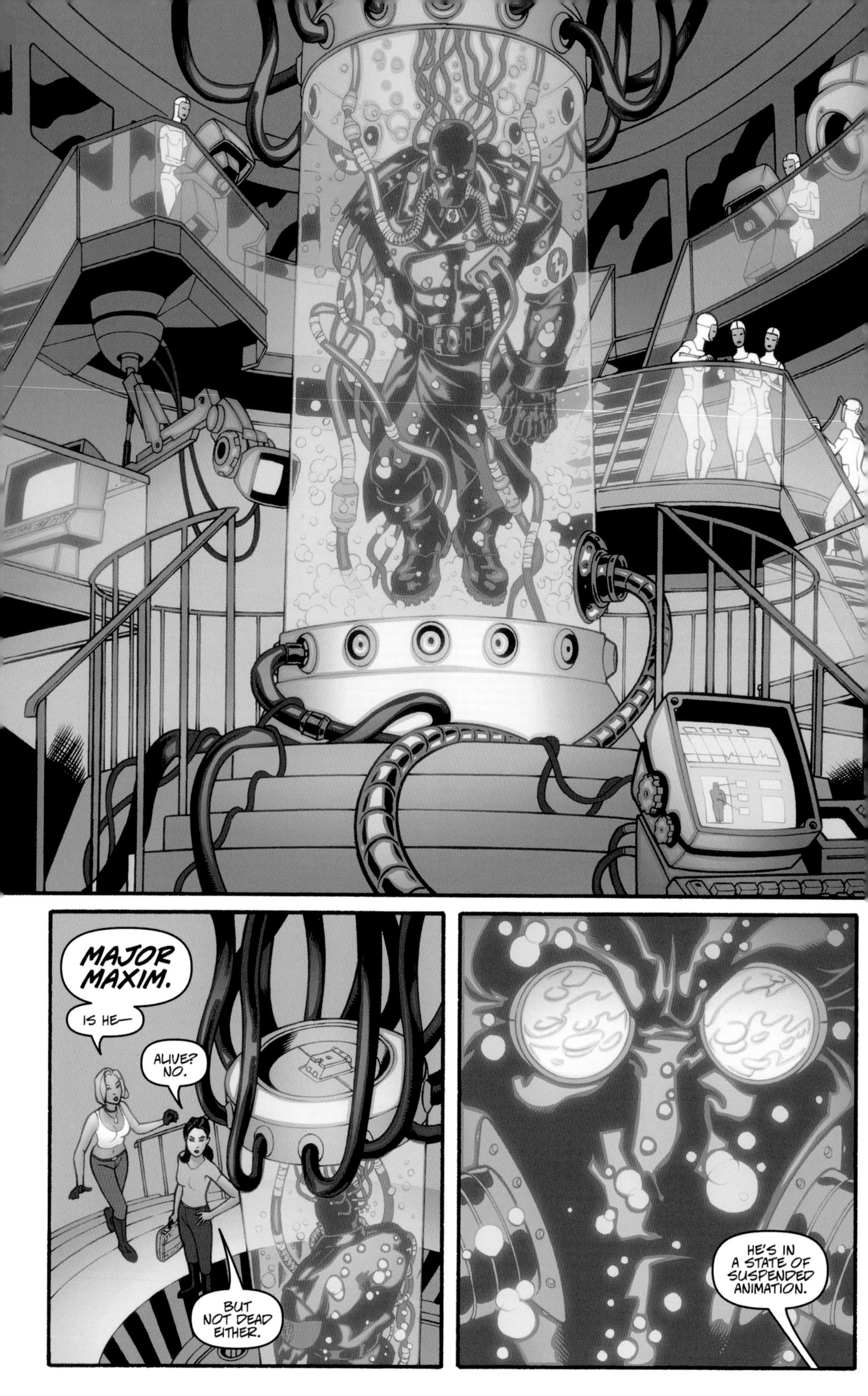
MAJOR MAXIM.
IS HE—
ALIVE? NO.
BUT NOT DEAD EITHER.
HE'S IN A STATE OF SUSPENDED ANIMATION.

MAXIM WAS A KILLING MACHINE. HE SERVED AS THE CHIEF ENFORCER FOR AN INTERNATIONAL CRIME SYNDICATE KNOWN AS *THE HAMMER.*

WE KNOW ABOUT THE HAMMER. WE ALSO KNOW THAT MAXIM WASN'T THEIR ONLY EXPERIMENT...

THIS IS MY FATHER'S HANDWRITING. THESE PAGES ARE FROM HIS JOURNAL.

WHY WAS HE WRITING ABOUT THE HAMMER?

HE'S BEEN SPYING ON THEM FOR YEARS, ABBEY. AND NOW, *THOSE PAGES,* ALONG WITH THE *BRIEFCASE* YOU RETRIEVED—

—THIS PROVES HE'S ALIVE!

DO YOU KNOW WHERE TO FIND HIM?

I DON'T THINK *ANYONE* CAN FIND HIM, ABBEY. AND AS OF NOW, THAT'S THE ONLY THING THAT'S *KEEPING HIM ALIVE.*

YOUR FATHER'S LATEST INTEL PROVIDES US WITH *NEW DETAILS* ABOUT THE HAMMER'S *ENDURING THREAT*—

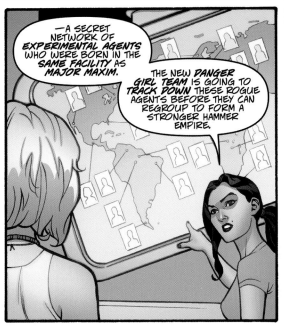

—A SECRET NETWORK OF *EXPERIMENTAL AGENTS* WHO WERE BORN IN THE *SAME FACILITY* AS *MAJOR MAXIM.*

THE NEW *DANGER GIRL TEAM* IS GOING TO *TRACK DOWN* THESE ROGUE AGENTS BEFORE THEY CAN REGROUP TO FORM A STRONGER HAMMER EMPIRE.

EASIER SAID THAN DONE, SARAH—THE HAMMER ARE INCREDIBLY SECRETIVE. DECADES WENT BY BEFORE ANYONE KNEW THEY EVEN EXISTED.

WE JUST DON'T KNOW ENOUGH ABOUT HOW THEY OPERATE.

WE DO NOW.

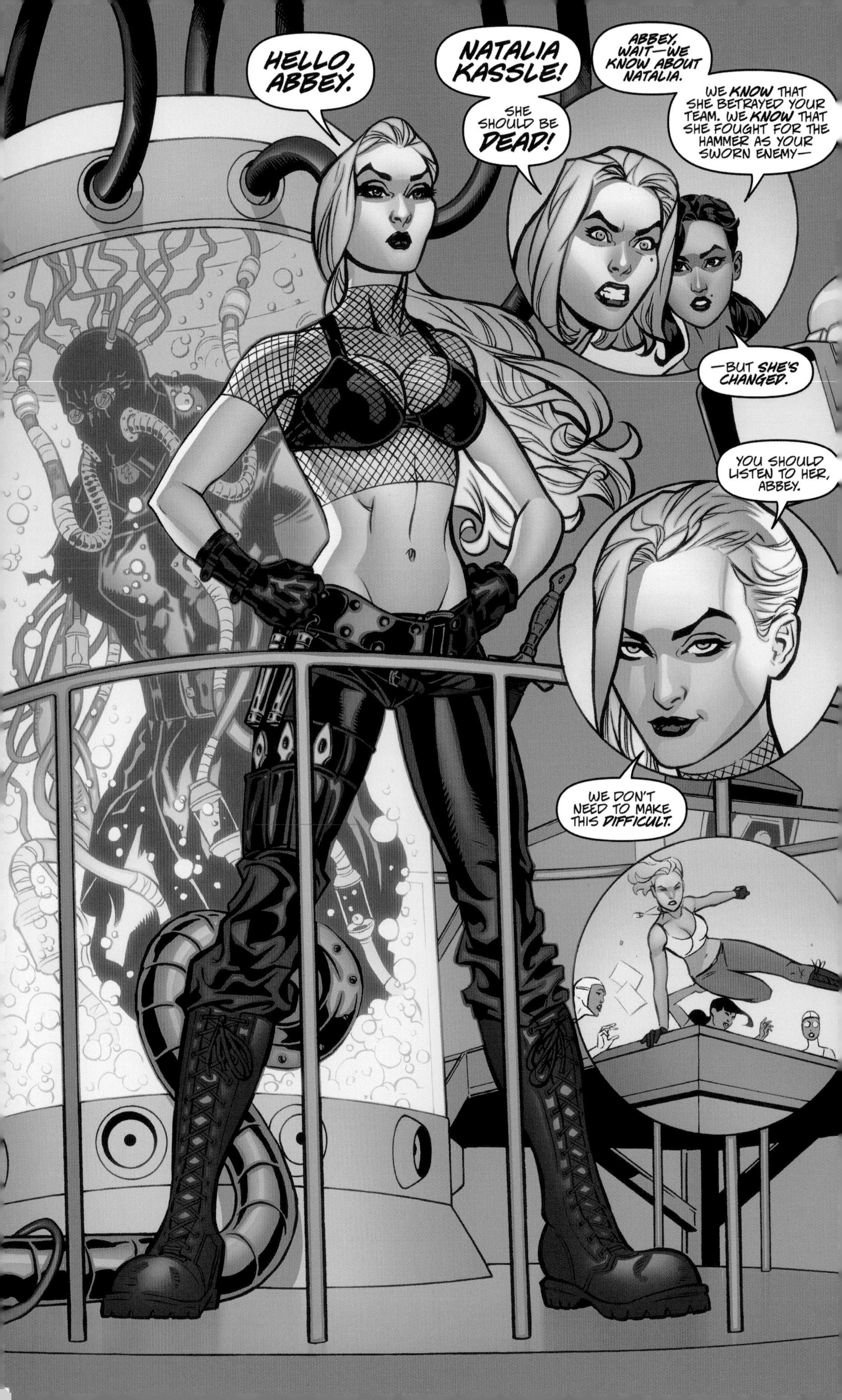

HELLO, ABBEY.
NATALIA KASSLE!
SHE SHOULD BE DEAD!
ABBEY, WAIT—WE KNOW ABOUT NATALIA.
WE KNOW THAT SHE BETRAYED YOUR TEAM. WE KNOW THAT SHE FOUGHT FOR THE HAMMER AS YOUR SWORN ENEMY—
—BUT SHE'S CHANGED.
YOU SHOULD LISTEN TO HER, ABBEY.
WE DON'T NEED TO MAKE THIS DIFFICULT.

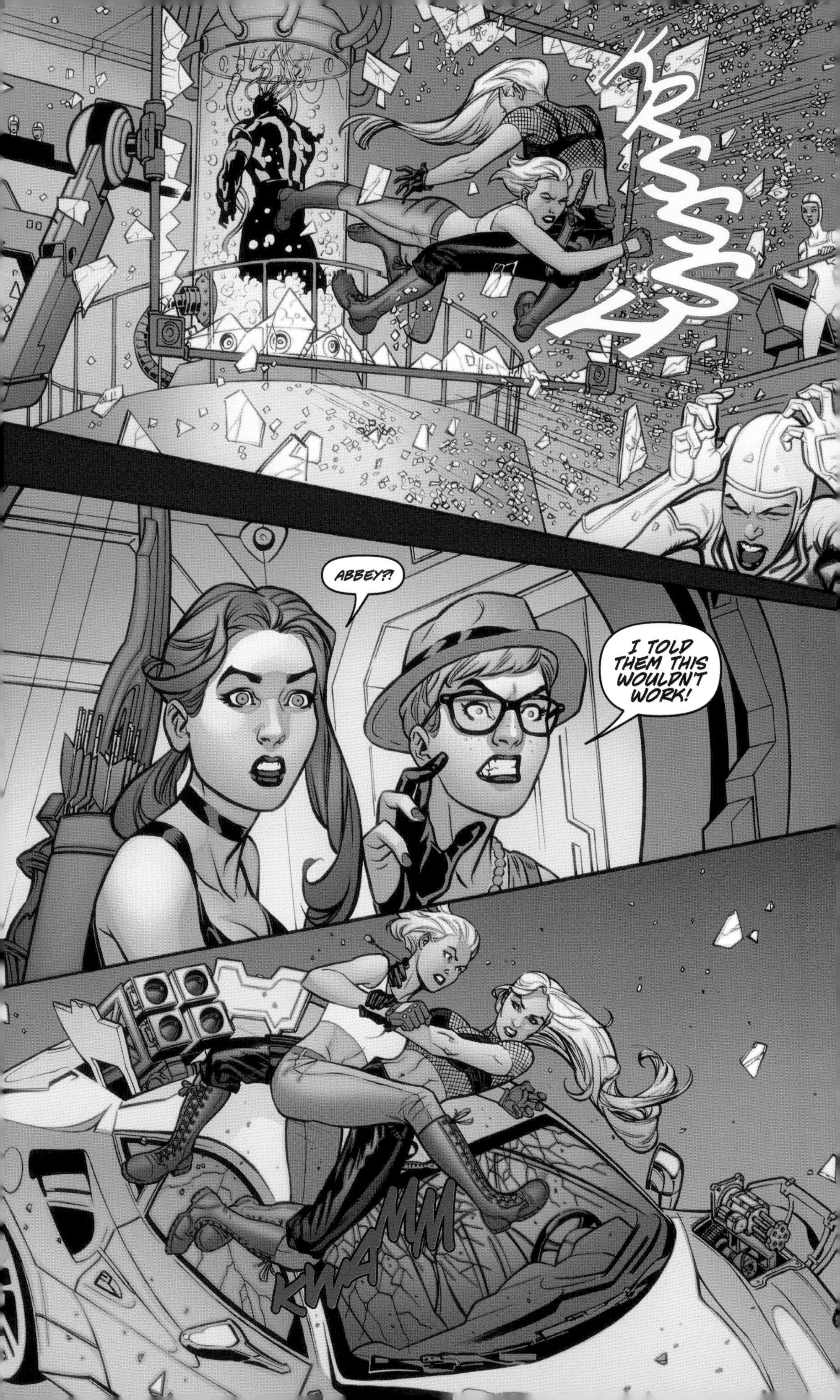
KRSSSH
ABBEY?!
I TOLD THEM THIS WOULDN'T WORK!
KWAMM

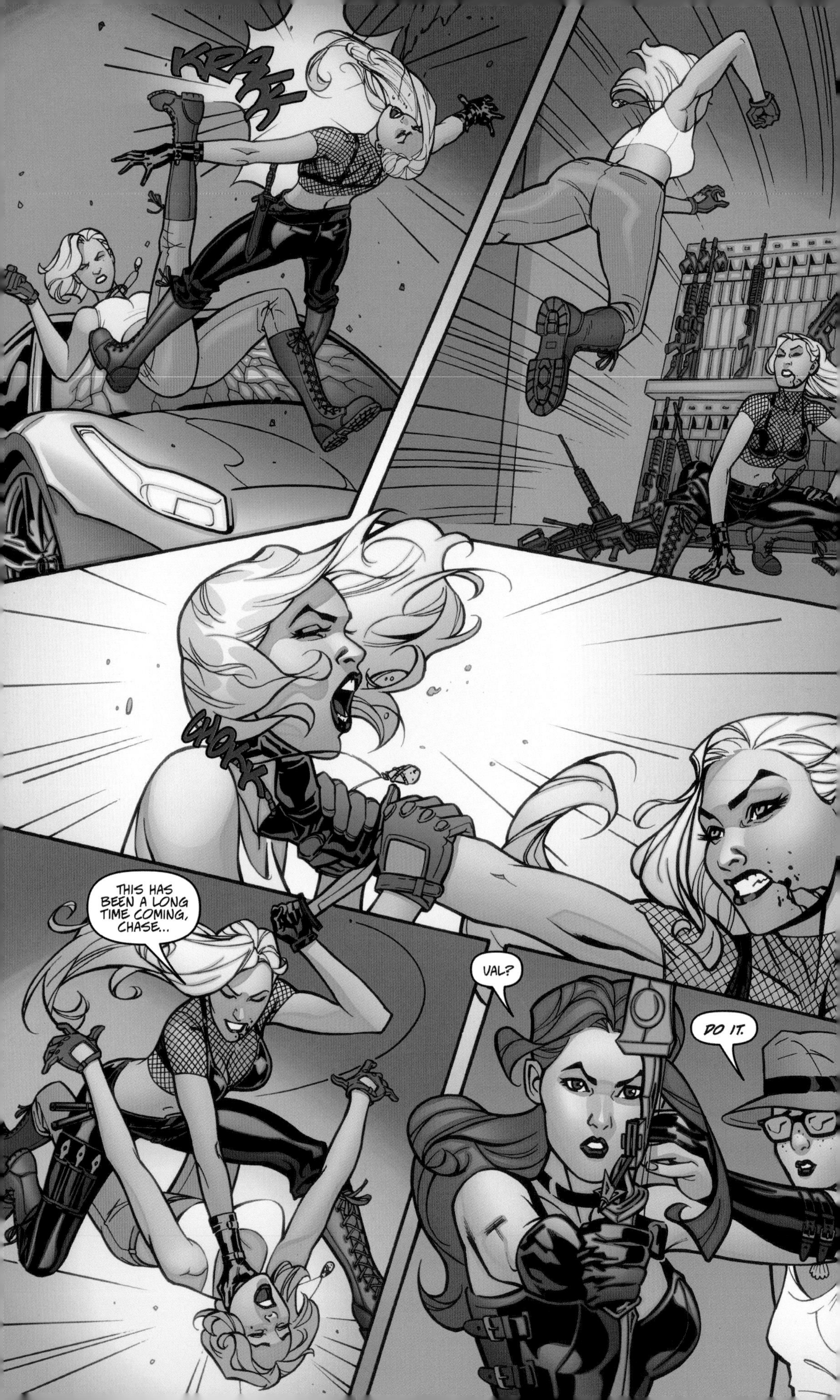
KRAKK
CHOKK
THIS HAS BEEN A LONG TIME COMING, CHASE...
VAL?
DO IT.

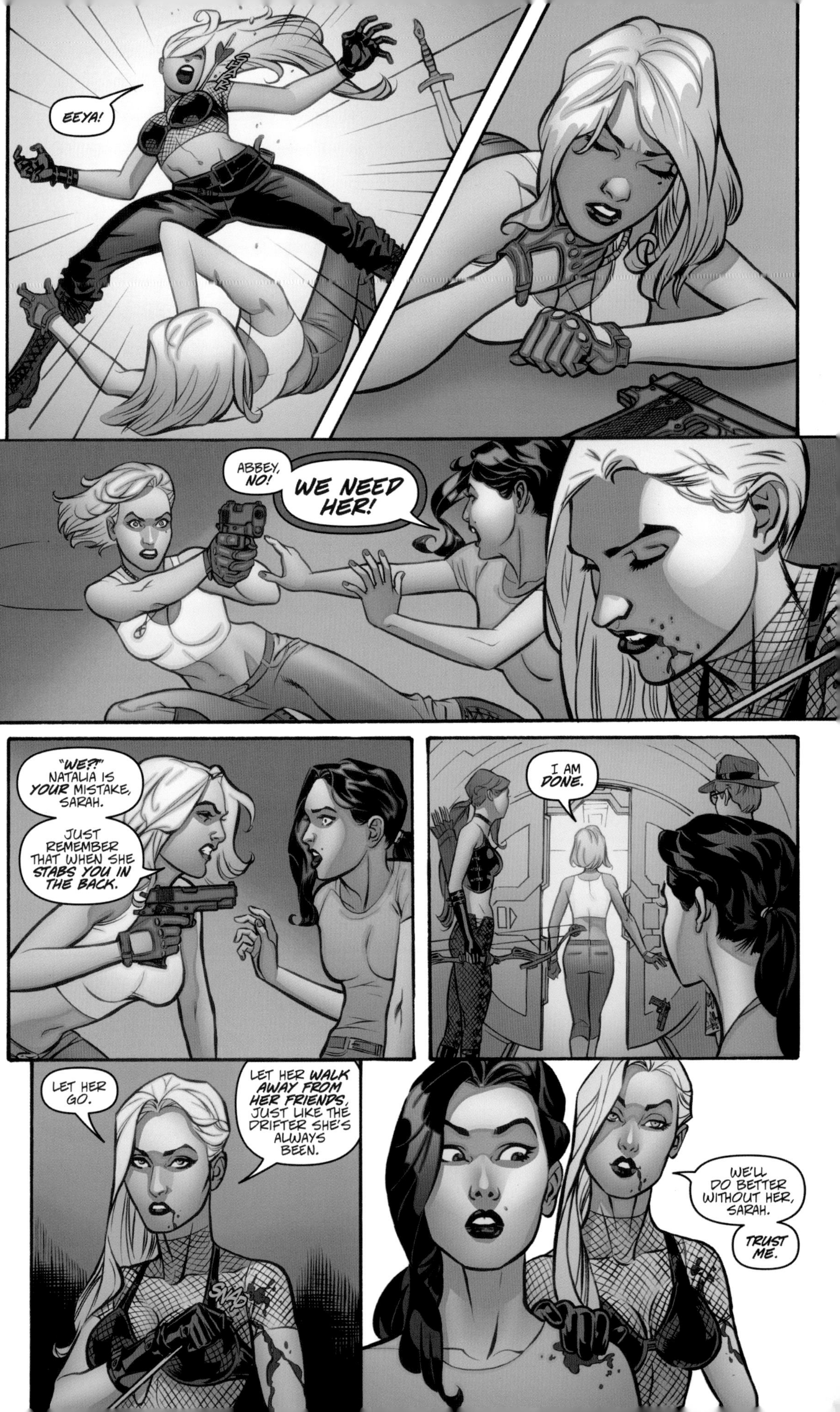
EEYA!
ABBEY, NO!
WE NEED HER!
"WE?!" NATALIA IS YOUR MISTAKE, SARAH.
JUST REMEMBER THAT WHEN SHE STABS YOU IN THE BACK.
I AM DONE.
LET HER GO.
LET HER WALK AWAY FROM HER FRIENDS, JUST LIKE THE DRIFTER SHE'S ALWAYS BEEN.
WE'LL DO BETTER WITHOUT HER, SARAH.
TRUST ME.

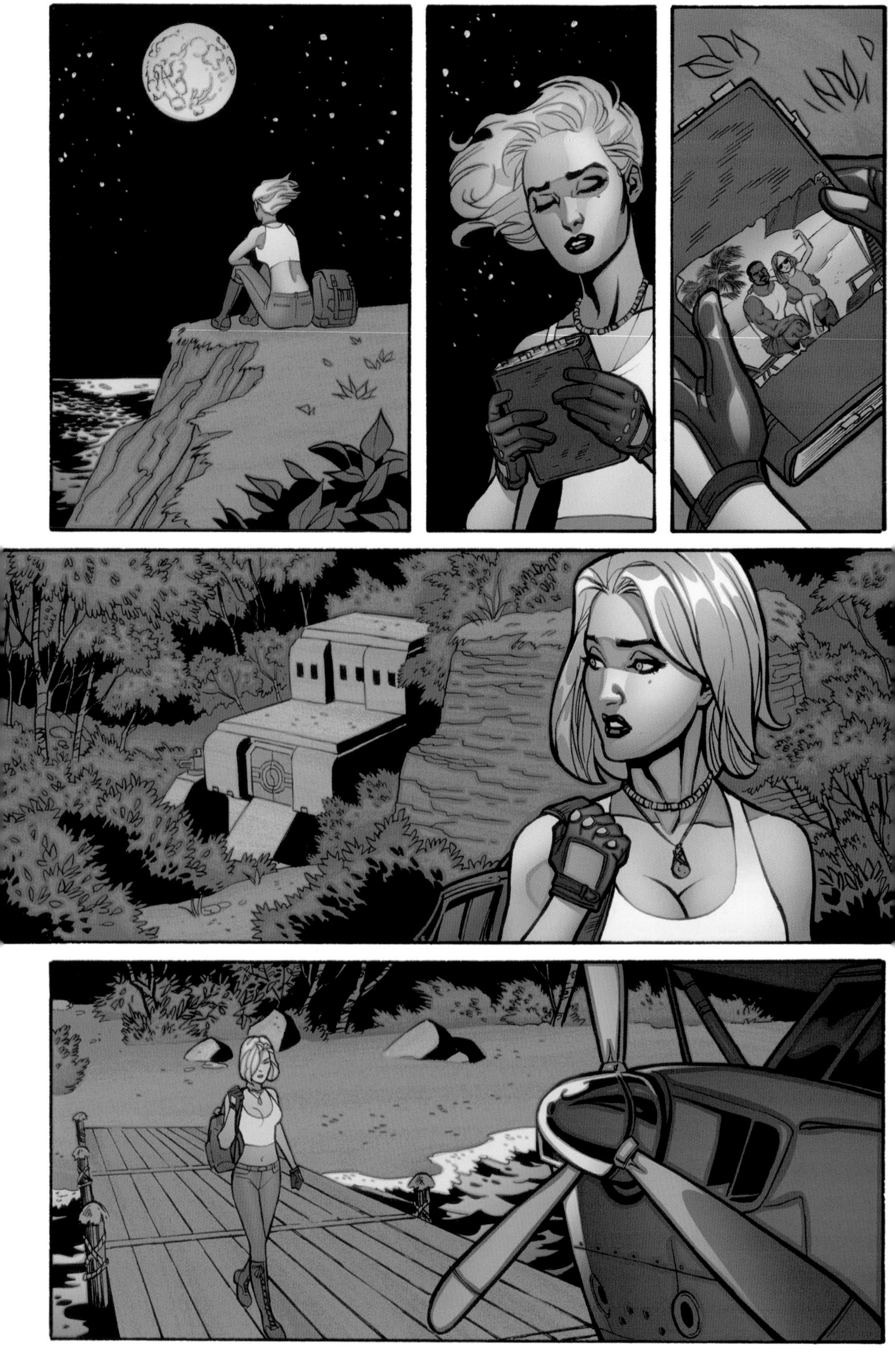

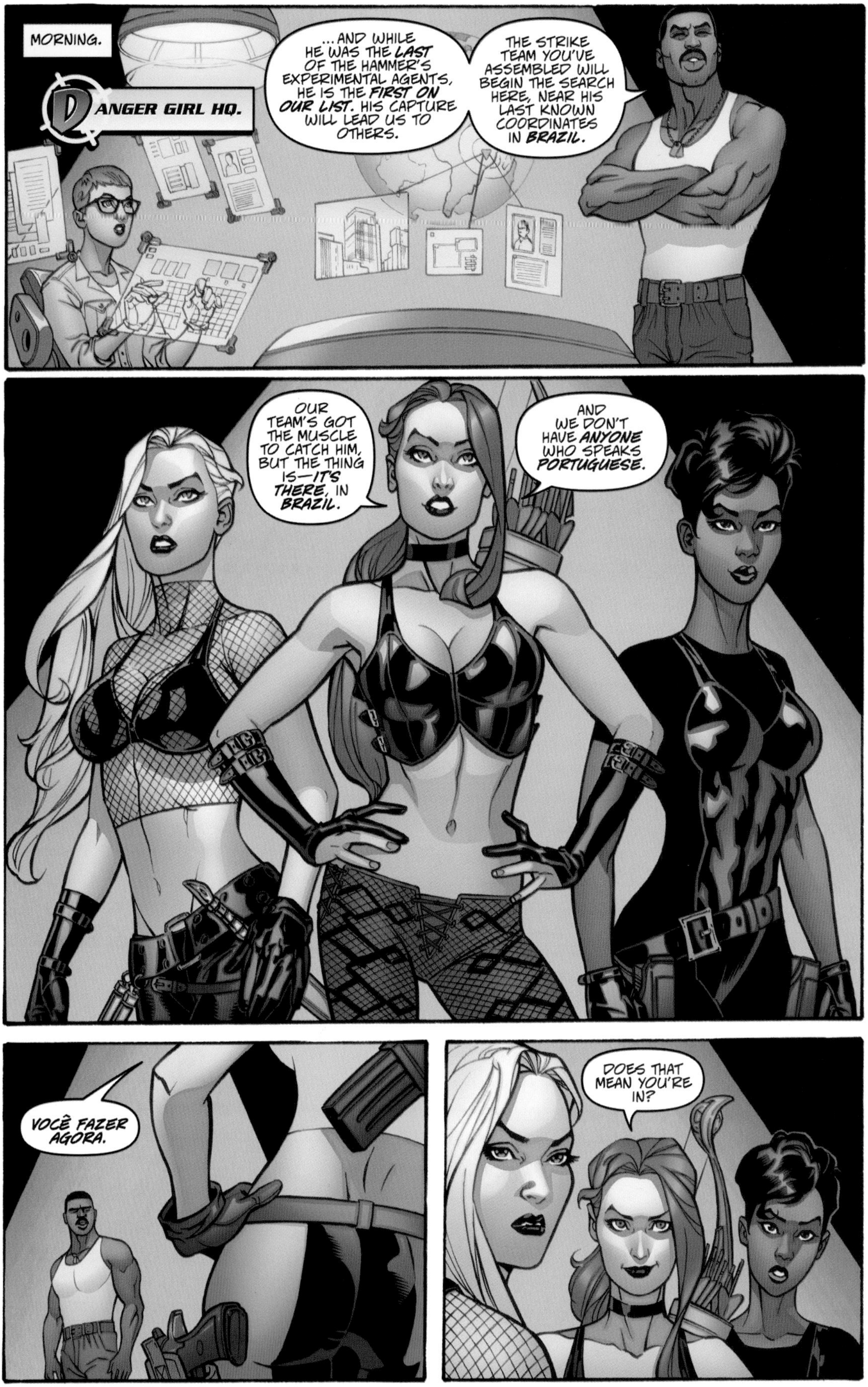
MORNING.
DANGER GIRL HQ.
...AND WHILE HE WAS THE LAST OF THE HAMMER'S EXPERIMENTAL AGENTS, HE IS THE FIRST ON OUR LIST. HIS CAPTURE WILL LEAD US TO OTHERS.
THE STRIKE TEAM YOU'VE ASSEMBLED WILL BEGIN THE SEARCH HERE, NEAR HIS LAST KNOWN COORDINATES IN BRAZIL.
OUR TEAM'S GOT THE MUSCLE TO CATCH HIM, BUT THE THING IS—IT'S THERE, IN BRAZIL.
AND WE DON'T HAVE ANYONE WHO SPEAKS PORTUGUESE.
VOCÊ FAZER AGORA.
DOES THAT MEAN YOU'RE IN?

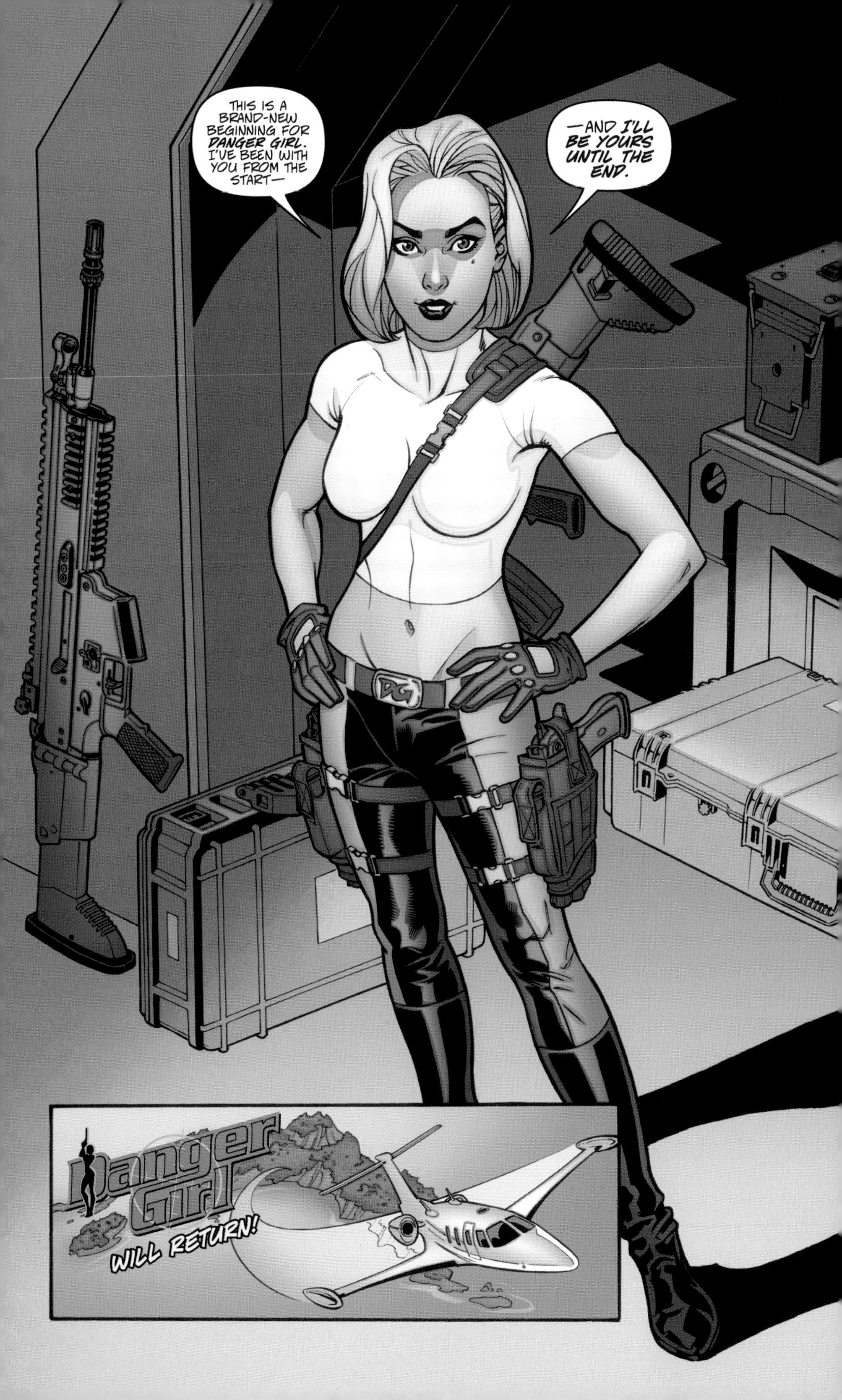
THIS IS A BRAND-NEW BEGINNING FOR DANGER GIRL. I'VE BEEN WITH YOU FROM THE START—
—AND I'LL BE YOURS UNTIL THE END.
Danger Girl
WILL RETURN!

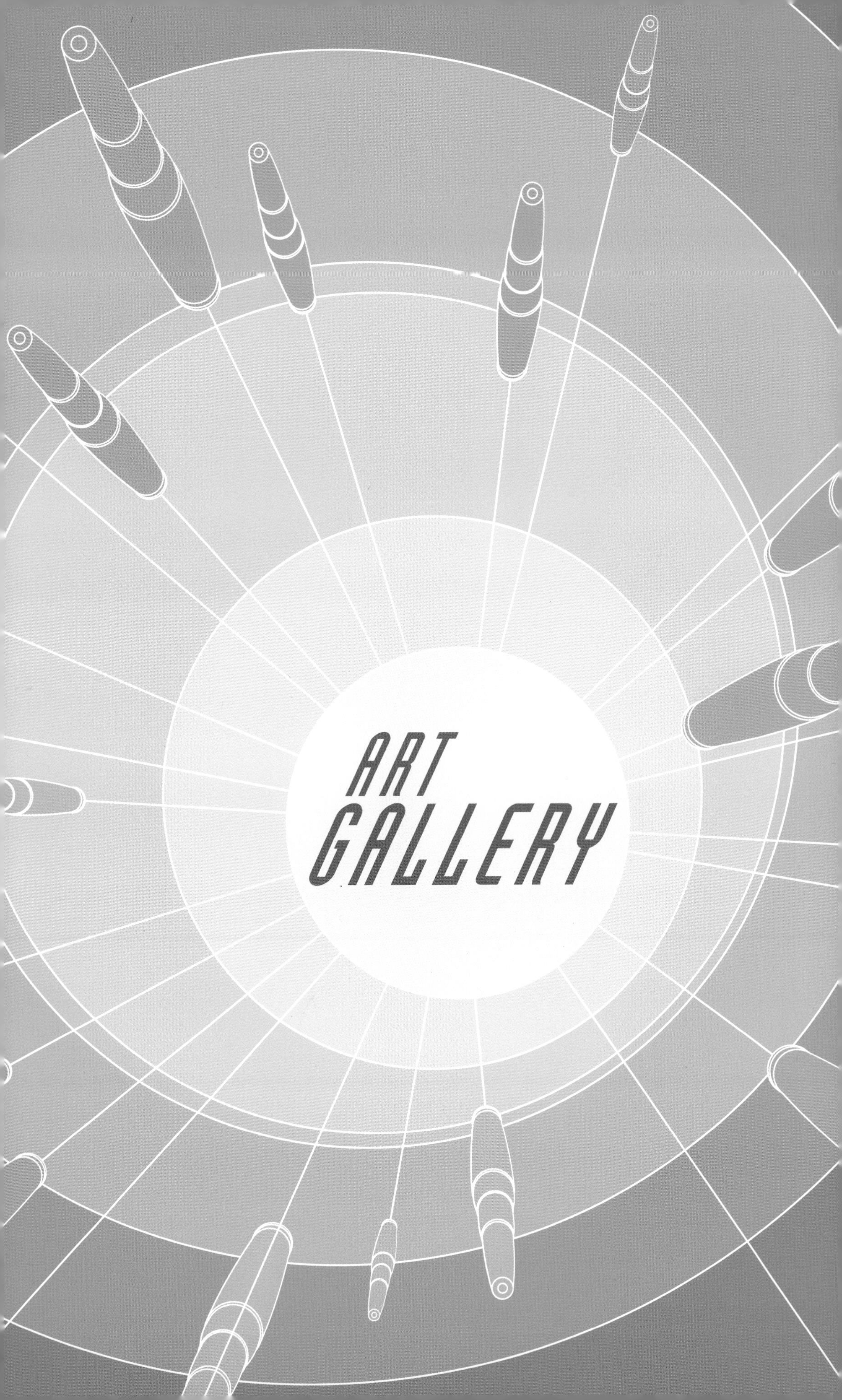
ART
GALLERY

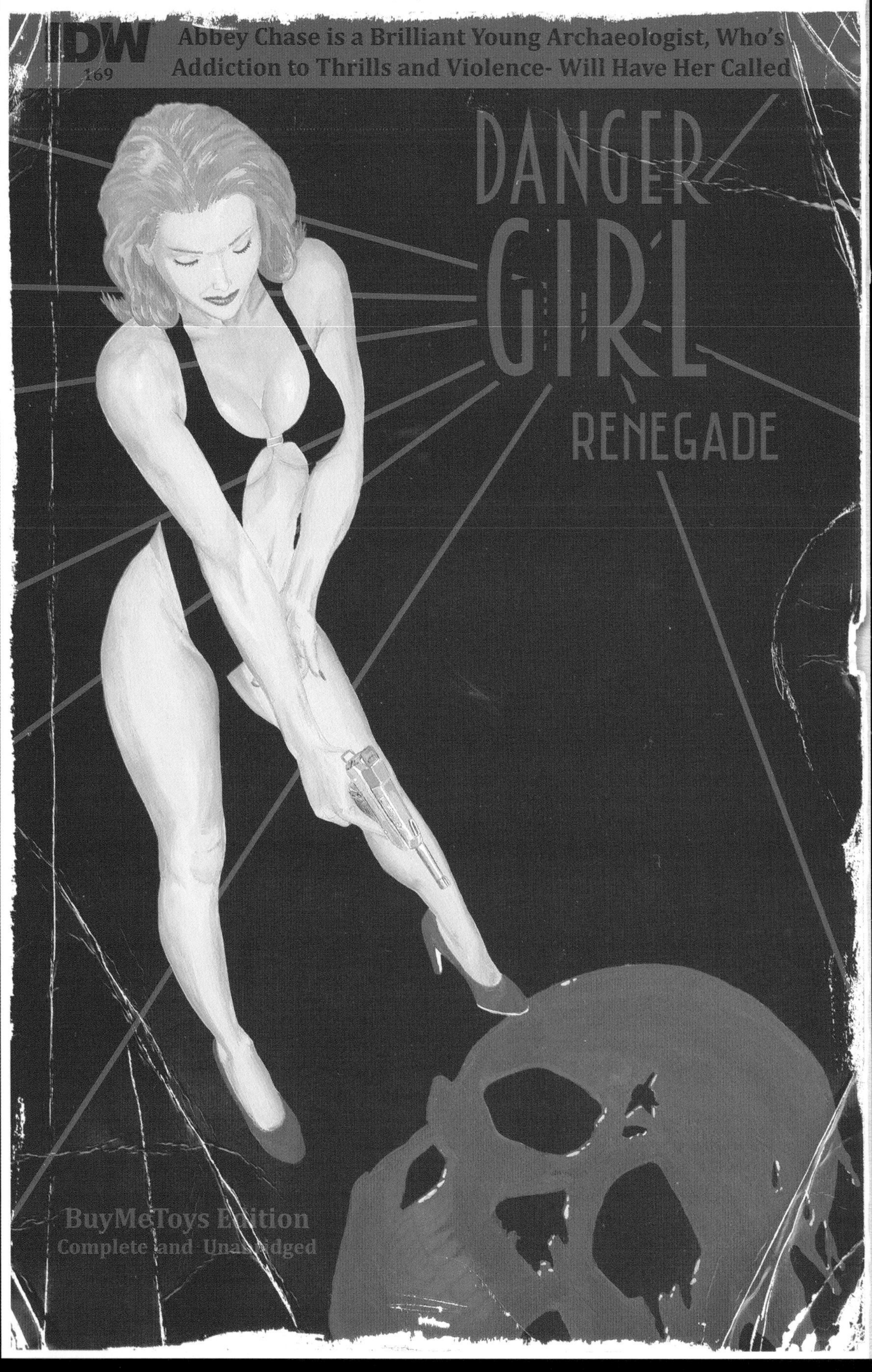
IDW
169
Abbey Chase is a Brilliant Young Archaeologist, Who's Addiction to Thrills and Violence- Will Have Her Called
DANGER GIRL
RENEGADE
BuyMeToys Edition
Complete and Unabridged

Art by Casey Heying

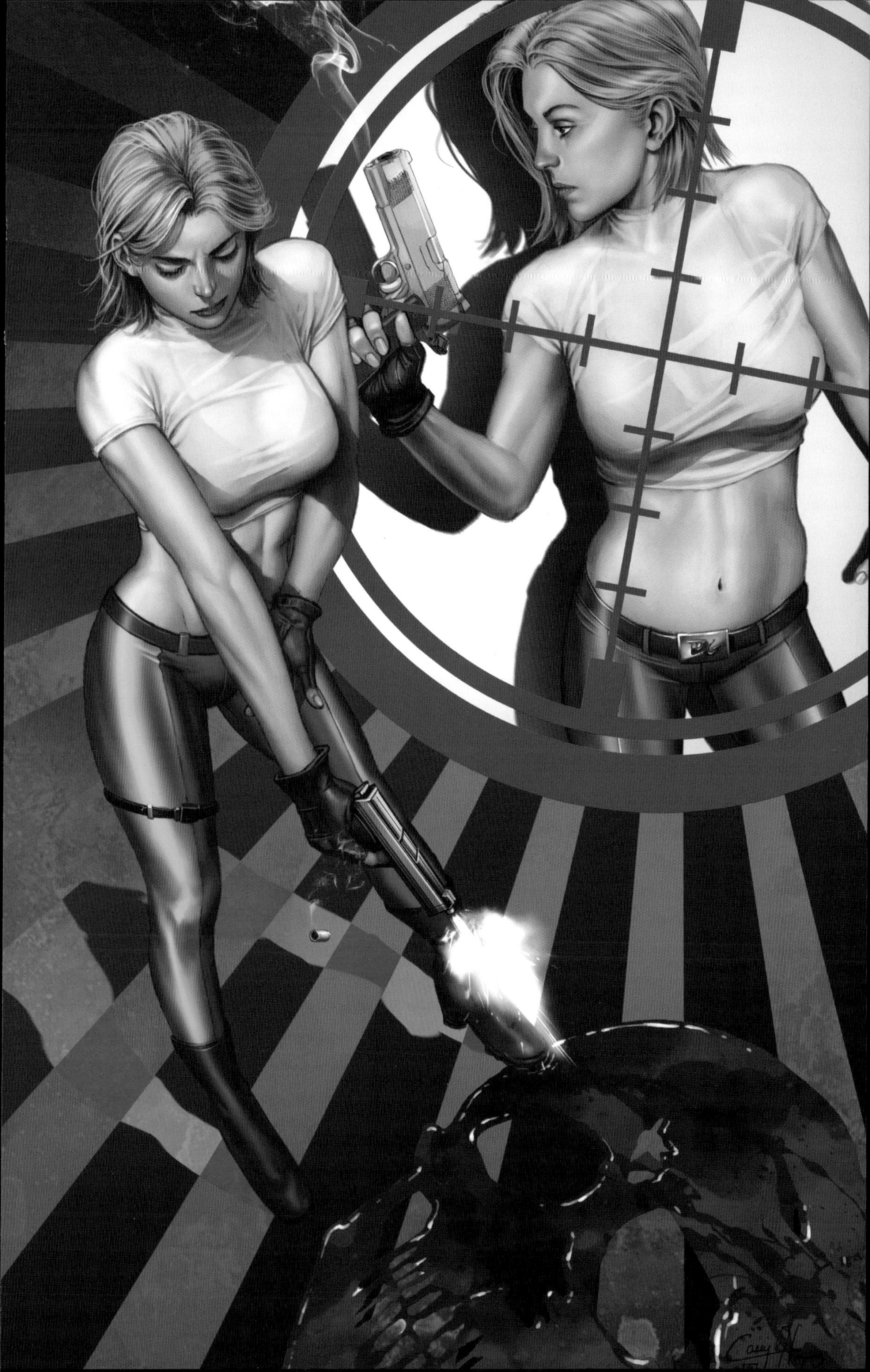

Art by Casey Heying

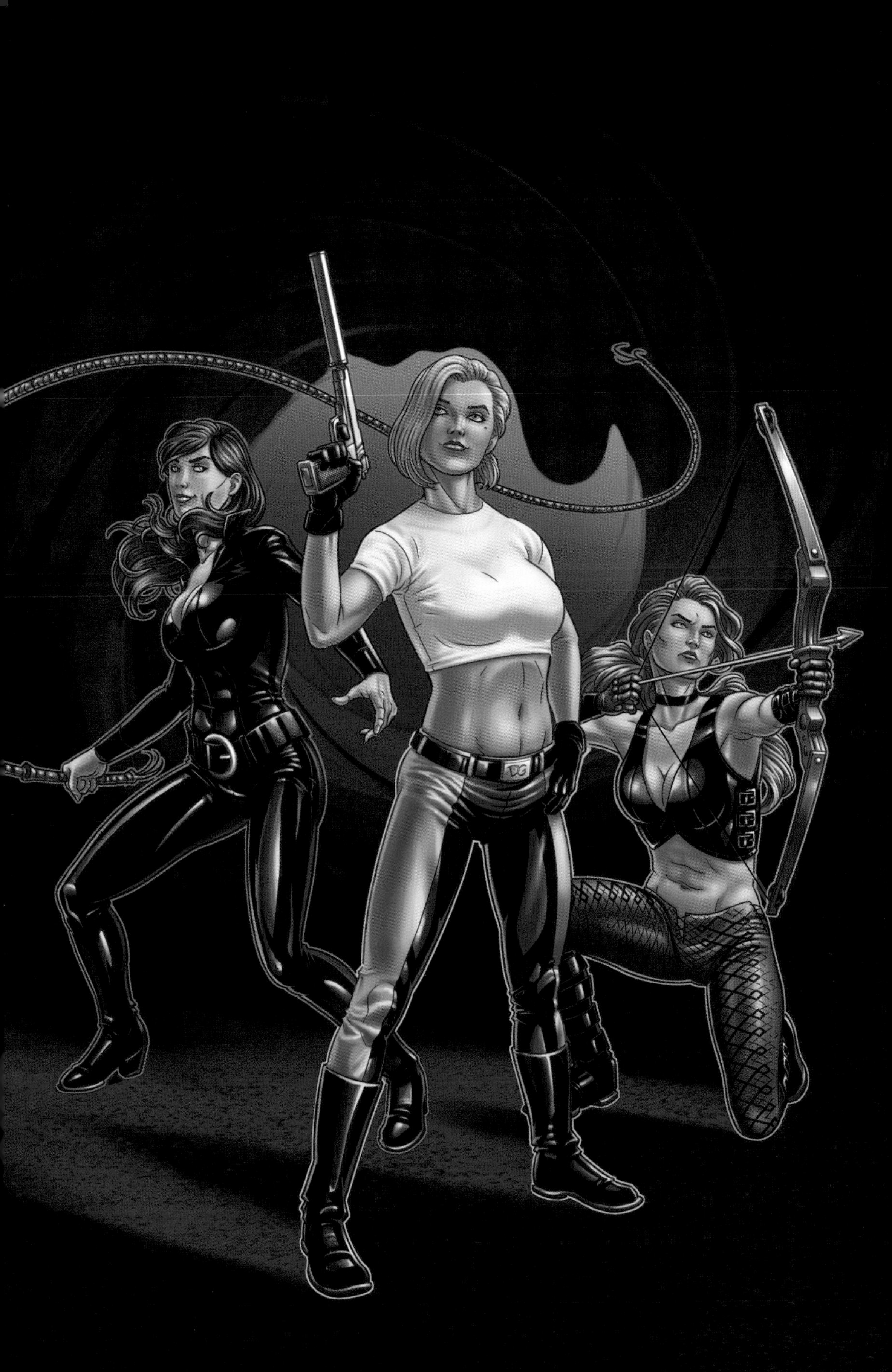

Art by Juan Cabal

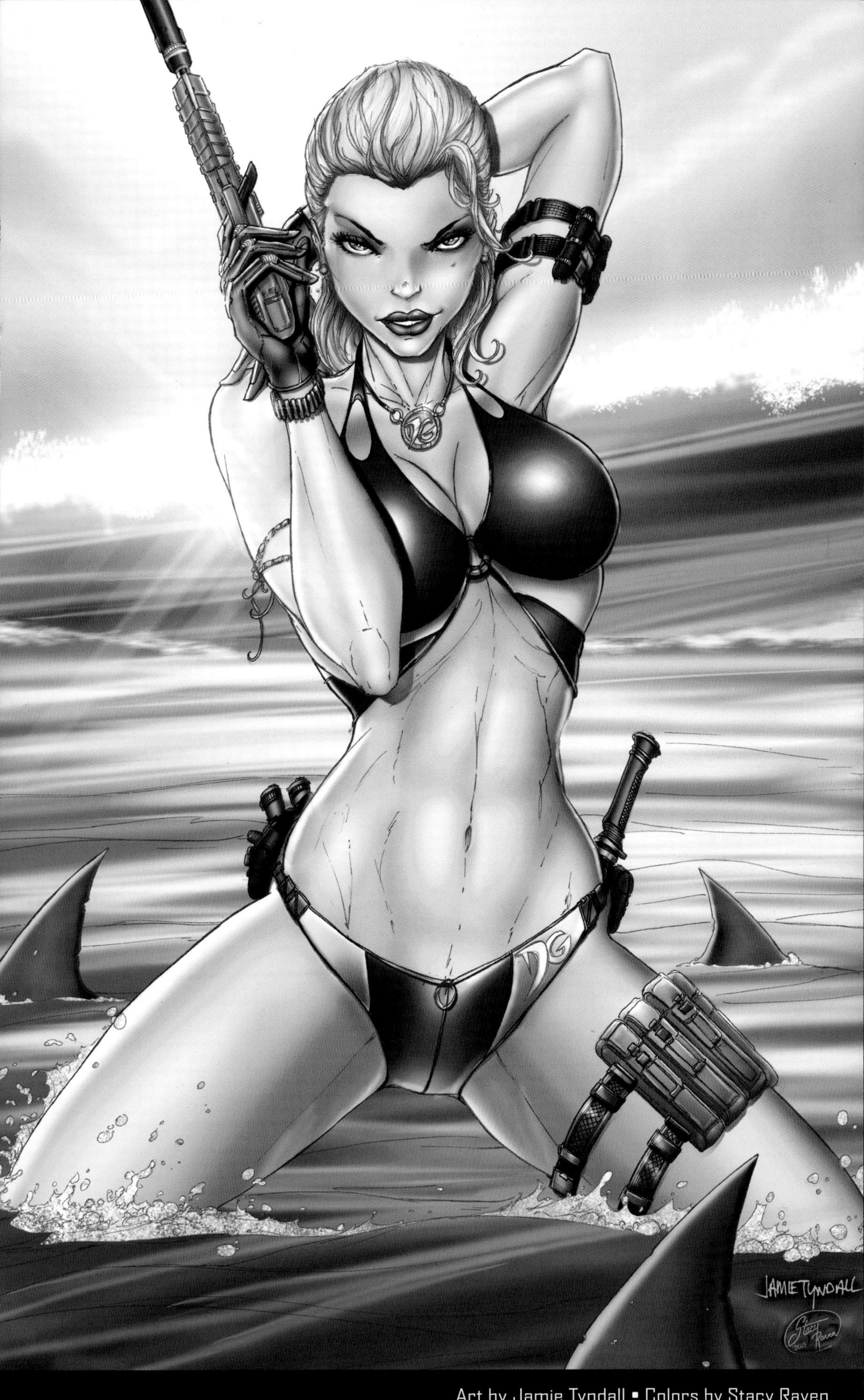
JAMIE TYNDALL

Art by Jamie Tyndall • Colors by Stacy Raven

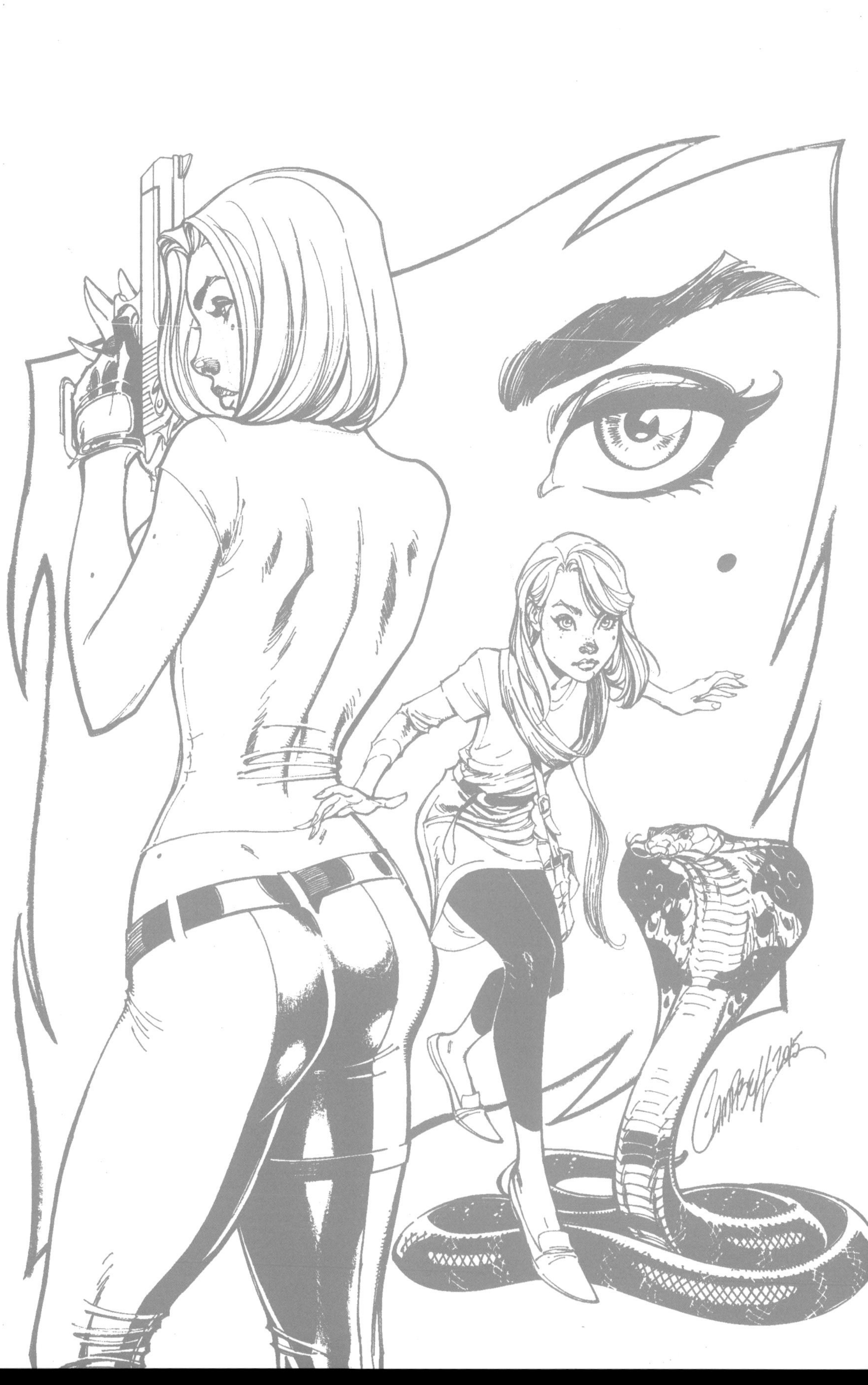

Art by J. Scott Campbell

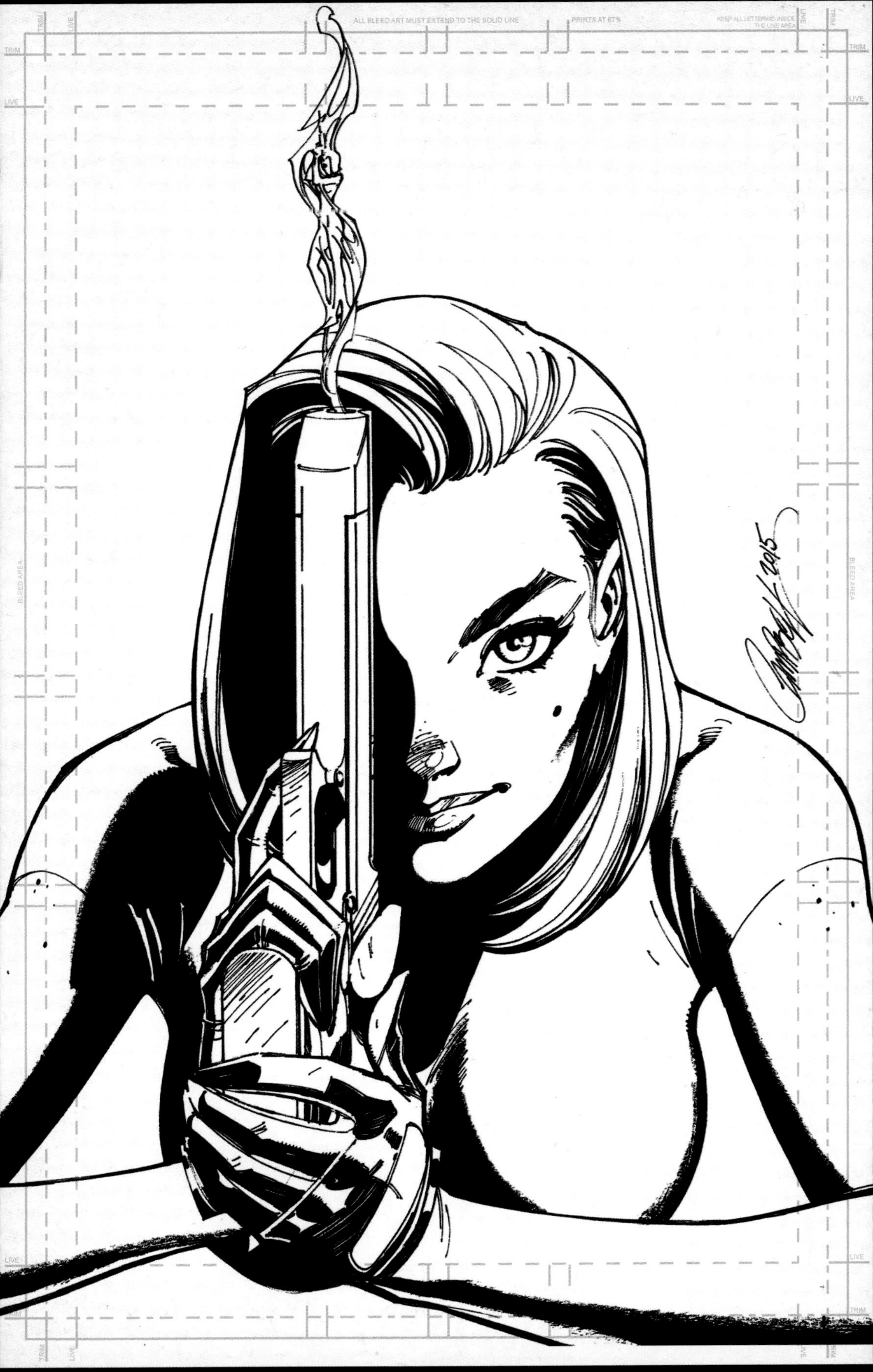
ALL BLEED ART MUST EXTEND TO THE SOLID LINE
PRINTS AT 67%
KEEP ALL LETTERING INSIDE THE LIVE AREA
TRIM
LIVE
BLEED AREA

Art by J. Scott Campbell

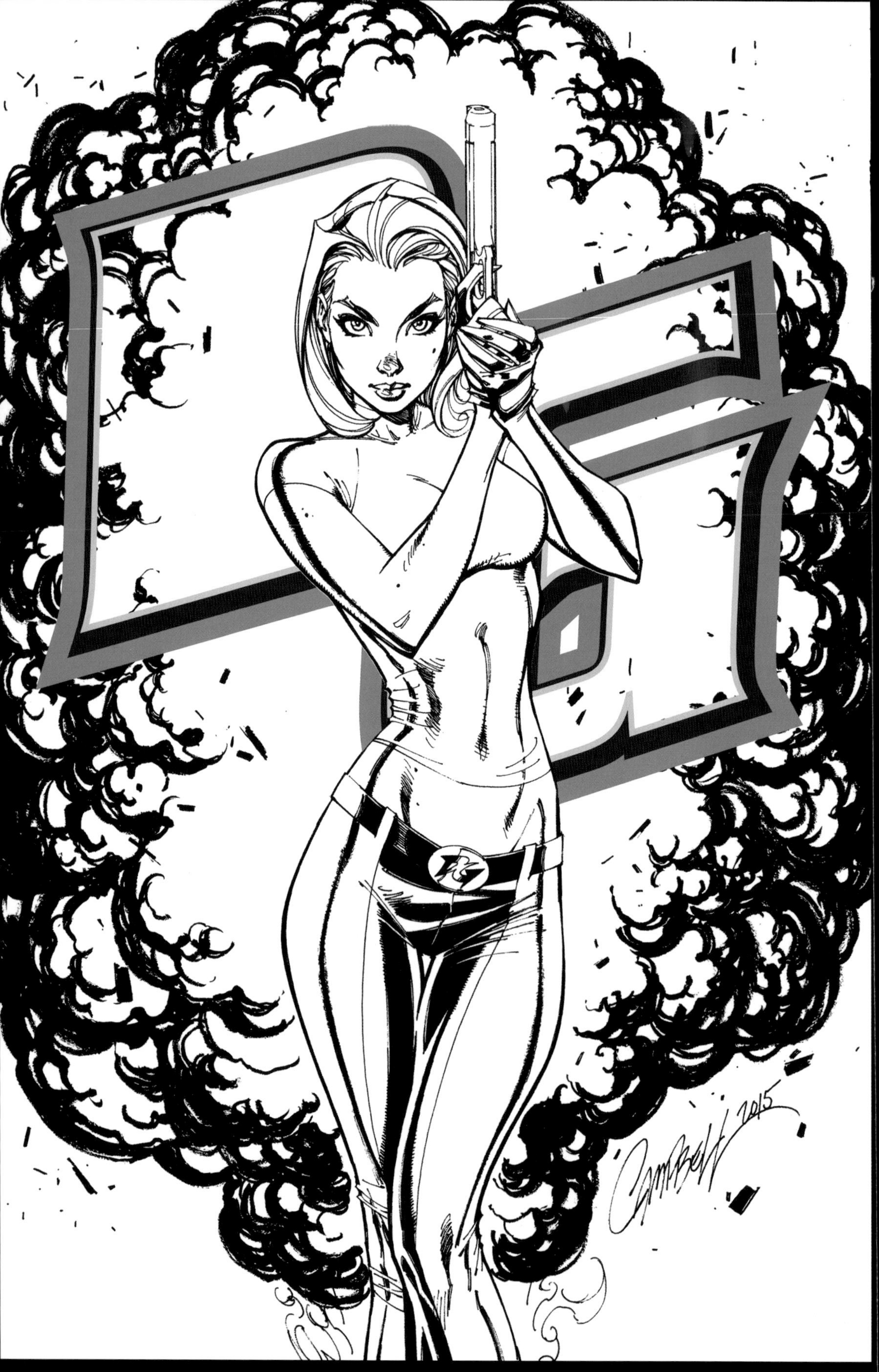

Art by J. Scott Campbell

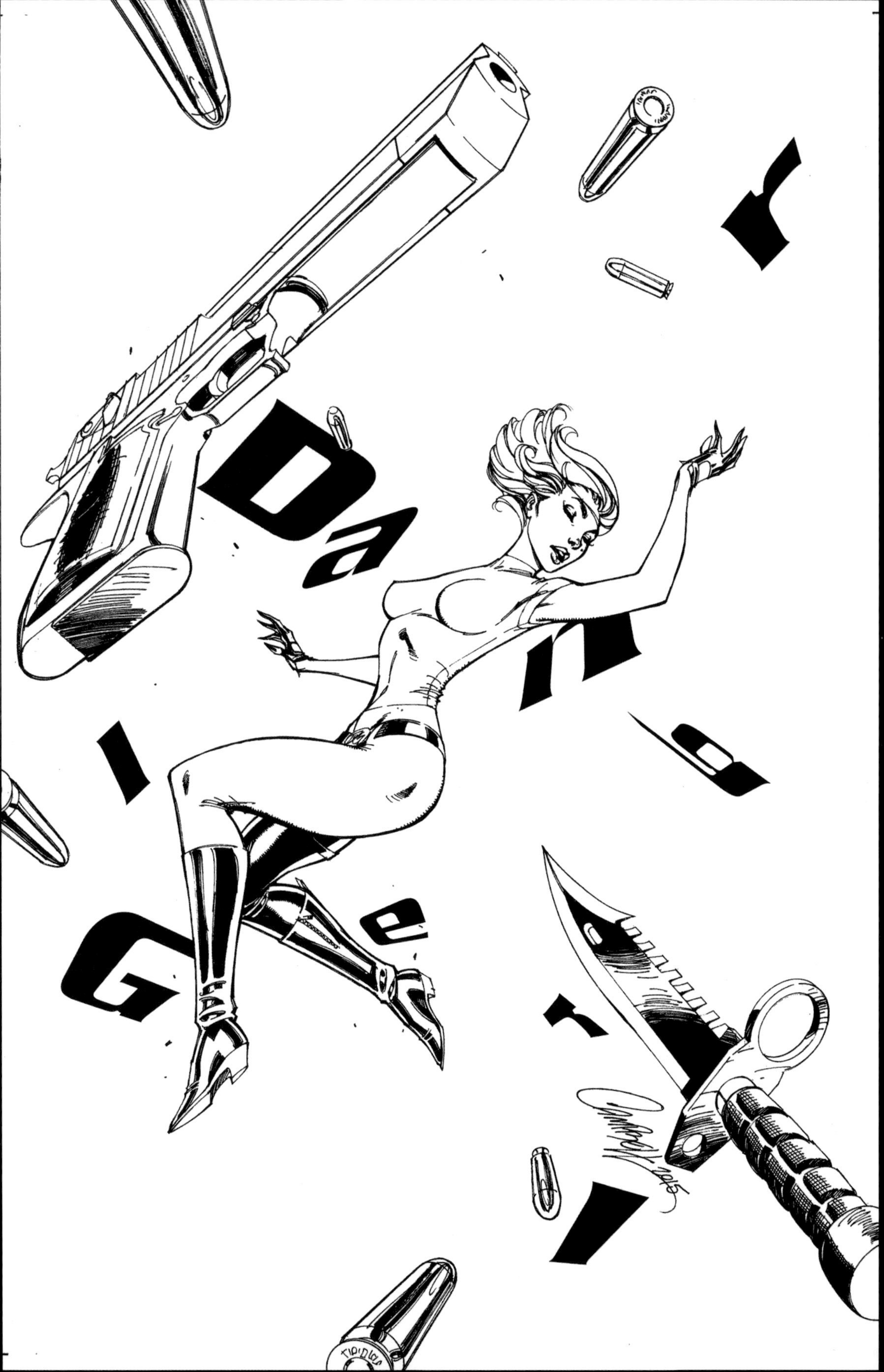

Art by J. Scott Campbell

GIRLS! GIRLS! GIRLS!

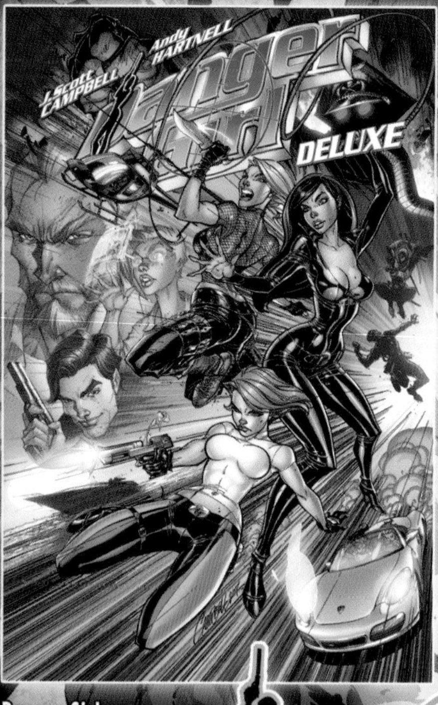
J.Scott CAMPBELL
Andy HARTNELL
Danger Girl
DELUXE

Danger Girl: The Deluxe Edition
ISBN: 978-1-61377-062-7

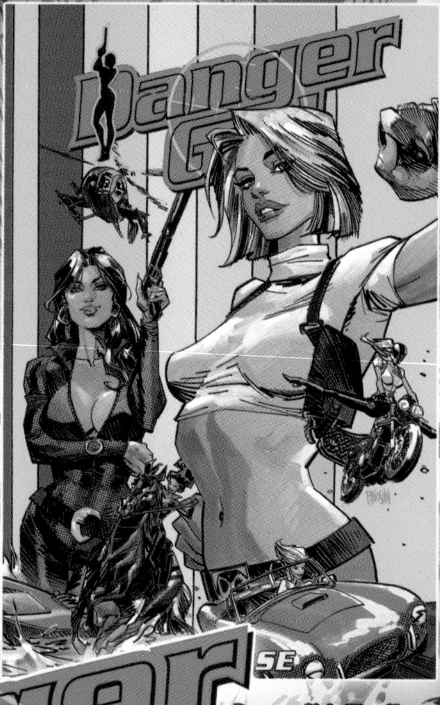
Danger Girl
SE

Danger Girl: The Chase
ISBN: 978-1-61377-904-0

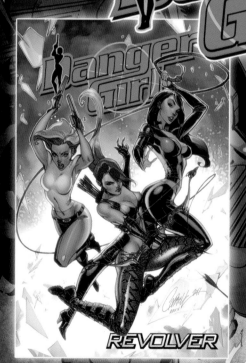

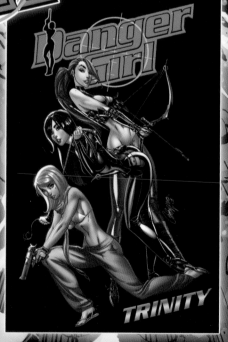

Danger Girl

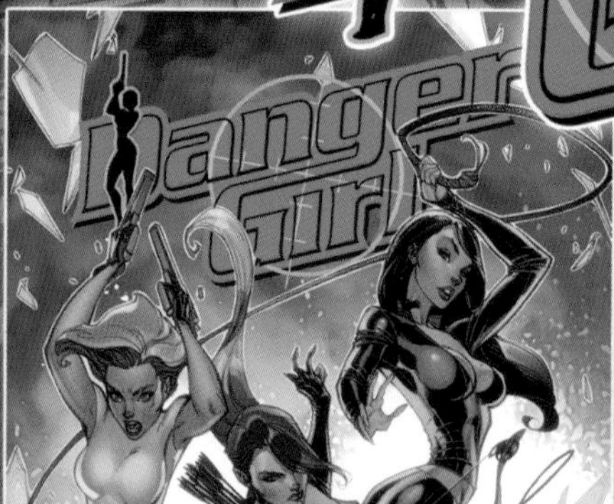
Danger Girl
REVOLVER

Danger Girl: Revolver
ISBN: 978-1-61377-215-7

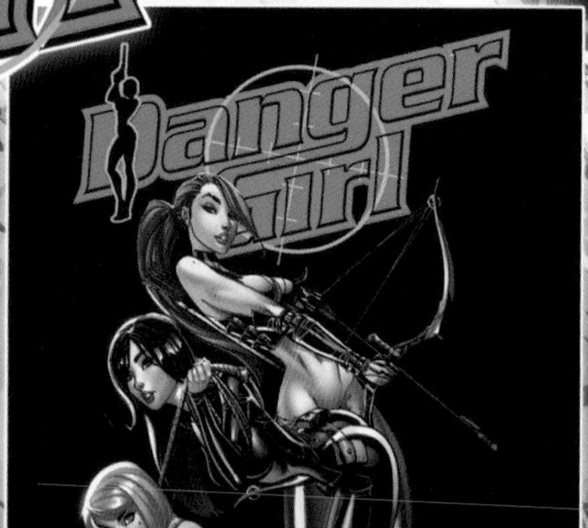
Danger Girl
TRINITY

Danger Girl: Trinity
ISBN: 978-1-61377-736-7

IDW

www.idwpublishing.com